CONVERGENCES, DIVERGENCES & AFFINITIES

The second wave of Free Improvisation in England, 1973–1979

Trevor Barre

Copyright © 2017 Trevor Barre. All rights reserved.
First paperback edition printed 2017 in the United Kingdom.

A catalogue record for this book is available from the British Library.

For extra copies of this book contact **trevorbarre@aol.com** or visit **improvmusic.co.uk**.

ISBN: 978-1-912009-56-5 PAPERBACK EDITION

No part of this book shall be reproduced or transmitted in any form or by any means, electronic or mechanical, including photocopying, recording, or by any information retrieval system without written permission of the publisher.

Published by Compass Publishing www.compass-publishing.com.

Edited by Deanne Greenwood

Designed and set by www.artdesk.uk contact john@artdesk.uk.

Printed in Great Britain.

Although every precaution has been taken in the preparation of this book, the publisher and author assume no responsibility for errors or omissions. Neither is any liability assumed for damages resulting from the use of this information contained herein.

Trevor Barre is a retired mental health practitioner. His first publication was *Beyond Jazz*, a study of the early years of English free improvisation in London, and he hopes to produce further works that gradually tell the full story of this most fascinating of musical genres. Trevor lives with his family in north London, his home for over 30 years. Although his tastes range over the full spectrum of jazz music, he prefers live free improvisation.

For more information on all things improv, and to follow my blog, visit my website at...

improvmusic.co.uk

COVER: Evan Parker (saxophone), David Toop (aquapipe) and Paul Burwell (drums) at a Gen One/Gen Two hoedown, 42 Gloucester Avenue on February 12th 1978. In this very early gig at the then new LMC HQ, Toop explores the element of water, in a fire bucket.

CREDIT: © JAK KILBY WWW.JAKKILBY.CO.UK

AUTHOR PHOTO: JANE FRANKEL

Please note that the dates accompanying the LP/CDs portrayed in this book are those of the recording of the material, not of their release schedule.

This is what people said about *Beyond Jazz: Plink, Plonk & Scratch; the Golden Age of Free Music in London, 1966-1972*, Trevor Barre's first book about early English free improvisation:

'Striking the right balance between entertaining and academically rigorous, the book is a pleasure to read and an invaluable history of 'Free Music'… he adroitly builds his case for these being the exciting formative years …a great primer and, for those already well aware of the history, offers wonderful insights and anecdotes fresh from Barre's painstaking research and personal communications.'

PAUL ACQUARO
Free Jazz Collective website

'This is a great read and reference. Making me dig deeper into the artists… really looking forward to Volume Two.'

JOHN PAZDEN
Free Jazz Collective website

'A succinct, personal, opinionated and ultimately insightful volume…a crisply written, well informed overview of the scene during these seven crucial years… without resorting to Gnostic angels-dancing-on-pinhead designations, Barre is able to trace and analyse the music of these advanced groups through deep listening to representative high quality music recorded at the time…with its wealth of well researched information, Beyond Jazz can serve as a suitable introduction to the music for those who have just discovered the genre through one of its hyphenated offshoots like Free-Rock or Improv Electronica.'

KEN WAXMAN
JazzWord

'It's one of the better reads in the sub-genre – entirely engaging and historic-informative, without too much dry chin-scratch academia dud-speak. A fine and welcome read that sources recordings for its discussions, something we here, as sick out-of-control record collectors, are perfectly fucking okay with.'

THURSTON MOORE
Bull Tongue Review # 2

'Enthusiastically copious, informative and decidedly welcome...without recourse to theoretical jargon, weighing up still-current debates concerning the relevance of this music's documentation while analysing its many political proclivities.'

SPENCER GRADY
Record Collector

'Free music crusader Trevor Barre deserves the gratitude of all intrepid souls curious to venture below the surface of this most subterranean and seemingly impenetrable of underground scenes, due to the considerable labour of love involved in researching, compiling and writing of the densely packed information overload that is Beyond Jazz...besides detailing the histories of key musicians and ensembles of the period, (it) includes in-depth analysis of significant recordings.'

GRAHAME BENT
Shindig!

'It's a highly readable appraisal of that most English of musical revolutions.'

DANIEL SPICER
Jazzwise

'Author Barre narrows the focus somewhat, a specific time frame, as single location...doing as good a job of describing the music as anyone who actually agrees that it is music could do...it's a fascinating read...this is, after all, a musical field that has been very poorly served by music journalism... it's a difficult book to put down.'

DAVE THOMPSON
Goldmine magazine

'My purpose is to simply say how satisfying it is, in an age of hyper-commercialism, to find that free improvisation is thriving...and that its history is being documented by people like Trevor Barre, themselves as ascetic and dedicated as many of the music's practitioners...nor do you have to be a free improv monomaniac to enjoy it...anyway, I read what we should all hope is merely volume one with great interest and enjoyment, and it left me feeling not just immeasurably more informed but also a better equipped listener.'

ALUN SEVERN
Letterpressproject

'It's the first book-length treatment of the first generation free improvisers…it's engaging and informative, without academic dryness, and there's a music family tree and valuable photographs of musicians, bands and album covers… a major plus are the quotes taken from his personal communications with musicians…there's genuine insight here…an honest, unpretentious book that makes the listener think and listen, or re-listen, to the masterworks it discusses.'

ANDY HAMILTON
Wire

'Overall, this is a good starting point from which to explore the world of free music.'

PETER STUBLEY
European Free Improvisation website

'I love it so much that I am reading it a second time and am seriously considering the third time round…his cross-reference to My Bloody Valentine, Merzbow, Alternative TV and many more, which one would NOT expect in a book more on the jazz side of things, connects me to him, thousands of kilometres away (Singapore).'

PSYCHMETALFREAK
Blogger

'A terrific overview of the key musicians…as an avid fan and spectator, Trevor Barre augments his research from all available published resources with quotes from personal correspondences with many of those involved, which gives it a far weightier aspect than a mere compendium of facts…it stands alone as an all-in-one reference for the music of the period. I hope he's writing a sequel from 1973 as we speak. Highly recommended.'

PAUL MORGAN
SpaceForEars e-magazine

Acknowledgements

Peter Baker
Steve Beresford
Ian Brighton
Janet Christianson
Charlie Collins
Martin Davidson
Terry Day
Jak Kilby
Richard Leigh
Paul Lytton
Will Menter
Evan Parker
Dave Panton
Blanca Regina
David Toop

Dedicated to: Jak Kilby and Richard Leigh, both of who have been most encouraging and facilitative in the process of writing this book.

Contents

	TIMELINE 1973–1979	i
	AUTHOR'S NOTE	vii
	FOREWORD	1
	INTRODUCTION	9
CHAPTER 1	THE LIVE NETWORK The Pioneers and the Settlers Derek Bailey and Evan Parker	41
CHAPTER 2	THE PIONEERS, CONTINUED Spontaneous Music Ensemble, AMM, Barry Guy, Howard Riley, Paul Rutherford	77
CHAPTER 3	SOME THOUGHTS ABOUT JAZZ IN THE 1970s	99
CHAPTER 4	THREE MAVERICKS	133
CHAPTER 5	COMPANY AND GEN TWO GROUPS	165
CHAPTER 6	LABELLING THEORY AND PRACTICE Free Improvisation Record Labels in the 1970s	191
CHAPTER 7	THE REGIONAL IMPERATIVE	205
CHAPTER 8	MUSICS: 'AN IMPROMENTAL EXPERIVISATION ARTS MAGAZINE' The 'Little Life' of the Free Improv Journal	237
CHAPTER 9	EPILOGUE Endings and New Beginnings	281
REFERENCES	BIBLIOGRAPHY, DISCOGRAPHY AND FILMOGRAPHY	289

Timeline

1973

▶ "I feel that I am living in a dream world at the moment." Tony Benn's diary entry on January 17th. (Sheen, 2009.)
Benn was an aristocratic socialist technophile, a difficult mix at the best of times. It seems that way now, from a safe distance – nobody owned mobile phones in 1973. *Absolutely nobody*. Yet. Go figure. It's only 40 years ago. The internet would have been seen as a sci-fi fantasy.

▶ January 1st: The United Kingdom joins the European Union (which we have now kissed goodbye to, for better or for worse).

▶ *The Smithsonian Collection of Classic Jazz* is released, a six-album retrospective of 80 'classic', soon-to-be canonical, tracks, which formed a template for future would-be tastemakers including the young Wynton Marsalis. There were to be no gainsayers when confronted with this solid wall of critically endorsed product.
This was the beginning of the institutionalisation of popular (and even non-popular) music. *Electric Muse*, in 1975, did a similar thing with psych folk, creating another *ne plus ultra* canon.
Eventually, the five-CD collection *Hey Ho! Let's Go* from 1999, with punk and post-punk, did exactly the same thing for that particular music. All ossified their particular traditions into easily digested 'classic' recordings, which is fine, to an extent, but which missed out much material that might have challenged the standard narrative (all three compilations are still essential, by the way).

▶ November 10th: *Balance* is recorded, the first 'Second Generation'

vinyl product with Ian Brighton, Colin Wood, Frank Perry, Rudu Malfatti and Phillip Wachsmann.
- ▶ The Spontaneous Music Ensemble's *Face to Face* duo recordings, made in this year in November and December, eventually appear on Emanem 4003. These also proved to be era defining.
- ▶ Ian Carr publishes *Music Outside*, the first book to feature free improvisers (John Stevens, Trevor Watts, Evan Parker, interviewed over two chapters) in any detail. And it was also the last, at least for several years.

1974

- ▶ Derek Bailey records *Lot 74*, perhaps his greatest solo achievement.
- ▶ Emanem Records launch – their first release is a Steve Lacy solo album.
- ▶ January 20th – 24th: The first ever International Festival of Improvised Music in this country takes place at Ronnie Scott's Club and the Collegiate Theatre.
- ▶ March 12th: The Unity Theatre in Mornington Crescent begins to feature free improv gigs.
- ▶ June 30th: Derek Bailey and Anthony Braxton play as a duo at the Wigmore Hall.
- ▶ Late 1974: Paul Rutherford records the material that will appear on Emanem 4019, and which is later recognised as one of the most peerless solo free improvisations ever brought to vinyl.

1975

- ▶ April: The first issue of *Musics* is published.
- ▶ May 2nd: The 'Young Improvisers' concert is held at the Wigmore Hall, which was sparsely attended but gave several Second Generation improvisers their first serious public exposure.
- ▶ June 17th: The original *Saxophone Solos* by Evan Parker is recorded, a landmark solo horn recording.
- ▶ November 8th: A fire at the Unity Theatre puts paid to that particular venue.

- ▶ 1975/6: The London Musicians Collective begins to cohere, following the example of *Musics*, and which anticipates Company.
- ▶ *Teatime* is released, the second Gen Two recording on Incus Records, featuring Garry Todd, Nigel Coombes, Steve Beresford, John Russell and Dave Solomon.

1976
- ▶ May 8th: The first Company gig.
- ▶ May 9th: The first Company recording.
- ▶ August 1st: The first London Musicians Collective (LMC) newsletter.
- ▶ September: The first LMC gigs.
- ▶ October 30th: Barry Guy records the monumental *Statements*, for solo bass and violone.

1977
- ▶ May 25th–27th: The first Company week, at the ICA, which is preserved for posterity on *Company 6 + 7* – a real Pandora's Box.
- ▶ Autumn: The Feminist Improvisers Group (FIG) form.
- ▶ September: The first LMC Festival, at Battersea Arts Centre.
- ▶ October 31st: The first FIG live appearance.

1978
- ▶ Early January/late 1977: The LMC move to 42 Gloucester Avenue as a permanent venue (at least for many years).
- ▶ April 30th: Evan Parker records *Monoceros* in Monmouth, Wales.
- ▶ June 22nd: The first Alterations gig.
- ▶ July/August: David Toop's 'Environmental & Contextual Music Festival' (Music/Context) which takes place in the Camden Lock environs and includes *Circadian Rhythm*, some of the material from which appeared as Incus 33.

1979
- ▶ Early 1979: Matchless Records is set up by Eddie Prevost, as is Paul Burwell's Actuel Music.

- May 3rd: Margaret Hilda Thatcher becomes Prime Minister, which is the most telling event of them all.
- November: The final edition of *Musics* is published, representing the end of an era as much as does Thatcher's victory. The avant garde will be further marginalised.
- November: The Bristol Musicians Cooperative curates a one-day festival (a noon 'til midnight affair) at 42 Gloucester Avenue, the LMC HQ, featuring over 50 improvisers from co-ops and collectives across the whole country. Ways of replacing *Musics* are discussed in one session, in the light of its concurrent demise.
- December: Recordings made at Tonstudio Bauer by AMM, who see in the new decade in a typically unpredicted way.

1980

The rock industry try to figure out some *fin de siècle* angles. Two examples: *1980: The First Fifteen Seconds* EP, (being four brief shots from Sheffield post-punk); the *NME* put Jayne Casey, the singer for Pink Military and, later, Pink Industry (which were great band names if nothing else), on the cover of their second issue of 1980. They make a *very* 1979-sounding EP and a subsequently well received album, before quickly disappearing down the 80s Saniflo, along with most of their contemporaries.

There was a merciless decade ahead, and post-punk was not long for this world. Free improvisation put its head down and got on with it.

Author's Note

The reader will notice that, occasionally, I have recourse to referring to texts from the world of psychoanalysis (on a very basic and, I hope, intelligible, level). This frame of reference is informed by a Masters course that I undertook between the years of 1997 and 2000, which was concerned with the application of psychoanalytical thinking to the world of mental health institutions. In my case, that of acute adult inpatient care.

I do hope that the reader will indulge me here, before dispatching me into Pseud's Corner. I think that the 'little life' (a term first used by John Stevens, about free improvisation) of analytic theory and practice, and that of free improvisation, can co-exist, especially because the former's applied theories of groups and group behaviour can help us begin to understand the world of the latter. Free improvisation was beleaguered, in the years that I have covered in this book, by some of the difficulties that can emerge in working with other people in groups, and in collectives and cooperatives more specifically. In fact, the little world of free improv always benefits from a sympathetic and unbiased approach to its challenges, difficulties and opportunities, given how impassioned commentators can become when confronted with a music that does not accept 'normal' rules and constraints. It can all too easily be confined to the 'naughty child' part of the art house, scolded and patronised by the taste arbiters.

Similarly, there will be those who feel that I have dwelt far too long on rock, punk/post-punk/new wave music, and do not accept some of the claims that I make as to the convergences and affinities between these genres and free improvisation. I make no claims that my views are the be all and end all of debate about this most challenging music: on the contrary, I hope that there will be books forthcoming that will, in turn, challenge my opinions and viewpoint, and will promote further discourse about these most slippery of sounds.

I would like to think that the divergences between the various musical genres have lessened, in the eyes/ears of music fans, in the years between 1979 and the present. In 1979, links between the music of, say, Derek Bailey and Evan Parker, and that of drum & bass, or Japanese avant rock, would have seemed unlikely at best, preposterous at worst. However, these links did come to pass in time, and the average young free improv fan of today would see these convergences as perfectly *comme il faut* and unexceptional. The world of the LMC, at 42 Gloucester Road and other small venues across the country, contained, ultimately, the acorns that seeded the forest of today's free improvisation landscape.

I could have focused more on the links with contemporary classical music, with the likes of Cage, Webern, Messiaen and Stockhausen, for example, or with those of early electronic music, or those of the myriad of non-European influences. However, the other little life of the post-punk *diaspora* is one that I have lived far longer, so I hope that other authors can tease out alternative connections far better than I can, and I sincerely hope that they will do so. However, I am also aware of comments made by AMM's Eddie Prevost with regard to the attitudes assumed, by some of the above, towards free improvisation: "A general dismissive and rather patronising attitude [that] improvisers met from many composers (e.g. Luciano Berio, Pierre Boulez, John Cage, Elliott Carter)...We (and by that I mean the improvising community) needed to ignore these responses to our work, or face them out." (Prevost, 2015, p.3.)

It is instructive to note, in comparison, that the responses from many well known and respected African-American jazz composers, such as Anthony Braxton, Leo Smith and Cecil Taylor to name only the most obvious, were very different from that expressed by the above composers, these being musician/composers who could, presumably, appreciate the power and relevance of the improvisatory. Cage, for example, despite the aleatory devices, appeared to remain ever the composer, set apart and paring his nails. The *droit de signeur* of the composers of the western classical tradition was not one that was ever likely to be easily relinquished.

This music is, after all, still essentially a hybrid music (just like jazz itself, of course), despite its undoubted originality, and there is still much about its early influences, and subsequent development, that requires further study. The arguments look set to continue…

Foreword

Before we start, I would like to share a few quotes, which have been taken from individuals who I feel have, briefly and succinctly, highlighted some of the 'convergences, divergences and affinities' suggested in the title of this book. In particular, these quotes highlight the notion that there were strong links, but also considerable differences, between the so-called 'First Generation' of free improvisers (or 'Gen One' in my own shorthand), which were fully described in my first book *Beyond Jazz* (Barre, 2015), and the one that followed it, 'Gen Two', both of which this particular work is concerned with.

The relationships between these two groups of musicians were gradually played out through the years under consideration in these pages, and throughout the book I hope it is understood that these 'generations' are acknowledged to be artificial journalistic conceits. Most of the musicians discussed here, ironically, are of a reasonably similar age, and several played across the cusps of the time frames that I have established in order to facilitate both comparisons and distinctions between the two groups.

"The Seventies were the time for the battling of antinomies that came out in the early years; the meaning of the music, its ontology and epistemology, which led to splits and realignments throughout the decades." (Wickes, 1999, p.306.)

"I believe that being 'non-idiomatic' is in itself an idiom." (Pianist Alexander Hawkins quoted in Antoine Prum's film about English free improvisers, called *Taking the Dog for a Walk*, 2014.)

"What starts off being really spontaneous and seems to come from nowhere, inevitably it's gonna become self-conscious, and you have to confront that head-on." (Steve Beresford, quoted by Corbett, 1995, p.196.)

"At a time when free music – despite its declared intentions – was starting to codify its own terms and taboos, these younger musicians offered a more porous sense of what the music might involve. The new, evolving language could accommodate impurities." (Steve Beresford, interviewed by Julian Cowley, *Wire* 322, p.56.)

"Free improvised music is not jazz…some of it sounds like jazz, but they're not playing it. It is a separate genre." (Beresford, interviewed by Cowley, *Wire* 218, p.25.) This is a point that I continually stressed in my first book, i.e. that the music mostly emerged from jazz but, over several years, and certainly by 1979, had ultimately moved well beyond it.

"We were traditional musicians, but the tradition had only been invented three years before!" (Beresford, again interviewed by Cowley, *Wire* 218, p.28.)

"Moving outside the known semi-private space of mutually recognised experience and into the wider imagined community necessarily involves a loss of the *purity* [author's italics] and rigour which marked that music." (Blake, 1997, p.197.)

I make no apology for including so many utterances by multi-instrumentalist Steve Beresford, who also gets his very own mini-biography within this book. His pithiness often cuts through much of the opaque nature of free improvisation's meta-language, and his keen good humour emerges in his music, as well as in his journalism. The quote from John Corbett is from his influential (and highly recommended) book *Extended Play* (1994), which was in itself an example of barrier breaking (the giveaway being its subtitle, *Sounding Off from John Cage to Dr. Funkenstein*). In my view, the Gen One musicians had produced and established a recognisable musical language over a seven-year period (1966-72), and the most pressing question for the musicians (aside from financial ones, as ever) was, by 1973 – did free improvisation have to change/develop in order to remain a vital creative force?

My view, to answer this question, is that the music had to, and did manage to change, over the course of the seven years under review in these pages. The convergences and affinities between the two 'generations' are perhaps best appreciated by listening to one of the most representative recordings by Gen Two musicians, *Three & Four Pullovers* (1975-8) on the Emanem label (Emanem 4038). The knitwear under consideration featured Steve Beresford, violinist Nigel Coombes and guitarist Roger Smith in its trio incarnation, with percussionist Terry Day joining to make it a quartet, which recorded its particular portion of the CD three years after that by the trio. As these recordings feature two of the Gen Two

Three & Four Pullovers by The Three & Four Pullovers, January 14th 1975, May 5th 1978

improvisers (although Day could legitimately claim to be of the first generation, given his age) to whom I have devoted separate sections in this book, the group(s) can lay a good claim to be an especial embodiment of that particular era in free improv – a time that could be described, variously, as 'transitional', 'consolidating' or maybe even just 'protean'?

As Charles K. Noyes says in his *Pullovers* CD notes: "This music is a more 'related' extension of, say, the work of Bailey-Parker or Parker-Lytton, and it seems to be moving quite beyond that."

This covers both the idea of the music of this period as being 'in the tradition' (such as it was, given that, as Beresford suggests above, the music was only a few years old) and to be 'moving on' to further challenges. I would thus broadly agree with Noyes' observation, but the music I am most put in mind of, when listening to the *Pullovers*, in terms of 'affinities', are those of the two great groups of the First Generation, The Spontaneous Music Ensemble (in terms of The Three Pullovers) and, with The Four Pullovers, AMM. The scope of free improvisation broadened and developed over these years, as I intend to describe, but the links with these two most important group configurations of the music's early history should become clear to listeners, when they hear Emanem 4038.

To briefly allude to the title of this book, and to offer some sort of explanation as to why it is so called: When reading John Corbett's more recent (2016) book on free improvisation (one of a few on the subject published in this year, its notional 50th birth year, as noted on the masthead of *Wire* 392, 2016, p.4), I was particularly taken by the expression Corbett uses on page 110, "...trying to decipher what is happening, the provocations and responses, the convergences and divergences". Martin Davidson highlighted the "disagreements and reconciliations" (personal communication, 2016) that marked the period, but I thought I'd add 'affinities' to my title, to reinforce the syncretic, combinative nature of the newer free music. A trace memory, perhaps, when finally confirming the title to myself, was its assonance with the names of so many Blue Note label classics from the 1950s and 1960s, which I thought, in my own hubristic way, might give this book some extra heft and/or allusiveness on the book shelves. Some examples to illustrate this: Herbie Hancock *Inventions And Dimensions*; Grachan Moncur 111 *Evolution*; Bobby Hutcherson *Components* and *Oblique*; Cecil Taylor *Unit Structures*; Sam Rivers *Dimensions And Extensions*; Larry Young *Contrasts*; Elvin Jones *Polycurrents*; McCoy Tyner *Expansions* and *Extensions*. Most of these titles share an almost architectonic flavour, replete as they are with references to both structure *and* change. The most obvious 'affinities' between these titles are, of course, that all these artists are African-American, which was initially the influence that the early English freedom seekers, ironically, most wished to transcend. (Barre, *op. cit.*, pp.46-7, p.101.)

In terms of transcendence, one development that I wanted the book's title also to reflect was the expansion, extension, evolution (to maintain these themes) of the free scene beyond London to other parts of the country. Hence the subtitle describes '*English* Free Improvisation', rather than 'Free Music in London', which was the case in my first book. The chauvinism that Londoners can display (or are at least *perceived* to display) is one of the attitudes that most annoy people who live outside the M25 motorway (or even outside the North/South Circular Roads), so I wanted to get things more balanced right from the title onwards.

In the same spirit, by July 1972 the editorial of Issue 6 of the very short-lived *Microphone*, a kind of early almost-fanzine for the music, stated quite clearly that the magazine "is being established in the provinces in an attempt to widen the audience for new music and decentralise the London 'scene'," (page 7). Unfortunately, that edition also proved to be the last in a full form: Issue 7 was stillborn and only consisted of a front and back cover. It is worth noting that *Microphone*s 1-3 were sub-titled *New Music in London*, but the remaining editions had *New Music in Britain* on the masthead, perhaps as an acknowledgement of the editorial revelation, in Issue 4 (in the Letters section, on page 2), that "Issues 1, 2 and 3 have sold more in the provinces than in London".

It is worth bearing this in mind when reading Chapter Seven of this book, and also being aware that England was not the only country to suffer from big-city chauvinism: "There was little question that the New York area constituted a significant advantage for attracting the attention of the National Endowment for the Arts [an equivalent body to our Arts Council, *author*] peer panels. For example, in 1980, artists living in New York and its environs received more than half of the 78 NEA individual artist grants to jazz musicians that year." (Lewis, 2008, pp.395-6.)

Before we start in earnest, I want to also comment on a trope that several readers have asked me about – the seven-year temporal division that I used in my first book, and am using again in this one. I would really just like to reaffirm my fascination with seven-year cycles, and think that this figure (just about) works with free improvisation. One of my literary heroes, Thomas Mann, shared a similar fascination with the number, for what it's worth: "No round number for devotees of the decimal system, and yet a good, handy number in its way, a mythic, romantic bundle of time, one might say, more satisfying to the soul than a plain half-dozen." (Mann, p.842.) Without getting too carried away with flights of fancy and inappropriate comparisons with a writer of genius: using Shakespeare's 'Seven Ages of Man' conceit from *As You Like It*, the first generation could represent the babyhood/early childhood of the music, and the second the tricky period of pre- and early adolescence. These are rather fatuous notions, I'm well aware, but they do, however, dovetail with the whole concept of 'Ages', with the 'Golden Age', especially, representing a mythical time towards which our own time looks with envy and awe, however irritating some of the musicians find such a concept.

I would like to further extend the fancifulness of these conceptual improvisations by citing the psychologist Erik Erikson's Seven Stages of Development (there is a reasonable Wiki entry on Erikson for those sufficiently interested). Erikson postulated that there are binary internal processes that are operant through each person's life, and which we all face, but the ones that are relevant here are the earliest: that of Trust vs. Mistrust (i.e. 'Is it OK for me to do, move and act?'), perhaps appropriate to the early pioneers of the music; and the adolescent Identity vs. Role Confusion (the stage discussed in this very book – 'Who Am I and What Can I Do?'). I have also always particularly liked Erikson's last conceptual struggle, that between Ego Integrity vs. Death (or 'Is It OK to Have Been Me?'), which was perhaps the stage that the music had reached at its own recent 50th birthday (2016) and which is reflected in the increasing attention that the music received in this year (in which David Toop also published a book on improvisation). The 'Mid-Life Crisis' seems to have been successfully contained, thankfully (apart from various practitioners' experiments with Noise, perhaps?).

If we take the First Generation to be a notional Golden Age (as I did in *Beyond Jazz*), perhaps we could stretch the metaphor further and describe the period of the next generation as being a Silver Age? This has a precedent, as readers of comics will know.

To digress even further, briefly: in his book *The Comic Book*, which is a history of the form, Paul Sassienie describes a Golden Age lasting from 1938 (the first *Superman* comic) through to the end of World War Two. Comics in good condition from this era are, of course, very, very rare and extremely valuable. An interregnum followed before the Silver Age of 1956 to 1969 emerged, which contained, among other delights, the contemporary *Marvel* filmic superhero(es) gang, from The Fantastic Four and Spiderman onwards. These have been such a delight to the adolescent (of all ages) film fan of today, not forgetting the boost they have given the Hollywood film industry in recent years. Thor, Daredevil, Doctor Strange, The Avengers, The Silver Surfer all emerged through the narrow birth canal of 1962-68, and those are only my own personal favourites.

Although it might seem spurious in the extreme to conflate the two art forms of free improv and comic books (and there are many who would dispute whether the word 'art' should actually be applied to either), I do think that there is some mileage in doing this. Both free improvisation and comic books have had their difficulties in being taken seriously, both by the public and by the art police. Both have undergone recognisable evolutions, and have their periods that are seen retrospectively as trail blazing and innovatory. Early artifacts from both forms are treasured and expensive. Both have key artists/musicians who have become cynosures of excellence in their field. Just as the public found it hard to take seriously a product that was originally sold for ten cents as disposable kiddie fodder, so some found it equally hard to take seriously grown men doing the washing up in public (see the front cover of this book).

We know better nowadays, of course. Don't we? But it took a lot of perseverance and courage from the artists concerned in both modalities to reach this point. This book is thus a tribute to those who stayed the course, and produced such great music (and comic art) throughout all the vicissitudes of those now distant year.

Introduction

Towards the end of that cinematic panegyric to the 1960s, *Withnail & I* (1987), Danny the Dealer (a magnificent performance from Ralph Brown) ruefully exclaims to Withnail (a role Richard E. Grant was born to inhabit) and Marwood ('I', deftly portrayed by Paul McGann): "They're selling hippie wigs in Woolworths, man. The greatest decade in the history of mankind is over and, as Presuming Ed [Danny's enigmatic Anglo-Caribbean sidekick, *author*] here has so consistently pointed out, we have failed to paint it black."

This seems to have been exactly what many disillusioned individuals felt by the early 1970s, and hence the need for nostalgia was beginning to emerge from the inchoate feelings that were around at this time. As I described in *Beyond Jazz* (Barre, *op. cit.*, Chapter One), a toxic 'comedown' pervaded the latter period and beyond, both in England and America. Experimental jazz had been well and truly sidelined (Barre, *op.cit.*, p.35); the major labels had terminated their very (*very!*) brief affair with free improvisation; free musicians were struggling to find regular venues to play in, and money was too tight to mention. In Issue 5 (Winter 1975/6) of *Musics*, the "impromental experivisation (*sic*) arts magazine" (this title remained on the masthead for the first two issues), Victor Schonfield, the promoter and journalist who had organised many inspiring free improv and contemporary classical gigs/concerts in the 60s, opined in a lengthy interview with Richard Leigh, who was one of the magazine's founders and editors: "The people coming up now don't have the tendency to hero-worship that someone like John Stevens has – I remember him lecturing an audience of mystified tourists at the Little

Theatre Club one evening." (Page 8.)

It's not clear whether Schonfield meant tourists in the literal or metaphorical sense. Richard Leigh, in turn, felt that "there's no one person that the newer players look up to, and whose approval means anything to them". (*Musics, op. cit.*, p.8.) This was highly unlikely, I would have thought, but this did add to the iconoclastic vibe. In retrospect, it's easy to see that improvising giants like Derek Bailey and Evan Parker, the Gen One founders of Incus Records, eventually filled these supposedly vacant positions (and most of the younger musicians, despite their alleged iconoclasm, *were* eventually very respectful towards the elders, despite Leigh and Schonfield's reservations), but these comments do reflect the feeling at that time that the contemporary free improvisation scene was somewhat rudderless and in need of direction.

The same could be said for the world of more mainstream modern jazz after the death of John Coltrane in 1967, and before the emergence of Wynton Marsalis *et al*, in the early 80s, as jazz's saviour and avatar incarnate. In fact, even in the hyper-trendy (at that point) *New Musical Express*'s (*NME*) quite comprehensive two-issue 'jazz-history-for-beginners' pullout, published in the summer of 1981 (*New Musical Express*, 1981), there was no mention of Marsalis at all (although the NY loft guys managed to get a considerable section all to themselves). This was approximately the time, from what I can gather, at which all the modernist efflorescence began to wilt in influence in the jazz world, and at which the neo-conservatives began to reify and dictate the canon of a much safer avant garde world.

To illustrate this, the great composer and multi-instrumentalist Sam Rivers "first made [the assertion]…in '78, one he repeated in interviews well into the 1990s; that the music of the 1970s was the culmination of the music of the 40s, 50s and 60s". (Bill Shoemaker, in the editorial of e-magazine *Point Of Departure*, Issue 57, December 2016.)

This brings us up to the notion that modernism had basically had its final flowering by 1980, and decreased in both popularity and influence thereafter. Shoemaker had, a few years earlier, suggested that by the late 70s most of the major innovators of the 60s had either passed over or somewhat reappraised their iconoclasm: "The passing of John Coltrane and Albert Ayler had left a vacuum, and precious few of the luminaries from the 60s were pointing the way ahead. Pharoah Sanders had developed into a pied piper of soporific two-chord tunes, Archie Shepp was consumed with recapitulating the tenor tradition [*In the Tradition* on Horo, for example, *author*]. And Sun Ra's Arkestra was increasingly reliant on Fletcher Henderson tunes." (*Point of Departure*, Issue 30, August 2010.)

Shoemaker's last accusation is perhaps best illustrated by Ra's 1980 recording *Sunrise in Different Dimensions*, which features numbers by Ellington, Monk, Tadd Dameron, Horace Henderson, Coleman Hawkins, Strayhorn, Noble Sissle and Jelly Roll Morton.

Oddly enough, Shoemaker's 'way ahead' seemed to invoke the very generation that was gradually fading forward into 'recapitulation'. It was finally given the name 'neo-conservatism' in the following decade.

Conflict or, more euphemistically, 'divergences', seem to have been in the air by the 1970s, which must have made the idea of a unifying leader seem so attractive. After all, there had always previously been hero-innovators in the music until now, even in free improvisation, hadn't there? English percussionist Roger Turner (born in 1946), in Antoine Prum's film *Taking the Dog for a Walk* (2015 DVD), speaks at length, and in even slightly disparaging terms (to these ears), about the First Generation and their mode of 'insect music' (a term that was originally coined by American bassist Kent Carter), and the need to move away from this model.

I will quote Turner at length, as his comments are an extemporaneous discourse (although his non-verbal communication is also telling) on the way that some of the Gen Two improvisers thought about the earlier pioneers (starts at 10:55 minutes into the film): "I was never a kind of student at the Little Theatre Club, doing my mental notes. I was not overwhelmed with knowledge about the so-called First Generation, as a brigade, you know…I was aware that there were differences, in any case, within the First Generation. I mean people were vying for their identities, you know, it felt all the time that everyone was intent on chiseling language and likes and dislikes, and it was very much an on-the-edge type feeling, there was not a…it was not a lovey-dovey kind of, we're-all-in-this-happy-family-together thing.

"I didn't give a monkey's about the first or second generation thing in improvisation, I don't think that it ever entered my head, that I had to do something different to these people…apart from which, some of them weren't much older than me, they just happened to have made a mark earlier in that world, but…[*exasperated pause*]… so be it…I was interested in playing, figuring it out on the terms that were immediate to me, not in the perspective of what someone else had done.

"Derek Bailey formed Company…because he saw the Second Generation were promiscuous in their interchanging of musical partners…it was this generation who were moving…the social activity and the in-and-out of each other's flats/bedsits, which also developed the music, those constraints that the Londoners had in their musical lives, bedsits with noise upstairs and the neighbours…[*mimics playing scratchy guitar*]… you know, your insect music…not much space, snare drum and that…and a small snare drum at that… guitar, violin."

This diatribe is conducted with an intense combination of exasperation and impatience, as if demonstrating that, even 40 years later, Turner was keen to both acknowledge and disconfirm the first generation's influence, which is an ambivalent stance not that unusual when looking at cross-generational relationships (even though, as Turner notes, he wasn't that much younger than most of Gen One).

Wire's then Editor-in-Chief, Tony Herrington, had this to say, in 2008, about Alterations, the second generation 'supergroup': "Crucially, the group formed at a time when improvised music's in-all-languages philosophy had hardened into a dogmatic vernacular form that was defined as much by what it didn't allow players to do or say." (*Wire*, No. 297, p.114.)

Dogma was something that Turner was presumably talking about as well, but I'm not sure how fair this is to the music's groundbreaking early free practitioners, and I'm not at all sure if I agree with the 'in-all-languages' conceit, but Herrington's observation about dogma is also reflected in Clive Bell's description of "scary outpourings of vitriol and the squealing of bruised egos" (originally in reference to the contents of the London Musicians Collective's December 1980 newsletter), an accusation that could be seen as being also characteristic of *Musics*, the genre's principal mouthpiece from April 1975 to November 1979 (in Bell's History of the LMC, *www.variant.org.uk*). It seems that positions were taken and accordingly held onto firmly, particularly around notions of what was permissible in terms of melody (not allowed, according to some), harmony (definitely none of that, thanks) and rhythm (no toe-tapping permitted). The cornerstones of western tonality, pitch and meter were things to be overcome, for some, in a Nietzschean struggle between the new modernity (which is itself a tautology, of course) and the forces of musical reaction represented by – well, most other forms, really.

The genial electro-acoustician and instrument maker Max Eastley, who was someone else at the centre of the London Musicians Collective/ *Musics* matrix, described, again in Antoine Prum's film, some of the rather inflexible attitudes that were around at the time (starts at around 73 minutes into the film): "There was a faction (in the LMC) that…at a meeting,…they'd say, 'I want to bring up a very crucial point…[*dramatic pause*]…someone played a tune last night'…other people, like Steve [*Beresford*] would deliberately play tunes, it was a point of contention in some ways…there was that sort of tension between different factions, which made it even more interesting, actually."

Beresford's later combo, if that's the right word, Alterations, *did* feature tunes, if of a ragged, improvisational nature, but this was, for some, far too much messing about with the holiest-of-holy precepts, that of the avoidance of traditional western tonality and harmony (and also that of African-derived rhythmic devices). The gradual reintroduction of these features into free improvisation marks one of the key features of Gen Two and its influence. To most people, however, this would seem to be the narcissistic tyranny of small differences writ large.

Also, to add to this picture, I want to quote the Birmingham-based improviser Dave Panton, who felt that he had also fallen foul of the more rigorous ideology of some of the 'purists': "I always had some difficulty with the notion of free improvisation as a style-specific concept, usually cited as being non-idiomatic, which by that definition is exclusive [some might say elitist, *author*] rather than inclusive, and therefore, for me, rather narrowly finite…I prefer to think of my idiosyncratic approach to be more about improvisatory freedom than a predetermined improvisatory style…This, at the time, was not, it seems, an acceptable attitude to adopt towards the music and, together with a couple of Self-Criticism articles in *Musics*, and what was perceived as a turning down of Derek Bailey's invitation for me to join a Company week, I once again came in for some censure, and so my association with free improvisation came to an end, until many years later, when attitudes had softened and broadened towards the diversity of approaches." (Panton, personal communication, 2016.)

Earlier in 2016, David Hepworth published his paean to the year 1971 called, appropriately enough, *1971*, and subtitled *Never a Dull Moment*, which must surely represent an offence under the Trades Description Act as that year, in actual fact, was full of such moments. Ah, the windscreen wipers of history! Another veteran pop/rock writer, Jon Savage, produced the same sort of retro-manic obeisance, published in 2015, with his book, which was called simply *1966* (no subtitle was thought necessary for this most eulogised of years).

The Stooges included tracks called, in turn, *1969* and *1970*, on their first two albums. Probably to come soon – a book on 'The Year of Revolution', otherwise known as 1968. My apologies if I have missed any music books that have been written specifically about this year: David Quantick's 2002 book, *Revolution: The Making of the Beatles' White Album*, does cover some of this territory, as do an inexhaustible supply of social-cultural analyses. Another mythopoeiac year that has been covered, to ever-diminishing returns, is 1967, which contained the 'First Summer of Love' (with 1987 being its 'slight return', occurring ten years after 1977, 'the Summer of Hate').

Even obscure pop-punkers The Record Players (revived very briefly on a *Messthetix* #1 compilation) recorded a single entitled '67, at a time (1978) when psychedelia was terminally unfashionable (a stance which, however, proved to be very brief, in retrospect).

The three sevens clash (1967, 1977, 1987)? It's that number seven again.

In the midst of all this, what did the 1970s years offer? Well, quite a lot, in actual fact: Glam, Pub-Rock, R&B, Punk, Post-Punk, New Wave, DIY Electronica, Roots Reggae and Dub, Disco, Industrial, Prog Folk, Prog Jazz, Jazz-Rock, Krautrock. An embarrassing wealth, in actual fact, and these were just off the top of my head. If one were so inclined, one could also include some of the genres that Tony Herrington mentions in his article on Alterations – Afrobeat, Loft Jazz, The Ocora and Lyrichord catalogues, Advanced Salsa (?), Funk, 'Absurdist Oblique Strategies' (i.e. Brian Eno + Robert Wyatt). (*Wire* No. 297, p.114.)

I'm sure that the reader gets the gist. These were vibrant years and the decade offered an even greater choice, and variety, than its more celebrated predecessor, which had its own fair share of banalities, perhaps best indicated by crooner Engelbert Humperdinck (his chosen stage name being as obscure a reference as Josef Holbrooke!) overtaking The Beatles' *Penny Lane/Strawberry Fields* (which has often been put forward as the best single of all time by list-makers) to the Number One spot in March 1967, with the backwards-looking, power-balled *Release Me (Let Me Go)*.

The 70s has always suffered from its own set of stereotypes, many created by the burgeoning nostalgia industry – 'prog rock' is usually mentioned with a retrospective sneer (ignoring the undoubted achievements of King Crimson and the early Pink Floyd, to take but two examples); similarly, 'fusion' (with the early work of Lifetime, Weather Report and the Mahavishnu Orchestra also conveniently forgotten) and disco (an immensely popular genre and eventually a very influential one, despite the 'disco sucks' propaganda purveyed by 'rockists' and homophobes, particularly in America). Punk culture was *partly* responsible for the proliferation, by some, of the negative stereotypes about disco and prog that abounded in the late 70s, and which promoted dichotomous thinking in general about popular music, and its various exfoliations.

Never had the tyranny of taste been as evident as when the concept of

'Year Zero' took hold (i.e. in and around 1977). Record collections were eviscerated and all evidence of heretical material quietly disposed of (only to re-emerge in the same collections, years later, often as expensive vinyl re-issues, by chastened middle-aged ex-punks, or punk sympathisers like myself). We re-bought albums that were felt to have been embarrassing or apostolic at the time, but which are now seen as essential aspects of the rock canon (another tyranny, that of lists).

The record companies appear to have had the last laugh, as they now recycle 40/50-year old material at 20-odd quid a pop, and it appears that vinyl is now outselling digital downloads for the first time (*Daily Telegraph*, December 6th, 2016), which is a 'tipping point', as 'someone in the industry' sagely opined.

Unfortunately, free improvisation classics do not tend to be on re-release schedules, unless the label is Emanem Records who have just put out, for example, the SME's 1967 *Withdrawal* in time for inclusion in *Wire*'s 2016 Top 50 Archival Releases (at Number 36). Into the perceived breach, at the time, stepped the free independent (freendies?) labels that were contemporaneous with the proliferation of the DIY/self-help philosophy that had become established by 1977. (See Chapter Six for more on this topic.)

In terms of the history of free improvisation, I would suggest that the initial print run of *Musics* (Spring 1975), or the first Company gig at The Purcell Room (May 1976), or the formation of the LMC (an unspecific time, somewhere in 1975/6), could all provide notional interfaces between the early and late 70s, for ease of exposition. After all, a lot happened in a very short period, as it tends to do in times of change, and some markers can be helpful. The 'hippie hangover' period (as predicted so mournfully by Danny the Dealer) and the later period of harder, more abrasive sounds (punk, industrial, disco), separated by the caesura of circa-1975/6, forms as convenient a temporal division as the pre- and post-*Revolver* (The Beatles' vinyl game-changer of 1966) does in 60s histories. These are all rather Procrustian beds, I am all too aware.

Or perhaps, as my wife opined when asked about this notional division between the 60s and the 70s, "it was when trousers went straight", which is as good a definition as any I've heard. Just have a look at Steve Beresford's loons on the inside cover of *Teatime* (Emanem 5009), as opposed to what he's wearing, a few years later, on the cover of *Company 6 + 7* (Incus CD07), and you'll see what she means.

THE WORLD AT LARGE 1973-1979

January 1st 1973 was an auspicious start to the period we are reviewing. It was the commencement of a cycle that has only begun to end recently, but was one that lasted 43 (and-a-half) years – a figure that is not even divisible by or a multiple of seven, so my usual 'pet' numerical trope can play no part here. On that fateful day, Great Britain joined the European Economic Community (EEC), known nowadays as the European Union (EU), a decision that was finally overturned, on June 23rd 2016, by a controversial referendum. It would have been hard to think of a more significant historical starting point for this book, at this particular point in time.

Taking a brief overview of these years, it is instructive, but also rather depressing, to consider how many of the serious problems that faced the world at large in 1973 still remain active today, like an unquiet volcano: the Middle East, Israel and Palestine, the malign influence of oil in these areas, especially with regards to the House of Saud, and its continuing economic and ecological dominance. At home, there was, in no particular order: the EEC, which was contentious even at the point of our joining it; the pressure to decrease public spending, especially following the huge wage rises in this sector over the years under scrutiny; housing problems; wealthy foreigners beginning to buy up sites in central London; our national debt; immigration and race relations – issues that were exacerbated by the influx of Ugandan Asians in late 1972 (just as Kenyan Asian immigrants had earlier flocked to this country, after the rise to power of Jomo Kenyatta in the 1960s), which was partly a result of the pursuance of the policy of 'Africanisation' in our former colonies. (Wheen, 1982, p.75.) The Empire Strikes Back, indeed.

Some seemingly intractable problems were addressed, if not 'solved', it should also be remembered – Watergate (although the USA now has a president who appears to be even more mercurial than Richard Nixon) and Vietnam (the great *cause célèbre* of the 60s), where the last American troops left on March 29th 1973; many civil rights issues in this country and in America were at least brought to the front of public consciousness, and practical legal interventions made to address these issues. These were achievements that were unspectacular but meaningful, over time, for millions of people. But other difficulties soon emerged from the many-headed hydra of world conflicts: the Iranian revolution and radical Islam by the late 70s; Cambodia/Kampuchea and the Killing Fields in SE Asia; increased sectarian conflict in northern Ireland culminating in the murder of Lord Mountbatten in 1979; American 'interventions' in Central America; the Winter of Discontent in England; and (a disaster in the eyes of some, a blessing in those of others) the beginning of Margaret Thatcher's many years in office, "perhaps the last Prime Minister who felt no need to hide her total indifference to contemporary popular culture". (Sandbrook, 2015, p.xxv.)

All in all, these were tumultuous and unsettled times (but, then again, aren't they all?).

I will just highlight a few of the significant events, both to show how distant, in some ways, these times seem, and yet how so many of its issues have fed through to our current era, and still remain germane to us all now. A brief year-by-year snapshot should suffice for this purpose:

1973

January: A young Harvard student called William Gates, and his friend Paul Allen, design a basic operating system for the first personal computer, the MITS Altair, which makes it on to the cover of that month's *Popular Electronics*. Their company, called Micro-Soft (*sic*), earns $16,005 by the end of the year. By the end of the century it was turning over $20 billion and Gates' dream of a personal computer in each household is now not as hubristic as it once seemed.

January 22nd: The justices of the US Supreme Court give judgement in *Roe v Wade*, striking down nearly every anti-abortion statute in the land. The Court would no doubt be perturbed if it knew that the issue would subsequently still be fought over four decades down the line and, under

President Donald Trump (November 2016), seem to be again under significant threat.

February 1st: In a sign of things to come, women are allowed into the formerly male-only playpen/club of the London Stock Exchange for the first time.

August 27th: The Saudi Arabian government announce cuts in US oil supplies to force a change in America's attitude towards Israel (which, under Trump, promises to be even more recalcitrant). On December 23rd, Iran's oil producers doubled the price of the product. On the fifth of that month, our government imposed a 50 mph speed limit to save fuel, a desperate intervention, which it repeated in March of the following year.

December 14th: Ugandan dictator and sit-down comedian Idi Amin starts a 'Save Great Britain' fund to help Britain out of its economic woes. An indication, for many, if it were needed, of this country's decline and humiliation, and which some saw, probably with some justification, as a revengeful gesture for our colonial exploitations of Africa over the centuries.

December: The American Psychiatric Association (which is generally more conservative than their English equivalent, the Royal College of Psychiatrists) announces that it will no longer classify homosexuality as a mental illness and removes it from their lexicon, the *Diagnostic and Statistical Manual* (DSM) – the American version of our *International Classification of Disorders* (ICD). A significant portion of the American public, however, appear to remain unconvinced.

▶ Ian Carr's *Music Outside* is published in this year, a book that, for the first time, prominently features free improvisation musicians, i.e. John Stevens, Trevor Watts and Evan Parker, in its pages, as well as other modernist players. It will still be another 20 years or so before further significant literature is published that features English free improv to any extent (and that will be Derek Bailey's influential title about the nature and practice of the music).

▶ Quote of the Year: "There will be no whitewash at the White House." (Richard Milhouse Nixon, April 30th.) Another budding comic tells his best joke.

1974

January 6th: A professional football match is cancelled, for the first time, due to power cuts, on a Saturday – in those days the traditional match day.

March 6th: A miners' strike ends with a 35% pay increase. On September 17th, the nurses get rises of up to 58%. As an ex-nurse, this seems incredible to me now. Nurses haven't received any significant pay rises in the current era for the past ten years, with wages perpetually frozen through 'austerity measures'.

March 7th: In Ethiopia, there is the first ever general strike against the rule of Haile Selassie, seen in his own country by many as an imperialist stooge. This is in striking counterpoint to the veneration with which he was held by the Wailers *et al* in Jamaica, at exactly the same time, in roots reggae lore, where he was seen as a demi-deity.

July 11th: The first big property deal is conducted with wealthy Arabs in Central London. On June 21st 1976, two buy The Dorchester Hotel. This, together with Amin's contemptuous gesture from the previous year, convinces many that Britain is slipping in the world power stakes ('going to the dogs', in less euphemistic terms), and perhaps lays the ground for the UKIP-type prejudices of today, the 'we want our country and our sovereignty back' type of retrospective idealisation of – when, exactly?

August 8th: Nixon resigns, as the whitewash fails miserably to stick to the wall.

September 6th: White Paper announces plans to outlaw sexual discrimination in the UK. Forty two years later, we seem to have regressed and misogynistic trolling on the internet, and in the workplace, is rife; often in the world of music, sad to say.

September 12th: Selassie-I, the 'Lion of Judah', is overthrown by army officers, just as the Wailers begin to hit their popular peak with *Natty Dread* and *Live at the Lyceum*. Little protest is heard from Notting Hill *trustafarians,* a burgeoning social stereotype of the time. This is a compound word to describe affluent white westerners taken with the rebellious image of rasta, many of whom lived in and around this bohemian area of London W11 (and many of whom were enabled by their generous trust funds, hence the name). All the political, and very violent, background of Jamaican politics, although easily available to those who wanted to hear about it, was conveniently forgotten by most *trustafarians*, who continued to gain counter-cultural currency from their 'look', but who conveniently ignored the truly dire Jamaican political situation in the murderous elections on the island in 1976 and 1980.

October 1st: The first 'Maccy D's' opens (in South London).

1975

January 9th: Pay rises of up to 74% announced for some 14,000 hospital workers (was this the same planet that we now live on?).

February 4th: Margaret Thatcher takes over from Edward Heath as Conservative Party leader, but not everyone in her party is happy with this, despite the party's later presentation of her unambiguously immense popularity and influence. Her gender worries some Tory grandees.

April 3rd: The first call on a handheld mobile phone is made in New York City by its inventor, Martin Cooper of Motorola, apparently inspired by Star Trek's Captain Kirk and his portable 'communicator'. Forty years later, the mobile is one of the most unavoidable facts of modern living.

July 24th: Unemployment reaches nearly 1.25 million, the highest since March 1940. 'Labour isn't working', as Charles Saatchi and his ad company will later famously assert (even though, ironically, the unemployment figures proceeded to hypertrophy, over the 80s years of the Conservative beady eyed watch). One thing that doesn't change over the years is the specious 'post-truth' of politicians, reliable as tomorrow's sunrise.

November 7th: Great Britain asks the IMF for £1000 million, to add to the nation's humiliation. It's a long way from 1965/6 and little is now 'swinging'. More like flopping.

▶ Quote of the year, from the now-forgotten media commentator Marshall McLuhan: "Television brought the brutality of war into the comfort of the living room. Vietnam was lost in the living rooms of America, not on the battlefields of Vietnam."

This is one quote that has only become more telling, in these days of the internet and social media. Who then could have predicted ISIS, 'the digital caliphate'? (Atwan, 2015.) McLuhan himself, perhaps? Or Alvin Toffler (another best-selling author, of 1970s *Future Shock*, who died in 2016 having lived long enough to see several aspects of his post-industrial vision realised)?

1976

February 18th: The Race Relations Bill is published. This was a significant step for civilised values, although overt racism appears to be on the increase. The ultra-right National Front start to gain some prominence at this time.

April 1st: (April Fool's Day) Steve Jobs and Steve Wozniac unveil the Apple 1 computer.

April 5th: 'Sunny Jim' Callaghan becomes Prime Minister, after 60s political icon Harold Wilson resigns, defeating Michael Foot (who was later to become the last truly left-wing Labour leader, before Jeremy Corbyn).

June 9th: Metropolitan Police chief Robert Marks points out the force's poor relations with black youth, which were prescient remarks given the series of racially related riots that pervaded England just a few years later, in 1981. Race relations still remain one of the most topical and serious problems of the present day, both here and in America. There are, of course, always newer UK minorities to demonise, which is a consistent feature of our society over the last several hundred years. The most recent serious riots on these shores, in 2011, were sparked by the police shooting of a mixed-race man.

1977

January 3rd: The IMF approves a £2300 million loan to Britain to halt the fall in the value of sterling.

July 11th: *Gay News* is, ludicrously, found guilty of blasphemy and fined £1000. The Establishment was far from finished in its attacks on the differently (or difficultly?)-orientated. This is one area of social policy where progress does seem to have been made since, however. Homosexuality had only recently been made legal (in 1967) and was still part of the British psychiatric lexicon, despite some progress in this area, here and in America. It was still diagnosed as a (curable) illness on these shores. Homosexuality was only eventually removed from the ICD in 1992. Lesbianism had never been debated over in Parliament, anecdotally because Queen Victoria insisted that such a thing could not possibly exist, so was not worth being made the subject of legislation. (Wheen, 1982, p.109.) So, never underestimate a firmly held Royal opinion. It can still have consequences, even now.

July 12th: The average London house price is £16,731. Nowadays (August 2016) it is £633,746, which is around a 400% rise. This was great news for estate agents, landlords and property developers, but hardly anyone else, and the situation had reached critical mass by 2016.

August 28th: The Notting Hill Carnival of this year is marked by violence and rioting, which The Clash reflected on their single, *White Riot* (the much misunderstood *"White Riot, White Riot, White Riot…a riot of my own"*). Scritti Politti produced a more rarified number on their first EP, called *28/08/78*, which included a radio sample of similar disturbances two years later, played back over a jagged guitar undertow of considerable anxious intensity (and which proved to be an influential blueprint for countless later post-punk scratchy soundscapes).

▶ The 'Battle of Lewisham', two weeks earlier, was another notorious racially orientated skirmish that became a mythical London encounter between two visions of England. These differing visions/versions of what constitutes 'England' continue to be fought over even today, when post-referendum aggressive attacks on minorities appear to have increased.

November 3rd: Industrial action blacks out the state opening of Parliament. "There may be trouble ahead…" This was the beginning of the end of the pre-Thatcher era, and of consensus politics generally. Previously, party rhetoric had disguised surprisingly similar cross-party agreement as to the role and purpose of government, something that is next to impossible to imagine now.

▶ Quote of the year, this time from Paul McCartney: "You can't reheat a soufflé."

This statement was made absolutely indisputable when John Lennon was killed by Mark Chapman on December 8th 1980, an unambiguous end not only to the 60s but to the 70s as well, and another caesura of huge significance.

1978

January 30th: Margaret Thatcher famously claims that many British people fear being "swamped by people with a different culture", a cry oft-repeated by the political right (and others) ever since, up to and including Nigel Farage *et al*.

February 13th: A seemingly minor event, but Anna Ford is also 'sworn in', as it were – as ITN's first female broadcaster. A small step, but a step nevertheless. In the word of *avant* music, the Feminist Improvisers Group and female punk musicians were also making similarly important small steps.

March 21st: In Salisbury (an aptly colonial name), absolute white rule finally ends as Rhodesia's first three black ministers are sworn in, thus beginning the process of bringing to an end decades of oppression, not, unfortunately, without much violence in the ensuing years. On May 29th the following year, Abel Muzorewa became Rhodesia's first Prime Minister (it is renamed Zimbabwe on August 26th of that year).

1979

January 16th: The Shah flees the newly radicalised Iran. There were echoes of Ethiopia here.

January 22nd: A 24-hour public employers strike hits hospitals and schools.

March 1st: The Ayatollah Khomeini, a new powerful foreign interloper for the west to fret about, says that there is no place for democracy in Iran (a position that was honest, it has to be said). The western powers found this difficult to accept as they tried, increasingly aggressively, to impose that very thing across the Middle East up to, and including, our present time. On July 23rd, Khomeini bans music saying it corrupts youth (perceptive cove, that man with the beard). Turning the clock back 1,500 years seemed to become the order of the day in Iran and elsewhere, which was, unfortunately, beyond parody for women who had to endure the strictures and judgments involved in this chronological rewind of history.

May 4th: Margaret Thatcher becomes Prime Minister and goes on to hold the position until 1991, thus becoming the longest serving PM of the

20th century, incredible though it might seem.

▶ The public employees strikes also eventually failed to sustain their momentum or objective, and this marked the beginning of government retrenchment: on May 15th, Thatcher announced lower taxes/lower public spending/cuts on union powers, and the fight began in earnest, if only slowly at the beginning stages. On July 23rd, the cabinet agreed to public spending cuts of £4000 million. Dark days were ahead.

September 14th: Plans are announced to revitalise Docklands in East London, portrayed cinematically in the film *The Long Good Friday*. We live with the results today.

December 20th: A Housing Bill obliges councils to sell their houses to tenants who want to buy them, a decision that still haunts us today like an unquiet spirit. It could be suggested that the gradually spiraling costs of accommodation in the capital, especially in areas like Soho, inexorably led to the unavailability of affordable accommodation to 'creative types' (including musicians) who had traditionally flocked there, over the post-war years, to establish themselves. (My thanks to John Jack, a Soho resident for over 50 years, for pointing out this particular aspect of what has become a crisis in modern housing.) This gradually led to an impoverishment of musical 'communities' and a diaspora of creative talent. Now the East End of London, ineluctably, suffers the same fate. There appears to be no end in sight for the (hopefully unsustainable) rise in both unaffordable rented and private property, which is one of the few boom areas in the British economy, sadly.

Information collected from the Longman Chronicle of the Twentieth Century (1988)

THE MUSICAL WORLD AT LARGE 1973-1979

The events described above formed a backdrop for very different types of musical expression, for example: naturalism/realism versus escapism/fantasy, a dichotomy which emerged over the years of 1973-9. Punk rock is a good example of the former, however bogus it eventually proved to be, and disco/funk/glam of the latter. Some of it (post-punk, roots reggae) could, however, be quite po-faced and serious (with Public

Image Limited, which sought to combine the two sub-genres, perhaps being the best example of this particular strain and of any number of dread apocalyptic-ians).

Free Improvisation at the time tried, in its own unique way, to include both camps, and the Second Generation, in particular, made a point of trying to inject some post-modern humour into the mix. David Bowie and Roxy Music could arguably be said to have started PoMo in popular music, in and around 1972, an approach which punk/post-punk maintained, in its high/low culture *smorgasbord*. However much some free improvisation purists might complain about the comparison, iconoclastic drollery did also have its place in free improv.

The rock critic Paul Du Noyer, at his journalistic peak in the late 1970s *New Musical Express,* the post-punk bible, claimed that punk "dramatically widened the criteria of acceptability" in terms of its "invigorating and liberating effects upon music". (Du Noyer, 2009, p.213.) This could include, presumably, *mutatis mutandis,* what became permissible in the world of free improvisation around this time (and which could be seen as the 'impurities' alluded to by Steve Beresford in his quote in the foreword of this book).

It is very instructive, in this context, to approach a latter-day product, such as the four-LP box set called *Just Not Cricket!*, which is one of the most lavish latter-day constructs, featuring the contents of a festival celebrating British creativity from October 6-8 2011. There is also a two-CD overview, one of which is *Taking the Dog for a Walk*, the film directed by Antoine Prum, and the other consisting of interviews conducted by Tony Bevan and Stewart Lee, with various improvisers.

This very worthy vinyl doorstop features many great modern improvisers, too many to enumerate here. But, apart from the baffling exclusion of Evan Parker (after all, two of his true peers, Eddie Prevost and Trevor Watts, were here, present and very much correct), there were only a few Gen Two players (although there were several from Gen Three, if I may be so bold as to suggest). No David Toop, no John Russell, no Terry Day (in performance, at least). Now, I am obviously aware that there might be myriad reasons, of which I have no cognisance, as to why these guys were not there (some are featured in passing, it must be said). But it seems at least rather questionable that none of the most famous Gen Two *provocateurs* were present at interview in the CD film (apart from Steve Beresford and Max Eastley). To be blunt, it seems that many of the players at that event represented the fruits of the Free Jazz mainstream, rather than the Free Improvisation tributary, which is fine as far as this particular Free Jazz fan goes. But it does, however, pose the question of where did the Gen Two puckishness go? It touched free improv briefly in our time frame of 1973-9, but it clearly outstayed its welcome, and isn't really that evident in Prum's film, apart from a clip of The Promenaders in action.

Let's go back a bit

The late 1960s 'underground'/'progressive' scene (in rock music, as it gradually came to be called) may have facilitated the opening of a wormhole for free improvisation's initial pseudo-acceptance by the English culture police, in a time where 'weird' music was welcomed by a few adventurous souls within the recording industry. It was almost certainly more accepted and promoted than it would have been at any other time, and it could be said with some truth, that it was indeed a 'product of its time'. An 'atmosphere', 'ambience', call it what you will, was created in these years, in business terms, and the long-term effect was a general opening of the mind to experimental musical forms (as one small example, see the creation of 'Free Improvisation' as a genre in itself in CD classification).

Another earthbound example of this liberalisation: the English pub gave free improvisation small and grudging, yet tangible, places to perform, just as it did later with the its own 'pub rock/R&B' scene of the mid 70s. As did the further education circuit of colleges and universities. The Jam, bizarrely, played upstairs at Ronnie's, as had many free jazz configurations, through the Musicians Cooperative principally, over the early years. Similarly, the 100 Club was an early incubator of punk, as was The Roundhouse (where The Ramones played their first gig on these shores 40 years ago) and the famous Marquee.

All of these venues had given room to free improvisers, often grudgingly, as had other 'psychedelic dungeons' (as defined by Frank Zappa in 1967) of the time – even if Amalgam were once paid NOT to play a second set by the management of the Speakeasy, according to Trevor Watts. (Personal communication, 2014.) According to later member John Tilbury, AMM had the complementary experience, when they were initially not paid by The Roundhouse (where they shared a bill with Geno Washington, a very popular live act on the soul circuit at the time, eclecticism in action) because they were seen/heard by the promoters to be only 'tuning up'. (Tilbury, 2008, p.327.) An interesting musico-philosophical point, perhaps, but it didn't pay the bills, unfortunately. Nor was someone like John Cage available to referee.

The 1970s was perhaps the last gasp of modernism in jazz, as it was in rock. Almost everything subsequent to these years can be described as 'revivalism' of some kind or another. Wynton Marsalis and Stanley Crouch in jazz, and the various mod/rockabilly/powerpop/ska/post-rock/grunge *et al* retro movements in rock were aspects of the same phenomenon, i.e. life's backward glance. Some sub-genres and key individuals/groups could be said to be Janus-faced, looking both backwards and forwards (Jazz-Rock fusion, Progressive Folk, Roxy Music, David Bowie), but generally the idea of music progressing ineluctably forward in a linear fashion slowly died out over the decade.

I propose now to itemise some key events that mark the head and the foot, or beginning and end, of my fanciful temporal Procrustean bed, and which mark its boundaries and limits:

The head (1972/3-1976)

▶ Music critic Simon Reynolds put forward a fairly common view about 1973:

"The critical year – regarded by some cultural historians as when the 60s really ended – was 1973." (Reynolds, 2016, p.410.)

Reynolds also cited the influential book *Rock Dreams*, by writer Nik Cohn and artist Guy Peellaert (the latter went on to paint the sleeves of Bowie's *Diamond Dogs* and the Stones' *It's Only Rock'n'Roll*), which emerged in that year, as one of the first products of what we would now call 'retro', as a counterpoint to the contemporary loss of faith in the idea of linear progress or, at the very least, an apprehension of what the future had in store.

▶ March 1972's *Microphone* (Number 2) features a blunt statement from journalist Michael Walters (the main financial clout behind Incus Records at its beginning): "By rights, the new music ought to have starved to death years ago, simply because few of those who make it have ever earned what anyone else would consider a living wage." (Page 2.) He reserved his particular ire for the people who "manage to win a fatter living writing and talking about the music and the musicians than the real creators themselves can hope to make".

It would be presumptuous to ignore this perspective, as lack of money and opportunity forms a real backdrop to this story, and explains quite a lot of the inter-group conflict and defensiveness that also emerges from any examination of the period. And also its suspicion, at times, of outsiders. It also suggests a low mood within the free culture at that point in time.

▶ The Musicians Cooperative organise a Free Improvisation Festival in early 1972 (overleaf), to celebrate its first birthday, at various London venues – a sort of coming-of-age celebration, perhaps.

▶ Released in 1973 as *Incus Taps* (eventually rereleased on Organ of Corti in vinyl), Derek Bailey's second set of solo guitar recordings, released originally as a series of three 3" open-reel tapes, represents the first of several groundbreaking solo recordings that established him as, almost certainly, the most influential free musician of the period. It also suggests that Incus Records was prepared to be adventurous in the presentation of its product.

▶ Gen Two musicians start to undertake regular gigs at the Little Theatre Club. A very early recording appeared on *Teatime*, Track 12 (Incus 15), an improvisation by John Russell (guitar) and Dave Solomon (percussion) from late 1973. *Balance* (Incus 11), by several of the younger musicians, is also recorded and released sometime in 1973.

▶ Emanem Records, the brainchild of Martin Davidson and his wife, Madelaine, is formed in 1974. It eventually became the most thorough repository of recorded English Free Improvisation that exists, both past

incus records
87 Third Cross Road
Twickenham, Middlesex.
Phone: 01-898 4095

Compatible Recording And Publishing ltd

Incus 1	"Topography of the Lungs"	Parker, Bailey, Bennink.
Incus 2	Derek Bailey Solo Guitar	
Incus 3/4	ISKRA 1903 Rutherford, Bailey, Guy.	
Incus 5	"Urban Collective Calls" Parker/Lytton	
Incus 6/7	"Ode" London Jazz Composers Orchestra	
Incus 8	Tony Oxley Solo Percussion (in preperation)	
Incus 9	Han Bennink & Derek Bailey	
Incus EP1	"AMM at the Roundhouse" Care/Prevost	

European & American imports (P.M.P., I.C.P., JCOA, ETC.)
A selection of records is on sale at the ticket office.

MUSICIANS' CO-OPERATIVE

JANUARY 20th, 21st, 22nd

international festival of improvised music

arranged with financial assistance from the Arts Council of GB & the German Institute.

The programme for the first International Festival of Improvised Music, held in London and organised by The Musicians Collective, in early 1974, which was this author's first exposure to this form of music

MUSICIANS CO-OPERATIVE

(extracts from 'Draft of Proposed Manifesto/Brochure 1973)

Formed in 1970

to change the balance of emphasis in musical programming in London

to assist and preserve the rights of the Improvising Musician

Since then

an established feature of the London Scene

Now

looking to expand its activities to benefit the whole sphere of contemporary spontaneous music

The future

ability to create and maintain itself administrative umbrella

growing membership
full freedom and opportunity

to further their musical aims

THE MEMBERS

active in
Improvisation

their concern for the spontaneous
far wide of
existing musical catagories

EVAN PARKER - reeds (b. 1944)

plays in duo with Paul Lytton and Alex Schlippenbach quartet

has worked with many SME, Music Improvisation Company, Instant Composers Pool, Chris McGregor

other activities include Incus Records, and Prototype for Improvisers Orchestra

PAUL LYTTON - percussion (b. 1947)

plays in duo with Evan Parker

outside of music?
"I repair musicians teeth - what a bore!"

HOWARD RILEY - piano (b. thirty years ago in Yorkshire)

pianist and composer with his own trio also with the London Jazz Composers Orchestra

has studied in Wales, USA and England, has three Masters Degrees in Music

a professor at the Guildhall School of Music and Drama

"Any alteration in the modes of music is always
followed by alteration in the most fundamental
laws of the state."

Plato - The Republic

... .

SUNDAY 20th January   RONNIE SCOTT'S

AMM with Strings
  Lou Gare   tenor saxophone
  Eddie Prevost   drums
  Marcio Matos   double bass
  Marc Meggido   double bass

FRANK PERRY
  "...alone yet not alone"
                     solo percussion

PETER BROTZMANN TRIO
  Peter Brotzmann   saxes
  Albert Mangelsdorff trombone
  Fred Van Hove   piano

MONDAY 21st January   COLLEGIATE THEATRE

ISKRA
  Paul Rutherford   trombone
  Derek Bailey   guitar
  Barry Guy   double bass
  with Liz Grigsby and Les Carter

ALEX SCHLIPPENBACH/PETER KOWALD QUARTET
  Alex Schlippenbach piano
  Peter Kowald   bass
  Paul Lovens   drums
  Evan Parker   reeds

HOWARD RILEY TRIO
  Howard Riley   piano
  Barry Guy   bass
  Tony Oxley   percussion

TUESDAY 22nd January   COLLEGIATE THEATRE

EVAN PARKER/PAUL LYTTON DUO
  Evan Parker   reeds
  Paul Lytton   percussion

DEREK BAILEY
                     solo   guitar

PETER BROTZMANN TRIO
  Peter Brotzmann   saxes
  Albert Mangelsdorff trombone
  Fred Van Hove   piano

IMPROVISERS ORCHESTRA
  Musicians Co-op & Friends

BARRY GUY - bassist/composer (b. London 1947)

  plays with Iskra and Howard Riley Trio

                also with Tony Oxley group
  and several contemporary music ensembles

              formed the
  London Jazz Composers Orchestra in 1969

              is principle bass of
  Monteverdi Orchestra, Richard Hickox Orchestra,
  Orchestra of St John's Smith Square and the
  Raglan Chamber Players

              professor of double bass at
  Guildhall School of Music

DEREK BAILEY - guitar (b. ?)

  plays solo and with Iskra

  "Once in khakhi suits,
  Gee, we looked swell,
  Full of that Yankie-diddle-dum.
  Half a million boots went slogging to Hell;
  I was the kid with the drum.

  Say, don't you remember,
  They called me Al.
  It was Al all the time.
  Say, don't you remember,
  I'm your pal.
  Buddy, can you spare a dime?"

PAUL RUTHERFORD - trombone (b. 29th. Feb. 1940, a leap year baby)

  main concern is Iskra, but also plays with
  London Jazz Composers Orchestra

              has worked with
  Mike Westbrook, Tony Oxley, New Jazz Orchestra,
  and extensively throughout Europe.

              other interests
  "...likes his pint of beer like the next man."

FRANK E PERRY - percussion (b. 1948 in favourable circumstances)

  works " alone yet not alone", also plays in
  Ovary Lodge with Keith Tippett, and in Balance

  "....at 16 became interested in
  music as a logical extension of finding
  'I AM who AM I'

              enjoys working with trees and
  metals in the creative construction of Aquarian form

EDDIE PREVOST - drums (b. 1942)

  plays in AMM

              committed to music in which
  improvisation is the primary process
  has produced improvisation 'frameworks' for
  large ensembles, 'Spirals' and 'Silver Pyramid'
              has performed lectured and
  taught in many countries including USA & Canada

LOU GARE - tenor saxophone (b. 1939)

  plays in AMM, committed to improvisation since
  the inception of AMM in 1965

              but has worked on graphic
  and verbal scores with Cardew, Wolff and Prevost

and present. In particular, it recorded very early Free Music, without which our understanding of the genre at that point would be severely diminished. The Emanem label will be discussed more fully later on in this book.

▶ Evan Parker's *Solo Saxophone* appears in 1975, the first of the family of a dozen or so such recordings. Parker's solo endeavours start at this point, and these represent Derek Bailey's only serious contender for the most exhaustive of all early solo improvised English free music, in recorded form at least.

▶ In January 1974, the first International Festival of Improvised Music is held in London, again organised by the Musicians Cooperative, and is, coincidentally, my first live exposure to the form.

▶ *Musics* first edition is published in 1975 and will be a thread through this narrative, until its demise in 1979. It is invaluable for its presentation of the issues that preoccupied musicians and listeners throughout these years.

▶ Both Company, the ever-changing troupe organised by Derek Bailey, and the London Musicians Collective (LMC), the informal 'replacement' of the Musicians Cooperative, form in 1976 and are concrete examples of the music's long-term intent. Company formally ended with Bailey's death in 2005, and his biographer Ben Watson (2004) has the last Company week as being in November 2002 at New York's Tonic club. The LMC wrapped up in 2008, so both ventures had proved themselves to be in it for the long haul.

The Foot (1979–1980)

▶ Neutron Records (a Sheffield concern) produces a 4-track single called *1980: The First 15 Minutes,* a title that is a smart, self-conscious comment on the expectations that the new decade brought with it. It was a post-punk thing (from what I remember, the first 1980 edition of the *NME* featured Jayne Casey from Liverpool band Pink Military on its cover – the fairly unknown face of a fairly unknown group). One of the bands on the Neutron EP, Vice Versa, became the pop-tastic ABC, and reaped considerable commercial success very shortly afterwards.

That was the story of much of the rock avant garde at the cusp of these decades: some previously bold experimental bands mixed and matched various forms of dance music (The Human League and Cabaret Voltaire being the most obvious examples), some just went for what they called a 'deconstructed' pop, i.e. pop with slightly oblique and self-consciously 'ironic' lyrics, *vide* Scritti Politti and ABC. What jazz got, in this country, at least, was 'The Jazz Revival', when contemporary hipsters began dancing to Blue Note classics (and non-classics) and Art Blakey (born 1919) became a septuagenarian dance floor magus. And Rip, Rig & Panic, an unusual dada-esque funk/free jazz outfit based in Bristol. The move towards 'danceable', i.e. more easily marketable, music was palpable throughout 1980 and 1981.

▶ The New York Loft Jazz 'movement', one of the great Free Jazz independent scenes in 70s America, along with the Association for the Advancement of Creative Musicians in Chicago (AACM) and the Black Arts Group of St. Louis (BAG), is a spent force by the end of the decade. (Heller, 2016.) One of its most stellar performers, David Murray, was taken under the wing of Stanley Crouch, which proved to be a most symbolic emasculation of that particular movement. Murray soon concerned himself with releasing a welter of 'in the tradition' material (one every week, it seemed at the time), although his Octet of the early 80s does remain sensational, and their recordings remain an essential document of the small group modern jazz scene of those years, along with Henry Threadgill's Sextett.

▶ In the notes accompanying the punk/new wave retrospective, *Hey Ho! Let's Go!* (which was the rallying cry of The Ramones), Pete Gardiner explains why the set concludes at the end of 1979: "At the end of 1979, a second wave of British and American punk was on its way and we were also witnessing the first releases of many significant post-punk acts...on top of this, ska was the first significant musical movement since punk, and took much of its influence and audience from the events of the past three years. It therefore seemed a perfect point to draw the line."

▶ It is worth mentioning, at this point, the genre-busting sound of Ornette Coleman disciple, electric guitarist James 'Blood' Ulmer's recordings of January 1980, *Are You Glad To Be In America?* This was initially lumbered with the label of 'jazz-punk', which was a ludicrously bathetic title given the musical 'chops' of the musicians involved. But this recording, which was released on these shores by the English post-punk label of choice, Rough Trade Records, gave further indication of the barrier-cruising *fin de siècle* mood of the time.

▶ This atmosphere seems to have established itself by December 1979/January 1980. In particular, ska is *the* most retrogressive style of the time (although The Specials manage to infuse it with a quotidian English urban feel), and it is accompanied with the similarly backwards-looking micro-phenomena of mod (through the influence of the hugely popular The Jam, in particular) and rockabilly (stand up The Stray Cats, at least for a very brief round of applause). The so-called 'powerpop' non-event was also an attempt to cash in with another anachronous set of moves (Memphis 'cult' trio Big Star became the name to drop in connection with this genre, not that it did them any good in the long term popularity stakes).

▶ *Musics* magazine eventually tanks in November 1979, with some recriminations and bad feeling, but it gets its own chapter later on in this book, so I'll save it all for those pages.

▶ On a more positive note, Matchless Records forms, under the *aegis* of AMM's Eddie Prevost, a label and imprint that was to produce many important free improvisation 'products' over the next 35 years, and which continues to this day. Prevost has also written several important books on the theory of free improvisation, if that's your bag.

All this conceptual baggage leaves 1976 as the interregnum, the pivotal point that separates the two separate periods of 70s English free improvisation.

As highlighted in the brief historical references above, it is clear that the Oil Crisis in the Middle East caused Britain to go into 999 *modus* on many occasions due to the massive hike in OPEC prices – petrol rationing, speed limits, power cuts, all resulted from the displeasure of the Arab states. Furthermore, 1973 proved to be a very difficult and b(p)athetic year for British jazz. (Wickes, 1999, p.290.) Many creative musicians moved away from the experimental scene because of its sheer financial instability. There were no AACMs, BAGs or lofts to fall back on for support, emotional or financial, except for the tiny Musicians Cooperative, which had a limited membership. Many had families and partners who needed more security than could be provided by the occasional pub gig and whip-round. The 'alternative' media had lost interest as there were easier genres, such as prog rock and heavy metal/hard rock, to promote as the 'next big thing'.

However, it is worthwhile remembering that the 70s still had a reasonably healthy avant garde, even if English free improvisation became somewhat fractured and indeterminate. In America, they had, as already mentioned, the AACM, BAG, the NY Loft scene, plus Anthony Braxton's many and various projects, those of Roscoe Mitchell, Ornette and Harmolodics, Henry Threadgill and Air, William Parker, the Lower East Side musical mafia, Cecil Taylor, etc, etc. The 70s were the last time that the avant garde got a fair shot at inclusion in jazz history 'trees', hence the importance of this period. By the early 80s, the neo-classicists had moved in. As Eric Nisensen said: "Neo-classicist hard bop is very similar to rock in that, despite having the outer trappings of free expression, it is actually a very limited and conservative form of music." (Nisensen, 1997, p.231.) Fusion had paved the way for this revival, in being hip (at the time) but not especially challenging.

In England, of course, as has been already pointed out, we had the 80s 'Jazz Revival', which further lionised hard bop as *the* modern jazz of choice. You could even dance to it, supposedly. Anybody remember the Tommy Chase Quartet? Wynton Marsalis and Stanley Crouch would have approved of both Tommy's music and his band's dark-suited attire (clothing being, of course, an important signifier of intent). It signified that he was a 'serious' modernist', unlike the *dilettantes* who infested the avant garde, the scruffy buggers who didn't know their Armani from their Arnolfini.

One of the recurring themes within Free Music is that of underwhelming funding and publicity. Valiant attempts were made to create musician-run organisations in English free improvisation – the Musicians Cooperative

(MC), the London Musicians Collective (LMC) and many regional organisations (Chapter Seven) – and in 1979, Actuel Music, which was set up by subsequent *Wire* founder Anthony Wood, to promote improvised music and to organise festivals and concerts (it ceased operations in the mid 80s). The 'official' organ for jazz musicians and enthusiasts was meant to be the Jazz Centre Society (the 'straight' alternative to the MC and LMC), formed in 1968, funded by the Arts Council, but it was apparently never particularly efficient at addressing or meeting the needs of free improvisers. (A good reasonably contemporary account of these funding issues is contained in an article by Brian Priestley in *Wire* 14, 1984, pp.38-9.)

Steve Beresford sent this excoriating letter to a LMC meeting in October 1980, a sad reflection on how problematic group relations had become in the world of English free improvisation by 1979: "The dynamics of the current magazine meetings depend more on pointed silences, emotional blackmail, mumbled asides and semi-sneers, than on direct statements. The *Musics* collective is frightened of growth, frightened of taking and using power. There is no sense of history, of where the music is from and why people play it. The collective is a morass of impersonality. We trivialise each other's contributions." (Bell, *op. cit.*)

This sounds very much like adolescent behaviour, and might fit in with the earlier allusions to Erik Erikson's stages: Silences, emotional blackmail, mumbled asides and sneers...no sense of history...

Those of us who have adult children will be familiar with this litany for sure, all of it part of the adolescent *armamentarium.* These are also the symptoms of demoralisation, as much as anything more abstract.

The popular strains of this end-of-decade period were jazz-lite: jazz-rock fusion; ambient; Wyndham Hill/New Age; CTI; jazz-funk.

The most serious and influential new jazz label of the 70s, ECM Records, run by producer and bassist Manfred Eicher, reintroduced and reinforced the creative importance of acoustic chamber jazz. But it also featured, at least in its early years, important free improvisation LPs, as well as significant recordings of the African-American diaspora. These recordings were criticised in some quarters for their 'iciness' and lack of affect, although this might have just been a reaction to Eicher's particularly exacting sound standards, which were the opposite of 'low fi'. He apparently added echo to what seems to have been a perfectly well-recorded live gig at the LTC by Bailey and Holland in 1971 (ECM 1013), for example, an early indication of a determination to get 'his' sound right. My own particular listening memories of the early/mid 70s contain a considerable amount of ECM material, which I found to be among the more exciting jazz records of the era, but also (by osmosis, mostly) of an equally considerable (and mostly unwanted) exposure to the likes of Grover Washington (*Mister Magic* was huge in my circle of friends), Tom Scott & the LA Express (*Tom Cat*), Larry Carlton (including his peerless work with Joni Mitchell at the time), Bob James (*Three*, in particular), the (Jazz) Crusaders (culminating in the massively popular *Street Life* from 1979). These musicians/bands were tight, tuneful and funky, but contained the seeds of neo-classicism, and their whole approach was essentially a conservative one.

Veteran jazz writer Brian Morton described the times using the image of Janus, the Roman god of doorways and gates, who was able to look both forwards and backwards simultaneously. The backwards-gazing Janus seems to be in the ascendant in the modern era: "The fear of anticlimax is a powerful driver in jazz and improvised music, and…it was one of the motor forces of the 1970s…it is that double awareness (of past and future) that, for me, make the 70s such a powerful and still exciting period in music: Janus-faced, retro- and avant- in equal and equally stretched measure, 'optimistic' and 'tragic' in historically unique combinations…it was an astonishingly creative time…the culture clashes of the time led to some of the most unseemly squabbling and pointless position-taking in the whole of history, but the apparent ossification of genre is belied, as any form of creationist thinking is belied, by the fossil record. What was left behind by the 70s was as rich a shale as any, and as richly various." (Morton in his *Far Cry* column in e-magazine *Point of Departure* 47, June 2014.)

Morton is making the case here, it seems, for the 70s being as creative and exciting a decade, if not more so, than its more widely celebrated earlier sibling. It would be hard, I suggest, to make similar claims for any of the subsequent musical decades.

In terms of delineating this period through its recorded artifacts, as I did in *Beyond Jazz*, I want to use a quote from Dominic Sandbrook's four-book history of the years 1956-1979 in this country – essential reading for anyone interested in this period. He writes the following in connection with pop music, but it could well apply to free improvisation: "What really defined...music in the early 70s, though, was its sheer fragmentation. No group dominated...in the same way that the Beatles and Rolling Stones had done a few years earlier...music had already lost the exaggerated, utopian associations of Swinging London and the Summer of Love." (Sandbrook, 2010, pp.354-55.)

Both the Stones and AMM continued throughout this period (and well beyond). Both bands have a roughly similar lifespan, but I am reluctant to draw any conclusions from this observation. Victor Schonfield was making the same point about fragmentation in the *Musics* 5 interview cited above.

There were no clear equivalents, in the period under analysis, to early free improv recorded masterpieces such as *Karyobin*, *AMMusic*, *The Baptised Traveller* and *Iskra 1903*. It seems likely that the second generation musicians made music that was less susceptible to permanence and repeated listening than these earlier pieces – *Balance* and *Teatime*, however enjoyable, seem fractured and discontinuous (as was the intention no doubt) and to demonstrate less valency, or disposition, for domestic listening than the earlier works. For me, the most sheerly enjoyable records of this period, over the long term, and for whatever reason, are those of the earlier free improvisers in the interregnum period of 1974-5 – *Solo Saxophone* (Evan Parker), *Wigmore Hall* (Bailey/Braxton*)*, *London Concert* (Bailey/Parker), *Lot 74* (solo Derek Bailey), *Dynamics of the Impromptu* (Bailey/Stevens/Watts), *Quintessence* (Spontaneous Music Ensemble) and *Discrete Harm of the Bourgeoisie* (Rutherford).

Many of the great recordings of the time were made in the solo format, or in duo or in trio, combinations that tend to favour virtuosity, and which the ECM 'chamber jazz' style also supported. Combinations of over five members tended to raise eyebrows as to how chaotic they might inevitably become (a concern which I hope the London Improvisers Orchestra [LIO] has eventually put to rest).

Interestingly, psychoanalytic group studies have found that a group of over about 12 members "is ineffective as a work group [i.e. one that is intent on achieving an effective specific task, *author*], and is ultimately incapable of useful debate and effective decision making". (Obholzer & Roberts, p.169.) The LIO and the LJCO (London Jazz Composers' Orchestra) thus have something to disprove (which they do, on most occasions). The Sun Ra Arkestra and the various big bands of the Swing Era also put in question the views of the psychoanalysts. But also, as importantly, this finding also reflected the disquiet of many fans of the music, who questioned how the free *modus* translated into large-group playing.

The *Smithsonian Collection of Classic Jazz* (1973) was a landmark for that year: "The compilation that helped set the agenda for two generations of jazz text books, many of which keyed their musical examples to the collection's unparalleled contents." (Anderson, 2007, p.182.) Together with the much more recent Ken Burn's *Jazz*, a mammoth 4-DVD box set, these two monolithic products set in stone the mummified history of jazz for time immemorial. Guess how much American, let alone English, free improvisation featured in Burns' Cecil Sharp moment?

This book is an attempt to provide some sort of counterbalance to the newly minted creation myths.

CHAPTER 1

The Live Network
The Pioneers and the Settlers
Derek Bailey and Evan Parker

I suggested in *Beyond Jazz*, (Barre, Chapter 3), that the most important free improvisation venue in London, and indeed the whole country, in the late 60s, was The Little Theatre Club in London's West End, where English free improvisation can be truly said to have begun. The venue was still operational in the 1973/4 period (January 1974 was the only time that the author ever attended one of its gigs), but its days were numbered even then. The Old Place, in Gerrard Street, the original site of Ronnie Scott's famous jazz club, had been made available by Scott for use by the more adventurous young players, until its lease ran out in May 1968, a very generous gesture by the bop tenor player, who had little affinity with this type of modernism. Various small pubs and clubs also gave space to the music and, occasionally, at the other end of the live spectrum, high-culture venues like the South Bank would give opportunities to groups like the SME and AMM, usually on bills with 'modern classical' heavyweights like Christian Wolff, Cornelius Cardew and John Cage, and often arranged by Victor Schonfield and Music Now. The free improvisers were therefore caught between an establishment rock and a marginalised hard place of small pubs and commercial clubs, neither type of setting being ideal for the presentation of this music.

Today, we have long-established small(ish) venues like the Vortex and Café Oto (in London at least) which seem popular with both musicians and audiences, but in those far-off days, musicians had to play where they could, often in spaces where they were patronised and/or unappreciated by the management (to put it mildly).

The Jazz Centre Society (JCS) was an early attempt by the establishment to provide opportunities for jazz musicians and audiences. It eventually spread its promotional activities to the regions, liaising with the statutory arts associations and plugging for funding for tours by, amongst others, the Musicians Cooperative (see below), particularly through the Arts Council-funded Contemporary Music Network scheme. (Annette Moreau, one of the Council's members, appears to have been particularly supportive of the music.) (See Wickes, *op. cit.*, p.252.) Clive Bell's opinion (Bell, *op. cit.*, 1999) was that, "the National Jazz Centre [the premises supposedly run by the JCS] in the 80s, by contrast [to the LMC], spent half a decade and untold sums of money not organising a single gig."

Weekly events were established at The Phoenix in Cavendish Square, the Hampstead Country Club, Putney's Star and Garter pub, the Seven Dials and the 100 Club. Bassist and composer Barry Guy's famously precise diary also contains several other small, but reliable, venues from these early years. (Barre, *op. cit.*, p.125.)

By 1970, dissatisfaction with the JCS and its poor record in promoting free improvisation led to the formation of the Musicians Cooperative (MC) by several prominent first-generation players (Barre, *op. cit.*, pp.277-9), which aimed to represent the interests of these musicians, and which promoted a significant amount of high-profile concerts in London, including international events. It was ultimately replaced by the London Musicians Collective, a more heterogeneous group of cross-generational improvisers, to which interested parties didn't have to be invited to join (which they did in the MC), as membership was open to anyone who was interested. The actual handover between the two organisations has never been clarified, if it ever happened, which sounds doubtful. One imperceptibly melded into the other, however different the two actually were in practice.

Looking at *Microphone*'s 'Live Music Dates' section, in the mid/late

1972 period, gives one a good idea of where 'the action' was, if free improv was your thing: Goldsmiths College in Lewisham, site of a well-regarded AMM recording in 1982; the Conway Hall, Red Lion Square (which is where I actually first saw AMM, in 1994); the Roundhouse, by Chalk Farm tube station (the venue for the ICES festival in 1972, which is discussed later); the Marylebone Institute; The Air Gallery on Shaftesbury Avenue; Janice Christianson's Albion Music, a mostly forgotten but important provider of live music at that time (just see the variety of gigs promoted by the Albion Music Series in *Musics* 18: Christianson was Derek Bailey's partner throughout the 70s); Bedford College NW1; the Whitechapel Gallery; Cecil Sharp House, which was more usually a traditional folk venue.

These are just a sample of the variety of venues that were available, but none were principally dedicated to free improvisation (Albion Music had to shift venues regularly). Eventually, the LMC settled at 42 Gloucester Avenue in Camden Town. Even later than these venues, the Red Rose Club in Finsbury Park and the Clinker in Borough emerged as semi-permanent sites for free improv, but in the early years, it was played wherever and however long promoters would tolerate it.

There are some gigs/venues/promoters that do deserve an especial mention:

▶ The Little Theatre Club was closed for much of 1975 and, shortly afterwards, left for temporary premises on the corner of Monmouth Street and Long Acre, very close to the original site of the Club, and which subsequently became Peter Stringfellow's famous/infamous night club. It was known by then as the 'New Little Theatre Club', probably the kiss of death, in retrospect. And then… oblivion. A sad end for such an influential institution.

▶ York University, alma mater of one Steven Beresford, who did his absolute best to broadcast the music on that particular circuit after being blown away by a solo Bailey gig there.

▶ The Davidsons (Martin and Madelaine) held events at the venerable Wigmore Hall, e.g. the famous Bailey/Braxton 'duo of the deaf' in 1974. Janice Christianson subsequently promoted the 'Young

Improvisers' evening of 1975 there.

▶ Christianson's role has, according to several of the musicians of that time, been grossly underestimated. Speaking for the first time about those years, she agreed to give me her account of Albion Music, its formation and cessation. I can find no mention of Christiansen in Ben Watson's Derek Bailey biography, so I will let her tell the story in her own words, and thus give her the chance to re-enter the frame from which she has been omitted for so long: "The starting was easy – I worked at the Old Place for a while and was so pissed off when it closed (that) I found a pub, The Albion in Hammersmith, where we opened, and it ran for five weeks. Mike Westbrook opened, I think – packed house – and others followed, but on the fourth week it turned out that the jolly landlord had been fiddling the books, so we were allowed the fifth week and got booted out in our turn. The end of the Albion Modern Jazz Club." (Personal communication, 2016.)

The name Albion was kept and the Holland Park venue, that she mentions next, was apparently a private house in this very opulent area of London: "I have forgotten the name of the next pub, Irish, in Hammersmith, by the tube, with loud music from below, at the top of really narrow steep stairs [just like the LTC, *author*] – we carried at least one wheelchair-user up and down. As my taste was for pure improvisation, the music drifted in that direction, and takings drifted down too. I can't remember how long we ran there as ALBION MUSIC, but opened, at the same time, somewhat pretentious Sunday afternoon sessions at Holland Park, the London Music Club – a nice grand piano and surroundings, and I think did Friday nights, too. Howard Riley played solo once – more to the usual punters' taste there. And poetry crept in too. But I remember that we had some really good sessions, and good turnouts. The West London bias was because I lived in Shepherds Bush."

The "certain bitterness" that she admits to feeling comes out clearly when she describes the entry of Derek Bailey into the proceedings: "I had no publicity. Derek chucked a lot of my belongings, and records, so I lost everything about Albion Music. And recently found, and threw away, two newspaper cuttings about the LMC gigs – so I can't even offer data.

We must have lasted a few years. The Albion Music thing grew out of that as Derek persuaded me – I had a fulltime (very) job in Forest Gate as a community worker – that the future lay in milking grants from the Arts Council, who were quite accommodating. So, under pressure from the arch manipulator/control freak, I organised more and more concerts/tours for the great Derek Bailey. He worked me extremely hard. I loved the music but found the pressure of holding down a job, servicing Derek, and carrying a lot of responsibility for use of public funds, very difficult. Then, when he found love with his Japanese girl, that was it, he asked me to leave. I bought a narrow boat and sailed away into the sunset – well, Tottenham Marshes, actually – just where the Olympic Stadium ended up. Handy for the train to get to East London."

The move onto the narrow boat coincides with the end of the time frame of this book, and she observes that the 'star system' manifested itself even at these margins: "There were so many 'big stars' about, that some of the lesser known musicians got badly neglected – I wish I had stuck to giving them the platform – *the original reason for starting the whole caboodle?* [author's italics]. I did meet and hear Frank [Perry?] the amazing [Buddhist] percussionist, later, and realised how much I missed the music, but once I left London, in 1981 I think [moved onto the boat in '79] I really moved into a totally different life. Out in the sticks, where I like to be, setting up an Eco Co-Homes group."

So, a long journey taken in just a few years, and hopefully to peace in a more restful setting than promoting gigs for three men (one in particular) and a dog. Let's hope that future histories of the music will give Janice Christianson a more prominent place than she has so far been given. "I got dumped by them all (the male-orientated scene) as soon as Derek dumped me, only one bothered to keep in touch. Apart from Derek. Until he died."

▶ The Unity Theatre, a dedicated left-wing venue, was based in a former chapel in Mornington Crescent that provided a safe house for free improvisation and the Musicians Cooperative, until it burned down, suspiciously near Bonfire Night (November 8th 1975). This had been a venue for regular Tuesday MC gigs, so was a considerable loss. Less missed perhaps was the repast provided: "I remember that the bar sold one sort of food – bread and butter pudding. Luckily, it was excellent." (Steve Beresford in the notes to *Teatime*, which was recorded there.) According to Richard Leigh, the Newcastle Brown was also excellent. Evan Parker surmises that this might have marked the final concerts of the Musicians Cooperative, and the informal cessation of that organisation. (Personal communication, 2016.)

▶ The Kings Head pub in Acton – venue for a rather bizarre split-AMM, featuring the duos of Eddie Prevost/Lou Gare and Keith Rowe/Cornelius Cardew. How odd this pairing of pairs was is demonstrated by an article by Rowe in *Microphone* 5, June 1972 (about John Cage's cultural imperialism – 'bourgeois-individualist', to be precise – and the forthcoming people's revolution) and by Prevost's (and others') exasperated responses in *Microphone* 6. The fact that they could still share a stage, after all the conflicted viewpoints, is testament to something, surely?

▶ John Stevens' Friday night sessions at The Plough in Stockwell, started in the late 70s, were apparently inspirational for a generation of improvising neophytes (and veterans).

▶ The ICA in Pall Mall, soon to become infamous in 1976 for its 'Pornography' exhibition by COUM Transmissions (who soon morphed into the professionally transgressive Throbbing Gristle).

▶ Upstairs at The Engineer pub, opposite the future LMC HQ, featured regular Monday night gigs.

▶ The LMC HQ in Camden Town eventually featured weekly sessions, festivals and was the base for *Musics*. The very first LMC Festival was, however, held at Battersea Arts Centre in September 1977.

▶ The 1974 first International Free Improvisation Festival took place over two sites, at the Collegiate Theatre, now the Bloomsbury Theatre (two nights) and Ronnie's (one night).

THE SECOND GENERATION GET STARTED

A young guitarist, John Russell (born in 1954), had been in receipt of lessons from Derek Bailey, which were paid for by the proceeds of

Russell's paper round. A meeting at Ronnie Scott's Club (that has the heft, to these ears, but in a minor key, of that between Mick and Keef at Dartford Station in 1961), between Russell and John Stevens, at the performance of *Ode* in 1972 by the London Jazz Composers' Orchestra, led to the former appearing in duo with Dave Solomon at the Little Theatre Club (LTC) in late 1973 (a small recorded amount of which appeared on the album *Teatime*). These two had been playing at the LTC, alongside some of the younger players like Steve Beresford and Nigel Coombes, throughout 1973. Russell has since proved to be one of the great free music practitioners, promoters and organisers through his Mopomoso events, which were ultimately to prove a successor to Company, which have been operational since 1991 and which celebrated their 25th birthday in 2016.

Disgracefully, Russell does not seem to appear in any of the jazz encyclopedias that I have come across, a fate shared by most of the younger generation from the 1970s. He claims that Derek Bailey got the idea for Company from the myriad discussions and playing situations that Russell and his peers got involved with in the 1973/4 period (suggested in the notes to *Teatime*). He, and his fellow young improvisers, naturally gravitated, in time, to the Unity Theatre, and furthermore he, along with Solomon and Steve Beresford, was also invited to join the Gen One 'hive', the Musicians Cooperative.

By the time that the LTC finally folded, Russell had found a regular weekly venue at the Art Meeting Place in Earlham Street, WC2, (a gig that sounds off-puttingly like the bohemian cafe in Jean Cocteau's *Orphee* movie), in the pre-makeover Covent Garden (just after the market itself had finally closed). This site was described in mid 1975 as "an open resource for artists, musicians, film-makers, poets, etc., which is controlled by its users. Anyone can apply to use the space…." (*Musics*, No 2, p.32.) This sounds very similar to the mission statement of the soon-come London Musicians Collective HQ in Camden.

Solomon also remembers (*Teatime* notes again) the regular Engineer concerts, and those at the Unity Theatre. These were the years of 1974-6, demarcated approximately by the closure of the LTC and the formation of the LMC: "A period that tends to be overlooked in the historical accounts of this period," according to Solomon. Not any longer; this was an important *interregnum* for the music.

THE PIONEERS AND THE SETTLERS?

It was almost inevitable that there was going to be some sort of a 'kill the father' scenario at some point, what with strident younger improvisers gradually emerging, many of them from outside London, and wanting their say and their play. (We have already seen this with Roger Turner, who hailed from Whitstable, and who is quoted at some length in the introduction to this book.)

I feel it's worth quoting at length from a letter from early LTC habitué Richard Leigh, who was writing retrospectively to the LMC magazine *Resonance* (a later product, which is outside our time frame) in the summer 1994 edition (Issue 2, Vol.2, p.46): "My memory of the Musicians Cooperative is that it was set up as a reaction to the Jazz Centre Society, which had clearly no intention of doing anything for improvised music. The Cooperative was set up as a pressure group to get work for a clearly defined set of musicians: more or less the people usually referred to as the 'first generation' of improvisers. These included Evan Parker, Derek Bailey (at least I think he was in it for a while), Paul Lytton, John Stevens, Howard Riley, Paul Rutherford, Barry Guy and Trevor Watts. After a while, John and Trevor left the group…In those days improvised music was officially non-existent, and the most urgent task was to improve its status. The Cooperative found premises in Camden Town [The Unity Theatre, I presume, *author*]. Boards once trodden by the likes of Paul Robeson and Alfie Bass were now occupied by the Parker/Lytton duo, AMM, Frank Perry, Terry Day with Charlie Hart and George Khan (an unforgettably daft evening) and a wide range of other players: the Cooperative never saw the place as a venue for themselves alone."

One somehow feels that the pioneers wouldn't have appreciated their efforts being described as 'daft' (Leigh has made it clear that he was only referring to the Day gig), however libertarian they may have been. The up and going generation did seem, however, to relish the idea. Frank

Zappa once asked, "Does humour belong in music?" We were about to find out.

One thing is clear, even from this distant vantage point. The pioneers had a profound impact on listeners, including this author. "I remember hearing Derek Bailey for the first time. He played a short solo spot between sets by the SME at the Little Theatre Club. I had never heard any music remotely like what Derek was playing – and how often does that happen? Twenty-six years later, I still don't know where he got it from. Twenty-six years later, also, it is still fresh." (Leigh, *op. cit.*, p.47.)

We would do well to remember this. The music's pioneers had created something *sui generis*. Trying to call to mind some equivalently original music, all my 25-year-old son and myself could come up with was some electronic music (Aphex Twin, Autechre, Squarepusher) and perhaps noise artists like Merzbow, but English free improv still emerged from 1966 as somehow shockingly new.

The MC had had its day by 1976 – Leigh felt that its main difference from the nascent LMC was the latter's "openness to anyone who wanted to join", an anti-elitist stance from the start, but it would seem that profound philosophical/sonic divergences soon began to establish themselves within the Collective, whatever its initial aims. The MC was clearly full of virtuoso musicians, formally trained or not, but the newer improvisers had differing visions.

One of the side effects of these divergences, in my opinion, is the lack of truly great recorded product by the second generation in these years (and generally just a shortage of *any* recorded product from that time by them). I have to confess that, certainly with regard to group configurations, some Gen Two recordings can make opaque and recondite domestic listening, the sound of which is perhaps best experienced in its natural habitat, for me at least – i.e. in the live situation.

David Toop, usually associated with the second generation, described "an overlap in the mid 70s, as various Musicians Cooperative members invited in the new boys and worked with them", whilst making clear, once again, that there was no overt or formal line of succession between either of the two organisations or their musicians. (*Resonance* Vol.2

No.1, p.34.) He further suggested that: "To narrow early improvisation to the same few names [which I have, perforce, done, *author*], or make rigid or wrong distinctions between generations (*mea culpa* once more), is to write a lot of musicians, groups and activities out of history [one of history's inevitable processes, with free improvisation being no exception? *author*]. Musicians such as Maggie Nicols, Jamie Muir, Dave Panton, Terry Day, Christine Jeffries, Frank Perry, Trevor Watts, Lol Coxhill and others cannot be squeezed into the semi-official view of improvising history, yet all of them made strong contributions and exerted a profound influence on events around them." (Toop, *op. cit.*, p.34.)

I hope that my conversations with Dave Panton and Trevor Watts, and chapters on Day and Coxhill, will make a small contribution towards correcting these specific omissions.

It is emblematic that one of the LMC's running (in both senses of the word) problems was that of obtaining toilets for their site in Gloucester Avenue, a facility that no-one managed to improvise into existence in over ten years, mainly attributable to lack of sufficient funds (which amounted to a few thousand pounds, even then) that would have been needed to install them. And so the venue had to use its outlier and pseudopodium, The Engineer pub, for this purpose, thus proving that boozers had their uses after all.

"The place often exuded the atmosphere of a secret cabal, which some of us strove to modify and others strove with equal energy to fortify." (Toop, *op. cit.*, p.35.) The truth is somewhere out there, I'm sure, and we will return to the LMC in fuller detail later on.

In the meantime, before going on to an examination of Gen Two and its primary organisation and venue, I want to look into what the early pioneers were doing in these years, as they hardly went quietly into the good night, to quote Dylan Thomas.

Evan Parker, Derek Bailey, John Stevens/SME, AMM, Trevor Watts, Paul Lytton, Paul Rutherford, Howard Riley, Barry Guy, were all at the top of their game at this point in time, and were producing recordings of the highest quality over these years. Interestingly, solo and duo recordings were, as noted earlier, becoming increasingly popular with these improvisers, and many of them released major statements in this format over the 1970s.

However, we should remember that there were those who had begun to challenge some of the fundamental notions of this newly established canon: "There has been a strong trend away from the Stand-There-And-Play convention of 'straight' improvised music [a key point here, and surely an oxymoron? *author*] to more visual uses of it, in combination with, for example, performance." (Paul Johnson of the Coventry Musicians Collective, quoted in the Bristol Cooperative magazine, *op. cit.*, 1979, p6.)

Already there were those that saw the Gen One improvisers, mistakenly, as out of step with the 'times'.

Let's now look at each of the early pioneers in turn. We will move on to the younger players in subsequent chapters.

THE PIONEERS

There was a problem, even as late as 1976. Or a *perceived* problem, in the mind of Peter Riley in *Musics* 6 (p.12). "All that remains is to note which so-called second generation English improvisers haven't yet been disc-ed [*sic*]. And there aren't so many. The urgency in that aspect now lies mainly with: Terry Day, Richard Beswick, Larry Stabbins...plus the inaudible on SMO (Roger Smith...), and also Roy Ashbury...Then there are the outside-Londoners."

Then the *coup de grace*: "The point being that with these records the territory is mapped, these records put us where we are, not just in terms of coverage but because they create the landscape we live in, they have enough spirit to do that." (Riley, p.12.)

This partly explains my 'pioneer' metaphor. The first generation was the Daniel Boone of English free music. Later musicians (post-1972) were *settling* on already established territory. The cross-fertilisation of the main two early families, the Spontaneous Music Ensemble/Incus/MC clan and the various AMM groupings, continued throughout our period.

Keith Rowe joined Amalgam in 1979, and offered an alternative model: "Having Keith Rowe in the band, with his special brand of crude speed [very appropriate for the time of punk-thrash, *author*] and eerie effects, seemed to have an effect on Trevor [Watts] similar to that of Pharoah Sanders on John Coltrane, inspiring him to his ecstatic out-est [*sic*], and at times in these performances, the group seemed possessed." (Wickes, *op. cit.,* p.237.)

Evan Parker and Eddie Prevost still play together today, as do Rowe and John Tilbury (of the later AMM). Watts and Guy occasionally still perform with their old peers. These pioneers represent formidable founding father figures (the four Fs?) in the music, however much they, and others, might be uncomfortable with this notion.

DEREK BAILEY

This might just be the moment to let the reader know that Derek Bailey was the musician who originally fascinated me enough to be impelled to explore the genre of free improvisation. He was my gateway drug into the whole subculture. This was in 1974, coincidently the year that he released *Lot 74*, in my opinion the best, and most fully realised (or maybe it was merely because it was the first of his albums that I heard?), of all his many solo guitar albums. His whole approach, the laconic inserts, the bluff Yorkshire shtick, fascinated me, as a Midlands teenager emerging out of a grammar school education and being used to categorising my listening, so far as it then went, as being somehow 'underground' and 'progressive', as was the then popular terminology. I was particularly stricken, at the age of 17, with the first few Mothers of Invention recordings, the 1970 Soft Machine (*Number Three*) and the Miles Davis of *At Fillmore* and *Live/Evil.* Hearing for the first time, the sounds of Bailey (in particular) and, later, severally, others like Evan Parker and Iskra 1903, opened up a world of sounds that I couldn't really initially accommodate, so, my defence mechanisms in place, I rejected them as 'rubbish', even though these sounds burrowed away in my subconscious like a psychic tape worm and wouldn't go away. In my teenage arrogance, I thought I would take this music on and demonstrate (Lord knows how, by some sort of de-worming treatment?) what a load of pretentious rot

Derek Bailey and Evan Parker at a Company concert, the ICA, on March 4th 1979
CREDIT: © JAK KILBY WWW.JAKKILBY.CO.UK

it really was. I decided to see Bailey at the Little Theatre Club in early 1974, which proved to be my epiphany, and I was soon disabused of these notions. Forget Hendrix, Clapton, Fripp, Zappa, authentic guitar masters though they undoubtedly were. I had found my true guitar hero, wearing a tweed jacket and DMs.

Bailey was something else, I finally understood. And he has never been supplanted, in my view, both in terms of influence and, especially, technique. I am not a musician, but his unique *sound* will stay with me forever. Thanks, Derek.

I still treasure memories of his live sets. Wry and unassuming in *persona*, he tended to start his sets with a little fanfare, and ended them with the sound of his alarm clock promptly ringing the end of the improvisation, an arch statement in itself, and that was usually accompanied by a dry comment from Bailey to conclude. Was the alarm there to merely remind him to bring the set to a conclusion, or was it a reminder of the dreamlike artificiality of live performance? I found the whole *drollerie* of his approach utterly fascinating at the time, given what I had become used to from the likes of Emerson, Lake and Palmer and Led Zeppelin, what with their bombastic intros and their interminable concluding 'jams'. Despite the formidably unusual sounds emerging from this middle-aged, staid-looking man, the artist also clearly had a sense of humour, which was sorely lacking at the time in live music.

At the same time, Bailey was casting a huge shadow over up-and-coming free guitarists such as John Russell, Fred Frith and Ian Brighton (and their American peers like Henry Kaiser and Eugene Chadbourne), some of whom had studied with him, and was providing a penumbra that was to prove very difficult to get out from under. No other instrument was so identified with a particular improviser in this music than the guitar was with Bailey. His technique can, and has been, academically studied, up to and including doctorate level (by bassist Dominic Lash, 2010, for example), but it's really like the very many exegeses of the Beatles music and lyrics – the sheer *quiddity* of the sound cannot really be captured by written, cognitive dissections (as is also the case with AMM, another doctoral favourite, for example, with saxophonist Seymour Wright, 2013). As we will see below, there are two, equally valid, approaches to describing this unique music, both of which, ultimately, tend to fall short of doing the subject full justice. All this also introduces the idea of improvisers becoming academicised and objectified, even mummified, along with the whole practice of free improvisation, something that would have seemed, to put it politely, improbable, a few decades earlier. Once the genie was out of the lamp, however...

This book is ultimately, among many other things, a tribute to Bailey's influence, and I am only sorry (and even perhaps somewhat relieved!) that he couldn't contribute directly to it in some way.

The 1970s were the years that Bailey, and several of his other peers, fully explored the solo format, and many of his most treasured recordings come from this period: *Incus Taps* (1973), originally three 3" open-reel tape recordings (but later released on Organ of Corti as a single LP); *Lot*

74 Solo Improvisations; Improvisations from 1975, released on the Italian Diverso label; 1978's *New Sights, Old Sounds* (Morgue 03/04) – an incredibly rare Japanese record originally, but re-released in 2002 as Incus CD 48/49. Bailey had, in many ways, started the whole solo thing off with Incus 2, back in 1971, his very first solo record on the nascent label.

It is at this point in my crypto-historic narrative, that I want to quote Peter Riley, a frequent *Musics* contributor and contemporary commentator. It is a rather lengthy quote, but one that illustrates one particular type of approach, that which seeks to negate the sort of historicising that writers like myself are essaying. It is also typical of the sort of pseudo-philosophical arguments that raged at that time, regarding the recording of the music. It concerns itself with the "recent music of Derek Bailey", and appeared in the Bristol Musicians Collective magazine of 1979, on page 32.

"But where was the recent music of Derek Bailey? Surely it was improvised music, which only occurs now. It is played, and then it stops, and what's left of it? As far as our ears are concerned, nothing. And since there's nothing left, what difference does it make how 'recently' it stopped? It isn't something left behind by the musician like a book or a carved stone, in fact, it isn't an object he creates at all, which we could see set in its place in the past like a milestone. What sense does it make, then, to talk about

ABOVE FROM TOP: *Lot 74* by Derek Bailey, Spring 1974; *Incus Taps* by Derek Bailey, 1973; *Improvisation* by Derek Bailey, September 16th 1975 its development in the past, as if were something we still had before us to study? Once it has stopped, it has completely stopped and our memory is of nothing but its general effect, whether it stopped yesterday or ten years ago. The actual details of the music, which are where its real quality lies, are available to us only at the moment of history. The entire past of improvised music is one past."

Where to start with this rambling, neo-Platonic, statement? Eric Dolphy, one of the few modernist reeds players possibly possessed of genius, managed to sum up Riley's position in just 18 words (which can be heard at the very end of his *Last Date* album), some years earlier: "When you hear music, after it's over, it's gone, in the air, you can never capture it again." But then again, Dolphy *was* a genius (maybe).

Riley's piece strikes me as an example of long-winded sophistry, which, frankly, doesn't make a lot of sense. No, music is not a book, nor is it a carved stone (AMM's *Nameless Uncarved Block* notwithstanding). Musicians, even free improvisers, are allowed to develop their sound over time, and these changes can and should be preserved by contemporary media. Or, if not, why not? By the end of the decade, arguments like Riley's began to disappear, mostly because, I would have thought, they didn't hold together as especially cogent or useful. Riley managed to spin this argument out over two more pages without, unfortunately, telling us anything about the actual recordings, a journalistic conceit that was very much of its time. (See also, Paul Morley and Ian Penman at the *NME*.)

Riley's Time Lord affectations are also manifest here: "I think that improvisation, by forcing the return of music as actual performance within time and nowhere else, has the possibility of relating directly to personal time-perspective, and of resisting the neurotic monumentalism of personal time, which we see at its grossest in such products as *This Is Your Life*, but which inform the entire politics and public spectacle of this society." (BMC, *op. cit.*, p.32.)

Riley clearly had a rather worrying preoccupation with this very popular TV show, which I trust he eventually resolved.

Seriously, however, these were exactly the sort of sentiments that alienated the public. Pseudo-situationalist poses that somehow positioned free improv as being superior to the 'grosser' aspects of popular culture, which so many innocent people ignorantly enjoyed.

Moving back to Bailey's "recent music", and the recordings thereof, Bailey was seen by his peers, by 1973, as being perhaps somewhat solipsistic in this chosen solo format, even at that early point: "Derek Bailey's own particular endgame has caused him to withdraw into himself, and concentrate on playing solo guitar... He is austere, uncompromising and formidably committed to exploring and expressing his own interior vision, and he emits a sort of feeling that this vision would be deformed or tarnished if it were made to fit in with the exterior landscape of group music...at least on a regular basis. He enjoys playing occasionally with other people with whom he feels a strong affinity, but such people are few and far between. With monastic vigilance he tries to avoid the habitual side of playing." (Carr, 1973, p.70.]

It is ironic, with the benefit of hindsight, or the 'retroscope' as I like to call it, that Bailey formed Company three years later, a 'landscape of group music' if there ever was one. *Company's 1-7* had all been released on Incus by 1978, featuring a polyglot collection of international improvisers, across several artistic modalities, which demonstrated Bailey's willingness to explore affinities that hadn't even occurred to many of us (see later for a full account of Company activities).

Derek Bailey's own performances over these particular years was, as with many of the pioneers' recorded output, outstandingly varied. To mention just a few:

▶ *Incus Taps.* Reel-to-reel tapes, a format and presentation that must have seemed cutting-edge at the time (with Bailey at his best as well). Ten years later, they were not only unavailable, but completely anachronistic and archaic in format, what with CDs about to emerge and render vinyl equally redundant (but history proved otherwise, as regards vinyl, at least). Whatever, these recordings, followed by *Lot 74* (1974) and *Improvisation* (1975) were probably Bailey's greatest, and most representative, solo sequence.

▶ The Wigmore Hall concert with Anthony Braxton, attended by the author in his *jeunesse doree* phase (as he likes to think of it) in 1974, both set a standard for the music's acceptance by the establishment (maybe) and, at the same time, its corresponding accord with the American avant garde (presumably). The links forged with the Chicagoan multi-instrumentalist who, despite all his conceptual freightage, was still basically a jazzer, led to further contact with other AACM-associated improvisers such as trumpeter/composer Leo Smith and trombonist/composer George Lewis, and all three joined in Company events in the forthcoming years. The way by which these two, very different, improvisers, found a duo-playing compromise, is well described in Martin Davidson's notes that accompanied Emanem 4006, the Wigmore Hall live recording release.

First Duo Concert by Derek Bailey and Anthony Braxton, June 30th 1974

▶ Bailey moved on, a year later, to playing on a programmatic recording by bassist/composer Gavin Bryars, his old foil from the Joseph Holbrook Trio in Sheffield. (Barre, *op. cit.*, pp.225-6.) *The Sinking of the Titanic,* backed with *Jesus' Blood Never Failed Me Yet* (which included Bailey) was Brian Eno's Obscure Label's first release (Obscure 1). The composition had featured in Victor Schonfield's *Music Now* series in the early 70s, designed to feature free improvisers alongside modern composers. Obscure 2, *Ensemble Pieces,* was even more intriguing, with AMM's Cornelius Cardew on cello and Christopher Hobbs on piano, together with Bryars on double bass, Eno on voice, and Andy Mackay from the original Roxy Music on oboe. This was pluralism in action.

▶ *The London Concert* (Incus 16) with Evan Parker, from 1975, was the first of three duo performances, recorded by almost certainly the two most important voices of 1970s free improvisation. (There are only two other duo recordings by Bailey and Parker, to my knowledge, a criminal under-recording of these masters of the genre in this format.) Their three duo recordings are separated by two five-year periods: *Arch Duo* (recorded in 1980), perhaps being a more appropriate appellation than *Compatibles* (1985), which was released just before the almighty bust-up that signaled the end of Bailey and Parker's working and personal relationship.

The Cook/Morton duo had this to say about this classic pairing: "Old associates who have been making this kind of music for decades [two, in actual fact, it just seemed longer, *author*], and yet they still find new means of communication each time they meet. Parker utilises ever higher harmonics and extremes of tone; Bailey's characteristic idiom [despite his non-idiomatic stance? *author*] is still a furious handscribble. Together, they create a unique language, not so much unintelligible to others as beyond simple decipherment." (Cook/Morton, p.69.)

The London Concert by Derek Bailey and Evan Parker, February 14th 1975

The linguistic metaphors here are telling – this *was* a new language and it was being spoken increasingly often, as demonstrated by the increase in musicians wishing to learn and speak it.

▶ *The Crust*, which was among the very first Emanem recordings (Emanem 304), and featured soprano saxophonist Steve Lacy, one of the most important American modernists in our story (along with Anthony Braxton, George Lewis and Leo Smith). Bailey asked these players from the States to participate in early Company events (see *Company 6 & 7* for evidence), and the participation of both Lacy and bassist Kent Carter in 1973/4 concerts seems, in retrospect, vital to the emergence of international free improvisation. The slightly earlier influence, in the late 1960s, of Ornette Coleman *alumnus* Don Cherry, Albert Ayler (who played extensively in Europe up to his death in 1970) and of John Tchicai, who featured on John Coltrane's *Ascension* in 1965, also cannot be underestimated in yoking together the American and the European avant garde, as the BYG/Actuel series, started in 1969, demonstrated and provided many examples of, in its 50-odd (and *odd*) releases at the cusp of the 70s. (See Johannes Rod's book on Free Jazz labels, pp.22-3.) Several leading American free musicians had left to live and work in Europe in the late 60s, including the Art Ensemble and Braxton, because of the hostility to their music in their home country, and many ended up recording for BYG, including Lacy, Braxton, Cherry and Musica Elettronica Viva. The BYG Actuel story is well documented on a 3-CD set on the Charly label, compiled by Thurston Moore and Byron Coley. (See Discography.)

With the release of the first Company album on Incus 21 in May 1976, Bailey's attention was increasingly drawn to his new project, including the organisation of Company Weeks (which eventually took place from 1977 to 1994).

Aquirax Aida (the Japanese critic and promoter, and dedicatee of Incus 40, *Aida*, Bailey's 1980 solo masterpiece), suggested, in a visit to England in 1977, that Bailey consider touring Japan. Sadly, Aida died the following year. However, thus began a fruitful exchange of English and Japanese improvisers, which continues to this very day. There was a Japanese Company event in Tokyo in 1981. Company also featured American improvisers, as we will see, and relationships deepened with musicians like guitarists Eugene Chadbourne and Henry Kaiser and, eventually, John Zorn and the New York downtown scene. These events are described more fully in Ben Watson's book, where Watson uses the term 'Improv International' to trace the outline of this particular aspect of the gradual de-parochialisation of English free improvisation.

EVAN PARKER

Still the *eminence grise* of the English free improvisation world, Evan Parker's recorded output is now huge in both size and scope. Only the work of Chicago modernist Anthony Braxton exceeds Parker's discography as far as I can tell (Braxton's output still makes even Parker's look like that of Scott Walker). Or perhaps the output of Steve Lacy, or Lee Konitz or Chet Baker…but the reader gets the idea, I'm sure.

Having started off slowly and steadily (at least in terms of release dates) after his debut in 1968 on *Karyobin* (which is discussed in detail, in *Beyond Jazz*, pp.145-50), Parker gradually accelerated over the next few years: over the period covered by this book, for example, he participated in nearly 50 record releases.

Much of the information in these pages regarding his discography is garnered from a 1994 edition of Francesco Martinelli's book on the subject, so the figures presented here are thus likely to be somewhat out of date. As a result of all this activity, this particular section on this unique improviser is fairly long – it reflects both the sheer amount of recorded material and the importance of the overall role of the man himself. We can tend to think of musicians such as multi-instrumentalist and second generation improviser David Toop when we think of musical polymaths, but Parker, whose music can sometimes be mistaken as having a very narrow focus, is actually a player with a very wide knowledge of what we today call 'world music', and which informs both his playing and his thinking. He and Toop share occasional evenings at Café Oto in the present day, playing to the audience examples from their vast knowledge of musical forms (and no doubt their equally vast record collections). Just a few examples to whet the appetite: Gagaku, the ancient imperial court music of Japan, which is its classical music (and where the word 'karyobin' originates); Sicilian bagpipe music and Scottish Pibroch; north African raita; Korean oboe; Buddhist chanting; Tuvan throat singing; LaMonte Young and the New York 60s minimalists. These influences moved away from the idea, expressed at one time, of a 'pure orthodoxy' of free music, which was felt necessary in order to ensure that the music remained unencumbered by history, and/or traditional 'limitations' of form and function (as espoused by the likes of Phillip Larkin, to take just one example). In reality, everything was grist to the mill from this point on. Free improvisation was never a *tabula rasa*, every musician brought something to the table, however little baggage people may have thought they might be carrying.

Contemporarily, Punk purported to develop the notion of 'Year Zero', a pure restart and which claimed, in its pomp, to have correspondingly shed all previous shibboleths, but it soon turned out to be the 'same old same old', in new clothes, unfortunately. But it did leave spores.

The second generation ensured that an increasing heterodoxy determined that any 'purity' was not maintained for any length of time (these were the 'impurities' referred to by Steve Beresford in his quote at the start of the Foreword of this book).

What I propose to do, in order to make some sort of sense of Parker's recorded output from 1973-9, is to divide it up into different sections, a method used by Martinelli (*op. cit.*, pp.40-3), and also on the European Free Improvisation site, *www.efi.group.shef.ac.uk*, (under 'Evan Parker'), but I have used a slightly different set of categories: (i) solo saxophone; (ii) small group (2 to 8 musicians, inclusive) recordings with (a) European peers (b) American modernists, or a combination of the two, including Company configurations; (iii) big bands; (iv) others. This makes a choice of four categories (including two sub-categories), another Procrustian bed, but a *relatively* simple one for such a complex output (but which is still more complicated than I would have ideally liked, with apologies to the reader).

Solo Recordings come into their own

Probably Parker's most well known technical accomplishment, his circular breathing technique, has been extensively documented in over a dozen or so albums. I discuss the technique in *Beyond Jazz*. (Barre, *op. cit.*, pp.202-5.) According to my calculations, there are nine soprano solo recordings, one on tenor sax (*Live in Chicago*), one multi-tracked soprano (*Process and Reality*) and one a solo processed soprano, accompanied by live electronics from Walter Prati (*Hall of Mirrors*), the latter prefiguring the direction Parker would later go with the Electro-Acoustic Ensemble. Martinelli, in his notes which accompany the re-release of *Saxophone Solos* (the very first solo exploration of 1975) on Parker's own psi label (psi 09.01), makes it clear that there are other lone recordings, but which are next-to-impossible to get hold of. Certainly, I have never seen or come across the 'Japanese LP', called *Zanzou*, which is a combined soprano/tenor LP, recorded in Japan in 1982, and which was the first release of the Japanese Jazz & NOW label. The latter also recorded equally obscure releases by a solo Barry Guy [*Assist*] and by a Parker/Guy live duo from

1985 (Jazz & NOW 3), named *Tai Kyoku*.

My favourite description of the circular breathing process, which is/was also practiced at an advanced level by Anthony Braxton, Roscoe Mitchell, John Butcher and Lol Coxhill, among others, is Parker's own: "It's a question of how you want to incorporate the cyclic, repetitive elements into the Heraclitian flux, the river you can never step in twice." (Lock, 1994, p.179.) This also puts me in mind of James Joyce's description of water, "everchanging, neverchanging" (from the penultimate chapter of *Ulysses*, 'Ithaca').

Given that one of the potential criticisms of this body of work is that 'it all sounds the same', these are useful images to bear in mind.

The period of the mid 70s is, as we have already observed, noticeable for the increasing popularity, in freely improvised music generally, of solo and duo recordings. Solo saxophone recordings were not, of course, unknown before Parker's innovations. Anthony Braxton had recorded his own two-record *tour de force*, *For Alto*, back in 1968, an incredibly precocious statement from the young composer/improviser, which challenged all adventurous reed players; Coleman Hawkins recorded *Picasso* even further back, 20 years earlier in 1948; Eric Dolphy had made tracks of unaccompanied alto saxophone (*Tenderly* on 1960's *Far Cry*) and bass clarinet (various live versions of *God Bless The Child* in the early 60s); Steve Lacy was increasingly chomping at the soprano mouthpiece bit, with only himself for company, at around this time, and he subsequently became possibly Parker's only real peer in this realm, both in terms of concentrated attention to one particular saxophone and the amount of recorded evidence emerging from this process.

Most of the important Little Theatre Club-associated free improvisers from our pioneer group put out solo material at this time: Barry Guy, Howard Riley, Paul Rutherford, Bailey (as described above), Tony Oxley (one side of Incus 8), Paul Lytton, with fellow percussionist Paul Lovens: entire solo percussion recordings, however, remain somewhat of a curate's egg and an acquired taste, as do solo bass products.

The two major groups of the First Generation, AMM and SME, both curiously became duos for much of the 1972-6 period, with percussionist leaders: John Stevens (with Trevor Watts), and Eddie Prevost with, firstly, saxophonist Lou Gare and, subsequently (post-1976), guitarist Keith Rowe. One possible explanation for the duo manifestation could be the suitability and sustainability of this format for virtuosic playing.

For the Second Generation, it was mainly (but certainly not exclusively) Lol Coxhill who availed himself of this solo mode of presentation. Although he was a multi-instrumentalist and an unusually sensitive group player, Coxhill is undoubtedly best known for his solo soprano work.

David Toop and Paul Burwell worked as a duo, called Rain in the Face, which operated in the mid 70s and was very well regarded. Toop also worked in a hyperactive duo with Steve Beresford called General Strike.

Synchronously, the fascination with solo work was mirrored in the rarified atmosphere of ECM Records, then reaching its first plateau of popularity at around this time with several releases by contemporary American modern jazz giants, a format that became an ECM staple: most famously and successfully in the early days, with recordings by American pianists Keith Jarrett and Chick Corea, Canadian pianist Paul Bley, and double bassists Barre Phillips from the USA and Dave Holland, who was English. ECM 1018/1019 was a double LP by Circle (for more on whom see Gluck, pp.113-131), a 'supergroup', consisting of Braxton, Corea, Holland and Barry Altschul on percussion, the first three of whom all recorded solo albums themselves (Corea and Holland both on ECM, and Braxton for a myriad of labels over the years).

This was all in contradistinction to the AACM school of Chicago (the Art Ensemble eventually hooked up with ECM by the end of the decade), the members of whom tended to eschew their solo virtuosity, to focus on 'group sounds', somewhat like the English free improv 'insect music' groups (but with very different results), including extensive use of 'little instruments' (ultimately influenced by John Cage), including toys, which was a challenge that Steve Beresford *et al* cheerily took up in England (Beresford led a 'toy orchestra').

Roscoe Mitchell from the Art Ensemble, and Braxton himself, were nominally alto sax players, but in practice additionally played the whole gamut of reed and percussion instruments, which littered their live stages in profusion. This hypertrophying of personal instrumentation represented a new polymorphous form and content, as opposed to the notion of classic jazz instrumental 'purity', i.e. sax/trumpet lead, and a rhythm section of piano, bass and percussion (the bebop Platonian ideal), which was soon promoted as the only 'real' jazz – its 'classical' distillation/quintessence, the 'black classical music'. The latter model soon won out. It was, after all, so goddamn seductive (see the 80s 'Jazz Revival'). However, the solo format remained a respectable one, probably because of the inescapable virtuosity involved in such a venture.

Evan Parker's solo recordings of the 1970s

These early years were the most productive of Parker's solo career, in terms of records that represented a single short period. Five solo soprano albums were produced to cover the years 1975-80, bearing in mind, though, that a couple were released some years later; in particular 1978 produced three recordings, two from a single tour. Circular breathing was in the air, as it were: for example, John Surman's interesting six-piece, recorded as Morning Glory, who released an eponymous album in 1973, featured a track named *Cloudless Sky,* a curiously appropriate avian title, which starts off with a two-minute soprano solo feature, using the technique, and this was on a fairly 'straight' modern jazz recording. It would soon become a required 'extended technique' for advanced soprano players to demonstrate their 'chops', as I believe it is called. Parker himself had been edging towards circularity within his duo (again) with Paul Lytton (Shaker, on *Collective Calls*, for example).

A useful arboreal image is that used by critic David Ilic, originally in connection with AMM recordings – "as like or unalike as trees" (original source unknown). *Saxophone Solos* is a bit like a tough sapling, growing in confidence and inching its way towards the full maturity of *Monoceros*. The former was initially released in 1975 on Incus 19, and greatly expanded on the psi CD of 2009. It is more episodic, explorative and somewhat slower, the circular breathing less integrated and more tentative than its successor, Incus 27, whose nomenclature suggests monumentalism and brutalism at the same time, a stampeding beast with its single horn.

The first record is a major initial statement of intent, the second an astonishingly mature announcement of ascendancy. The language is fully formed on Incus 27, with the multiphonics and tongue techniques all present and correct, along with the feeling that you are actually in the bell of the instrument, hearing all the layers of sound that circular breathing creates. Its relentless nature sets it apart from *Saxophone Solos*, churning and unstoppable, especially on the long track on the initial LP first side, with the three shorter tracks on side two acting as miniatures. This mimics the structure of the later *The Snake Decides*, arguably his greatest solo soprano statement, from 1986.

Musics 21 (March 1979) featured two reviews of, and two approaches to, this kind of music (pp.26-8). David Toop spends some time describing the particular recording methods of *Monoceros*, the direct-cut process, which are also outlined on the back cover of the record, and then describes the sounds in technical terms, to wit: "The vocabulary of this music is deliberately limited and includes the above mentioned sustained high frequency combinations either in isolation or overlaid above a more deliberately articulated mid-range repetitive phrasing or glissing. The possibilities seem to range between a rapid staccato with an unusually harsh voicing and a relatively long sustain on one or more pitches which although well within human hearing are 'high' for music. Other features of the vocabulary are more conventional techniques such as multiple tonguing and multiphonics. The interaction between any and all of these elements certainly gravitates towards a strongly rhythmic approach which often

ABOVE FROM TOP: *Monocerus* by Evan Parker, April 30th 1978; *Vaincu Va* by Evan Parker, November 8th 1978

develops into regular patterns of repetition."

In particular, Toop has described here the piping effect of the 'mid-range repetitive phrasing', which underlies the 'sustained high frequency' overlay, resulting in the 'strongly rhythmic' drive that characterises this sound. This was a very modern 'swing' sound.

Richard Leigh, on the other hand, who didn't particularly like the "cold, though no doubt impressive" *Saxophone Solos*, did enjoy the "warm and natural" *Mononeros*, partly helped by the recording process. His approach towards analysis is different to Toop's, at least in this instance: "I haven't said much about the music on the record, beyond the fact that I like it. I don't intend to. A catalogue of the sounds heard on it would tell you nothing of importance. The vocabulary of approval is limited, and vague, pointlessly vague. It's nice music. There, that's done it – subjectivity."

This, in a nutshell, is one of the challenges of writing about music, especially music like this. Does one try to break it down into what is happening technically, or use metaphor and simile to communicate this? Or both together? It is impressive to read Toop's breakdown, but also refreshing to hear Leigh's alternative to this type of approach. The listener, in the end, has to access and listen to the music himself, which, in these days of YouTube, is not as difficult as it once was. At that time, one relied on journalists much more when deciding which recordings to investigate and, especially, which ones to purchase.

Evan Parker himself told me (personal communication, 2016) this, about his initial thoughts regarding solo playing: "I was at first sceptical about solo improvisation. I felt that two minds, as a minimum, were needed in order to generate the necessary 'chemistry', and that solo improvisation was close to 'composition'. Listening to Derek Bailey's solo work and Anthony Braxton's helped me change my mind. Later it became clear to me that the use of 'composition' and 'improvisation' as antonyms (still a common practice) was a category error. The writings of Busoni helped me clarify this, but I still struggle with the conventional usages."

This is controversial for those who still tend to think dichotomously about the notional separation of composition and improvisation.

Evan Parker's solo soprano work from this period is represented on two further recordings, both live, from his late 1978 North American tour of 29 cities, arranged by Martin Davidson and each one recorded within 24 hours of the other: *At the Finger Palace*, a San Francisco gig, on the obscure Beak Doctor label, and *Live at the Western Front*, from the following night and only released in 2013, and which took place at the Vancouver venue (hence the sub-title *Vaincu Va!*).

I'll take a leaf out of Richard Leigh's book here, and just state that these are two of my favourites from the solo collection. The two records have just one track per side, so each one weighs in at around 20 minutes, and are a consolidation of the confidence found on *Monoceros*. In the notes to the Canadian concert, Parker says that duration was one of his preoccupations at that time: "I wasn't that concerned with user-friendliness back then." Nowadays, he tends to insert just a few minutes of circular breathing into his live playing, but in many ways, this sort of musical experience needs longer than this to fully surrender oneself to 'the Heraclitian flux', at least in my experience. Probably the best way to approach this sequence of records is to treat them as a river, which one can dip into at any stage, bearing in mind that one never steps into the same river twice, as the saying goes.

Big Bands

At the other end of the scale from conversations with oneself, are conversations with the hydra of large (more than eight players) configurations, usually a tricky proposition in free improvisation, with chaos potentially always lurking around every corner. During the period under scrutiny, Parker made recordings with Alexander von Schlippenbach's Globe Unity Orchestra (several appearances over the mid 70s, Evan Parker being, by then, a major contributor to the European scene in general) and to Chris McGregor's Brotherhood of Breath. McGregor's fellow South African, Louis Moholo, still playing strongly to this day, recorded Parker in his own octet (*Spirits Rejoice* on Ogun 520) in 1978. Parker's loyalties, of which there are so many, also extend to Moholo's Dedication Orchestra, which aims to keep the music of

McGregor and his peers alive, many years after they passed over.

Finally, he contributed to Kenny Wheeler's Big Band (on some tracks) on 1973's *Song for Someone* (Incus 10). One feels duty bound to also mention Parker's long-term commitment to Barry Guy's London Jazz Composers' Orchestra, even though he didn't actually record with them, as far as I can ascertain, between 1973-9. His interest in John Stevens' ideas and playing abilities led him to appear in the Spontaneous Music Orchestra, the Ensemble's younger and more chaotic brother, which featured untrained musicians – a bone of contention to some of the Musicians Cooperative members, apparently.

Small groups with fellow Europeans

I have shoe-horned duos into this slot to avoid even further sub-division, even though it could be contested that dyads could constitute a separate group. There are many duo records, as there are with Derek Bailey, and I am sure than the financial aspects of only including two improvisers was attractive to producers, as well as the aesthetic and musicological potentials.

In particular, Parker's pairings with Bailey himself (as itemised earlier) and, in particular, with percussionist Paul Lytton, with the Parker/Lytton configuration, which constitutes exceptional examples

Three Other Stories by Evan Parker and Paul Lytton, June 27th 1971, June 6th 1973, July 19th 1974

of the form. Five LP/CDs were recorded during these years by the latter duo, which played across Europe in Germany (where *Ra* was recorded in 1976), Italy, Holland, Belgium and Switzerland. The two were eventually joined by Barry Guy in the early 80s, to make Parker/Lytton/Guy, who still play and record today, a preternaturally self- and group-aware trio combination of talent, as is the also still extant Schlippenbach Trio, with Paul Lovens on the traps, which Parker has played in for 44 years now. Parker's loyalties run deep.

The final duo, which absolutely *must* get a mention, is *The Longest Night*, recorded with John Stevens on the winter solstice of 1976 at

Riverside Studios in west London. This was subsequently paired with 1993's *Corner to Corner* (another studio date, this time in Islington) to make a twofer of recordings on Ogun Records, which is one of the essential examples of 'insect music' from those early years. Like Bailey's date with Anthony Braxton, the music is atomistic, *pointillistic* even, scratchy, discontinuous, microscopically detailed, with Parker on soprano and Stevens on an incredibly small, basic kit – no bass drum, two hi-hats, a child's snare, the notes to the records tell us. This is music pared back to a minimum, yet dense with

Corner To Corner/The Longest Night by Evan Parker and John Stevens, December 21st 1976, June 8th 1993

thickets of glutinous sound, like being dragged through a hedge forwards. The photo on the cover, by Jak Kilby, of the two improvisers, is, in itself, priceless, with Stevens portrayed chewing the ear off a clearly bewildered/ exasperated Parker, about Lord-knows-what. This is a telling picture, which suggests a lot about Stevens' personality (from what I've picked up over the years of writing this stuff). Another giveaway is Stevens' famously immodest description, of himself and his colleague, as being "two of the most skilled interpreters (along with a handful of others...) of this highly specialised form of improvisation." Well... if you've got it, flaunt it, as they say.

The many and varied Company records will receive attention in a subsequent chapter, with special mention given in the meantime to *Company 6 & 7* (Incus CD 07), an early collision/collusion between first generation improvisers and those of the second (in the guise of Steve Beresford), and also of our American colleagues of the time (in the less genial guise of Anthony Braxton, Leo Smith and Steve Lacy, some of whom did *not* like aspects of Beresford's shtick at all (see later).

To conclude this section, three small group sessions, which portray a round robin of first generation creative musicians that were thrown together under various individual aegises, but were essentially interactions of mainly SME and LTC-associated improvisers, all of which demonstrate mastery of the freshly hewn language of English Free Improvisation. These were, chronologically:

▶ An actual SME album (eventually released as a double CD, Emanem 3401-02), called *Eighty-Five Minutes*, previously *Quintessences One* and *Two*, mostly from February 1974. This was faultless first generation improvising, with Parker accompanied by Bailey, Watts, Stevens and American Kent Carter. These recordings could have been called *Karyobin, Parts 2 and 3*; they are that good.

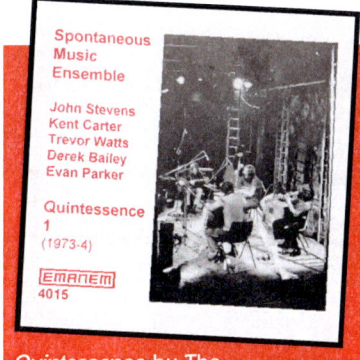

Quintessence by The Spontaneous Music Ensemble, February 3rd 1974

▶ *The Ericle of Dolphi* (surely near or at the top of bad pun lists?), recorded for Paul Lovens and Paul Lyttons' German label, Po Torch, in March 1976 (at a Total Music Meeting), and featuring Parker (as nominal leader), Paul Rutherford, Dave Holland and Lovens himself, a real collection of great talents. The second record of this double release was recorded in 1985.

▶ Another invaluable release is *One Four and Two Twos* (Emanem CD 5027), a CD that features the original quartet of Parker (who asserts that it was John Stevens' date, despite its earlier ascriptions to himself), Stevens, Barry Guy and Rutherford again. This recording was known, in an earlier incarnation, as *4,4,4,4*, (recorded in 1978) but previously unreleased tracks by Rutherford/Guy and Stevens/Parker, from slightly later on, were added to the original record, as is Martin Davidson's way, to ensure that we get value for money.

One Four and Two Twos by John Stevens, Evan Parker, Paul Rutherford and Barry Guy, August 31st 1978

All of these records are releases I would point neophyte listeners towards if they were interested in exploring the 'atomistic/*pointillistic/*

group music/insect music' styles that I describe in *Beyond Jazz* (pp.129-31).

Small Groups with American free improvisers

I feel that this section, although relatively small, deserves attention in itself, as a harbinger of things to come, as we slowly head towards 'improv international'. America was, after all, where it all began, and from under whose shadow British improvisers were trying to escape by the middle of the 1960s. Hence the birth of a specifically *English* free improvisation mainly situated, in the early days, in London.

We have alluded to Bailey's defining duo work with Braxton at the Wigmore Hall in 1974 (and a trio with Braxton and Parker on *Company Two* from August 1976 on Incus 23). I would add, rather cheekily, a disc from outside our time frame (just!), *From Saxophone and Trombone*, Incus 35 from May 1980, featuring Parker and Chicagoan George Lewis, a tremendously empathetic duo that yoked together two musicians who also had an interest in electronics (ominously for the 'purists'), a pointer to future developments, even at this early stage.

Having acknowledged the practical influence of Americans like Don Cherry and (part-American) John Tchicai, who had lived and played in Europe in the 60s with English and European improvisers, possibly the most influential and hands-on giant from those shores was Steve Lacy, who attracted Martin Davidson to make him the contributing musician to the very first Emanem recording from 1972 (Emanem 301), a solo soprano venture, which predates Evan Parker's first by three years. Of particular interest is *Saxophone Special*, now available as Emanem 4024, originally released as a LP in 1974 (Emanem 3310), and featuring a real mixed bag of quintet and sextet material with Lacy's long-running band of Steve Potts (a fellow alto player) and bassist Kent Carter. Early 'noise' contributor, Michel Waisvisz, also present, will be discussed further along in the narrative.

Both Bailey and Parker, as well as the SME's Trevor Watts, were involved in these early gigs recorded on this disc, from July 1973 and December 1974, and, although there was apparently an inadequate amount of rehearsal time, these gigs stood for an increasingly positive, and growing, relationship between the English improvisers and their American allies, who were (perhaps?) finding the adjustment to the English free language less than straightforward, and certainly more challenging, than they might have thought at the outset.

Cheating again, but only a few months into 1980, we have *Fables* (Incus 36), a tremendous quartet of Parker, George Lewis, Derek Bailey and Dave Holland, which, as far as I know, was, along with *Ericle of Dolphi* from four years earlier, one of the last 'pure' free improvisation records this most open-minded of bassists appeared on.

Other

This is the section that would be amplified in Parker's later discography (after 1980) – recordings with the likes of Jah Wobble, Spring Heel Jack, David Sylvian, Mark Hollis, Scott Walker, Robert Wyatt; all of them 'popular artists' who were trying something different (sometimes to the detriment of their careers). In the 70s, however, such a crossover was very unusual.

According to Martinelli (*op. cit.*, p.15), there are two solos on a 7" EP, with John Huscroft and Andy Bruns (probably from 1976), "overdubbed to poetry readings" just as, back in the day, Parker had provided a soundtrack to a short film, *Future World Channel*, that provided him with an introduction to John Stevens and his world. (Barre, *op. cit.*, p.207.) Multi-disciplinary, as this sort of interchange became known.

The other 'other' is *Circadian Rhythm* (Incus 33, now a very rare, anomalous and hence collectable Incus disc, as it doesn't feature Derek Bailey and has thus resisted re-release on that label). This was a recording of some of the sounds from the LMC-related event/happening from July 1978 and, according to Richard Leigh, David Toop and others, a pivotal event of the time, summing up both its ambitions and its absurdities. This originated in the "Environmental and Contextual Music Festival", proposed by Toop as a multi/mixed-media (as it used to be called) experience. Part of this event was *Circadian Rhythm* (which was Parker's idea) and which was originally intended to unfurl over a 24-hour period (the idea originating perhaps in the famous '24-hour Technicolor Dream' at Alexandra Palace in 1967?).

There had, ironically, been a 24-hour sound-athon at the Solihull Technology College – "where sound had to be continuous…and so inevitably anyone could pick up an instrument and make a noise…" – in 1977. This was organised by the future members of the post-punk band Swell Maps, school kids essentially, which does sound like an incredibly 1977 thing to do (quoted in the booklet that accompanied the *Messthetics* compilation of DIY bands from the Midlands). So the LMC weren't the first to do this, I'm afraid (plus they only managed 13 hours in the end). This was an adventurous time.

Musics 17 (May 1978) advertised the 1978 Festival thus: "The Festival will be based in the new premises of the London Musicians Collective…over a week in late July. [It occurred over nine days in the end, *author*.] The Festival will include performances, environmental events, seminars, tape/record recitals, film/video documentations, open-music sessions and exhibition (*sic*)." Toop's name was given as the coordinator.

Musics 20 featured mostly material from the festival and had a study of Lol Coxhill on the cover, of himself and his soprano, in what looks like Camden Lock scrubland. This event awaits a proper reappraisal of its contents, qualitative and quantitative, but we do have Incus 33, if you can find it. Parker involved his percussive friends, the Pauls Lytton, Lovens and Burwell, as well as Toop, instrument makers Hugh Davies (from the Music Improvisation Company) and Max Eastley. Most tellingly, the LP also featured artist/filmmaker Annabel Nicolson from the London Film Cooperative, which shared the premises at 42 Gloucester Avenue, on, variously, "charcoal, sparks, branches, twigs, fire, pine needles, draughts, smoke". This is instructive as it both reveals and reflects the probable influence (on Paul Burwell, in particular) of the pyrotechnic artist Steve Cripps, who died in 1982 aged 29, and who lived in a shed on Butler's Wharf in London's Docklands, before being moved on by developers who were/are ever keen to make it more and more unaffordable for struggling artists to find anywhere to live in central London.

It also proves Clive Bell's assertion (Bell, *op. cit.*) about the resilience of the LMC's performance space: "The floor was as hard as you like, you could flood it, light a bonfire on it (luckily!), bounce rocks off it."

As the expression went, when I was in the NHS, to describe unforeseen emergencies: "Fire, Flood and News at Ten." It is very hard to imagine this sort of event being allowed nowadays, with our modern focus on health and safety legislation. Perhaps us leaving the EU might make this sort of thing possible again, who knows?

The Festival continued with various 'events': 'Wheeled Music' (more dire puns), with "anyone with a wheeled instrument welcome to participate"; 'Circular Rhythm', "an attempted 24-hour marathon"; canalside 'happenings' (a good opportunity to see Lol Coxhill 'in the wild', on the Regents Park Canal towpath). It all looks like jolly good fun, if a bit like a weekend with The Woodcraft Folk.

The cartoon on page two of *Musics* 20 seems somehow apposite, in a good-humoured way: a punter asking for some tubing in a sailboat shop (the usual unlikely initial joke setting) for his 'water pipes', the shopkeeper saying, "Oh...you're a musician then?" and the punter answering, "Er?! No...it's for my toilet."

Boom, boom. It's just a shame that the LMC didn't have the luxury of a toilet to mend.

We've strayed somewhat off the main track here, as is my wont, I'm afraid. Evan Parker was, by this point, actively involved in the next generation's 'thing', and has continued to be on top of developments ever since. We will now move onto the other 'pioneers', as I have called them – the groups SME and AMM (and the individual musicians within), and the other principal early innovators, Barry Guy, Howard Riley and Paul Rutherford.

CHAPTER 2

The Pioneers, continued
The Spontaneous Music Ensemble, AMM, Barry Guy, Howard Riley, Paul Rutherford

Moving on from probably the two best known free improvisation practitioners, to two of its best known groups, the Spontaneous Music Ensemble (SME) and AMM, it is worth reiterating the curiously synchronous similarities between the two in these years. They had both spent the early 70s as duos: the SME of John Stevens and Trevor Watts, and an AMM of Eddie Prevost and Lou Gare. Both, by and from 1972, had downsized themselves from larger configurations, and both experienced a caesura in around 1976, where the membership was re-examined. AMM remained as a duo, with the replacement of Lou Gare by another original member from 1965, guitarist Keith Rowe. The SME expanded to slightly larger configurations, trios and quartets, with the inclusion of second generation players. The core members of both remained the same, however, Eddie Prevost and John Stevens, both of them drummer/percussionists.

It is noteworthy that the second generation tended to eschew fixed, long-term groupings, on the whole, and the ones that did emerge have been largely forgotten today, probably as much because of a paucity of available recordings as any other single factor. Derek Bailey's Company project reflected this generation's interest in mix-and-match entities. The SME ended with Stevens' premature death in 1994, but AMM is still a living entity and enjoying its 50th birthday (as a recording band) this year

Barry Guy (double bass), John Stevens (percussion) and Trevor Watts (alto sax) blowing up a storm at the Bracknell Festival, South Hill Park on July 7th 1979

CREDIT: © JAK KILBY WWW.JAKKILBY.CO.UK

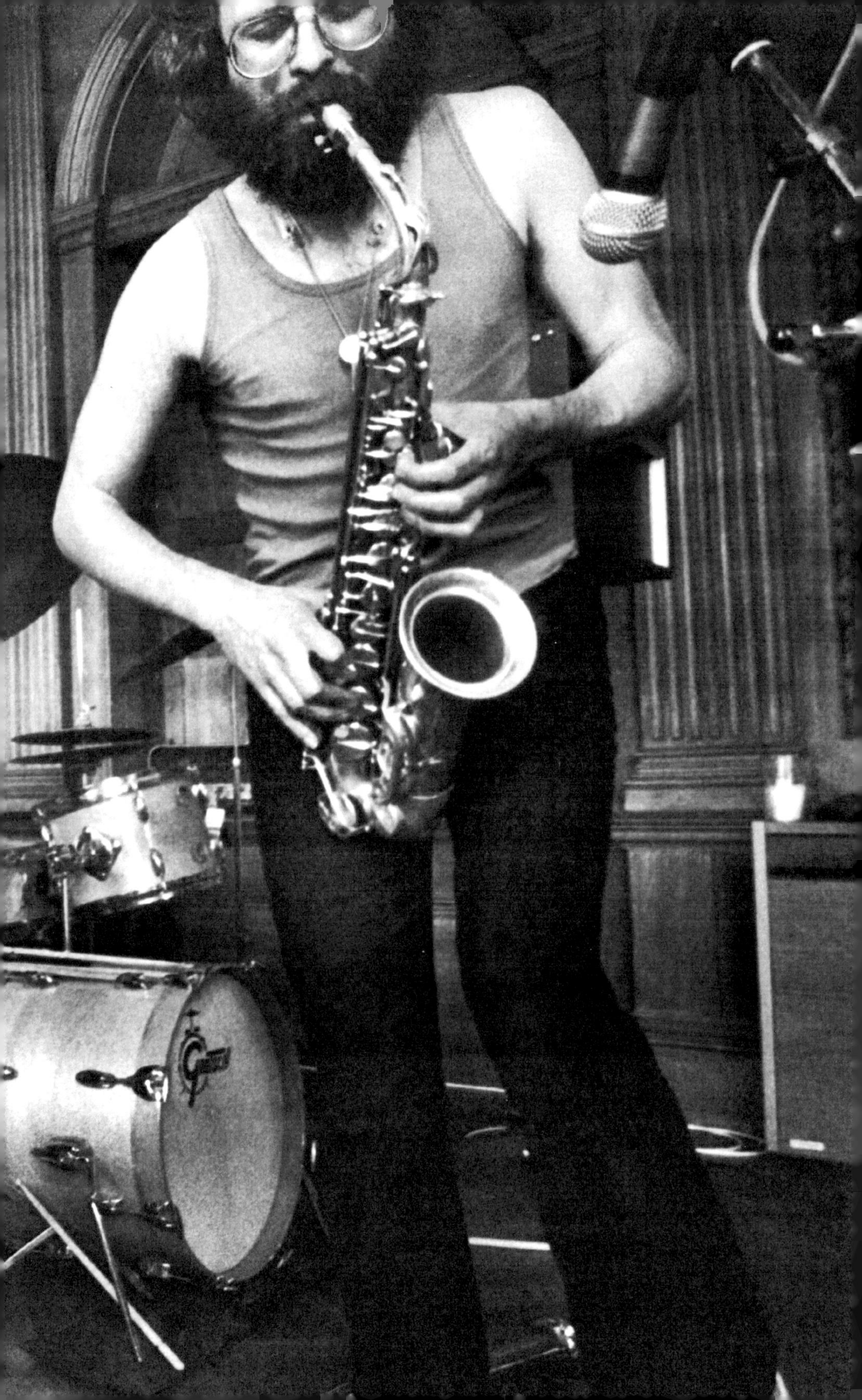

(2016). The SME continued to play in the '*pointillistic*/atomistic' style, which was pioneered by the Stevens/Watts/Rutherford original trio, in a series of recordings over the mid/late 70s, whereas AMM's 'laminar' sound was perhaps inhibited by its considerable reduction in size, making it a less layered cake? The incredibly dense striations of the Cardew-era AMM were replaced by something different, but still with a recognisable AMM soundfield.

THE SPONTANEOUS MUSIC ENSEMBLE

"For many improvising musicians, the *Face To Face* duo of John Stevens and Trevor Watts, for example, made a far bigger impact at the time than AMM." (David Toop, *Resonance*, Vol.2, No.1, Winter 1993, p.34.) This is maybe a reflection on the quasi-hermetic status that AMM had developed, even by that time (1973), as well as on the lack of recorded material, i.e. only *AMMusic 1966*, which had been deleted quickly and was, even then, hard to find, and an EP (Incus EP 1) from the 1972 Roundhouse ICES gig (discussed later), had been produced for public consumption by this stage, which was not a lot to show for seven years of intense musicianship.

It is satisfying to find that, at this point in time, an important influence on the next generation was, according to Toop, an English group as opposed to the overwhelmingly American authority that had prompted the earlier pioneers of the first generation.

John Fordham made the following eloquent summation of John Stevens' contribution in his *Guardian* obituary of September 16th 1994: "Stevens' balance of guileless exuberance, technical sophistication and encyclopedic knowledge of all kinds of drummers and drum styles was at the core of the communicativeness of his playing, but his love of musical communication in general led him to a second career founded on the conviction that music could be a force for social good. He won a Thames TV award for his community music work in 1972, and directed the former National Jazz Centre Outreach Community Music Project from 1983."

Stevens is fondly remembered by his peers and students, even though he was by all accounts not the easiest of men, who had his own not inconsiderable demons. His duo work with Evan Parker has already been remarked on in the previous chapter. The return of Trevor Watts to the SME, which resulted in the *Face To Face* recordings so eulogised by David Toop, and made at the Little Theatre Club in November and December 1973, produced "music of astonishing harmoniousness" (Cook & Morton, 2004 p.1495), a description that might appear somewhat disingenuous on first hearing the music, but *Face To Face* should be heard alongside the Bailey/Braxton and Stevens/Parker duos in order to 'get' the nature of the interactions, which are outside the standard rhythmic/harmonic/melodic rulebook but which are, nevertheless, examples of deep-listening empathy and response. This is an essential recording, as are the other records cited in this section, for those interested in 70s free improvisation.

In the end, Watts had had enough by 1976 (he'd been involved in the band for ten years by then, to be fair) and departed from the SME for good. Stevens, in turn, left Watts' band, Amalgam, which was more of a free jazz configuration, and the two rarely worked together subsequently. Like Evan Parker and Derek Bailey, and Eddie Prevost and Keith Rowe, personal 'differences' eventually split asunder a tremendously creative pairing. Watts apparently got tired of free improvisation's more arcane posturing and felt that his muse would be better served by playing music that had more rhythmic heft. This topic is still a source of some irritation for him. "He [a person who was very involved with the scene at the time, *author*] said to me, 'I heard you'd left the scene and abandoned everyone.' I was wondering why it bothered him, rather like a bit of gossip after all this time, and also I wanted him to hear my reasons why I did leave London, and in any case, what's it to do with anyone else? That's the kind of ownership people felt they had over you. I just find this very strange. He's kind of thinking that I copped out, which is the most ridiculous thing someone has said to me…I *never* stopped improvising. It's because I was playing with Africans [presumably the Drum Orchestra, Moire Music and the Celebration Band? *author*], it couldn't possibly be improvised. But it was, and the guys I was playing with were much better than the so-called free musicians who were often playing in their own self-imposed boxes." (Watts, personal communication, 2013.)

The racial aspect of this comment is impossible to ignore. Watts stuck to his guns, however, but, over the past few years, seems to have returned to free improvisation, often in the duo format once again, this time with pianist Veryon Weston.

What I think Trevor Watts was getting at here is the clannishness that characterises small-group behaviour, whether in political parties or in artistic sub-genres. Also, he is describing a reductive view on what constitutes improvised music. One thing that could be said about the Watts/Stevens SME is that it was austere, sober and somewhat forbidding, free improvisation at its most 'hair-shirt severe'. 'Plink, Plonk and Scratch' *in excelsis*. Watts clearly wanted out of this particular sound into something more rhythmically accessible. That he felt others were less than sympathetic to this apostasy is an indication of how emotive this choice of musical expression was and still is. Again, the notions of 'purism' and 'impurity' raise their heads, but the greatest improvisers easily transcend this artificial dualism.

After Watts departed for pastures new, Stevens ditched horns for over a decade, until John Butcher joined the SME in 1992. Butcher is now one of this country's most adventurous free horn players. Instead, Stevens favoured a kind of 'string-driven thing', and he was joined by Roger Smith on guitar and Nigel Coombes on violin, with yet another string player joining them on *Biosystem*, cellist Colin Wood. *Biosystem* (Incus 24) was subsequently re-released on psi, the first release on that label that didn't feature Evan Parker, its founder. (Ironically, Incus now seems to release only recordings that feature Derek Bailey, making it somewhat of a 'tribute label'.) It was recorded on June 28th 1977, at the height of the punk summer, so barely registered with style-makers at the time. However, it is, in itself, ample proof that Stevens' 'group music' did not depend on particular instruments or individuals (just as AMMusic was an independent 'thing in itself'). Clear linkage was audible with previous SME incarnations, in particular the "focused, coherent, telepathic group improvisation" (Eyles, 2008). Some listeners found that there was a danger of the music being cluttered and rather airless, what with so many stringed instruments. There was also a danger of it being lumped into some sort of 'pseudo modern-classical string quartet' ghetto, but the music was ultimately strong enough to transcend this.

'P.R.' (Peter Riley, I assume) wrote this rather patronising, in my mind, overview of Stevens in his joint review of *The Longest Night* (discussed above) and *Biosystem,* in *Musics* 18 (p.23). "The remarkable thing is that Stevens is still there: that having spent so much time playing jazz-rock and other pseudo-improvisational music [this is perhaps the sort of attitude that had riled Trevor Watts so much? *author*], he can still operate successfully in total improvisation, sitting there rattling and squeaking without a touch of nostalgia, entirely in accord with what the younger musicians are doing [Stevens was 38 at the time, *author*], or entirely supportive to Evan Parker's virtuosic flights. This must be a feature of his openness of spirit. I don't think it would stand up on its own, as in a solo concert, but in these groupings it is fully integral."

Talk about damning with faint praise. Riley should have been reminded of Stevens' 'integral' part in some of the most successful recordings of that era. These include:

▶ *Quintessence* (later released as the two-CD *Eight Five Minutes*). These recordings were briefly alluded to in the previous chapter. Two separate CDs, mostly from the same source (late 1973 and early 1974), were released as Emanems 4015 and 4016; this was an SME with a retrospective cast – Stevens, Parker, Bailey, Watts and a visiting American, Kent Carter (filling fellow countryman Barre Phillips' previous role in 1967/8), who had come to these shores with Steve Lacy (and who apparently first described this sort of playing as 'insect music'). Both bassists Phillips and German player Peter Kowald had fitted in seamlessly with English free improvisation, as did Carter. To contradict Riley's assertions, Cook and Morton counter-claim that "the stereo separations of the two sopranos, cello and guitar leave Stevens' kit very much in the foreground, and there are moments when the performance sounds almost like a concerto for percussion". (Cook/Morton, *op. cit.*, p.1496.)

Brian Morton goes even further in his (post-Cook) *Jazz Guide*, describing this recording as: "In so far as any record can capture a group as protean and evolutionary as SME, *Quintessence* is the key text, triple-distilled, rarified and raw...With virtually no preparation, the group, which had no prior history, created a series of improvisations that have no parallel even in Martin Davidson's extensive Emanem archive... the level of interplay borders on the uncanny...Many recordings of the SME survive, from before and after this time. All have something to recommend them, but none has quite the presence or has such an air of importance as this one, not as an 'historical document' but as a musical moment that replicates its searching energy and air of continual surprise with every fresh hearing." (Morton, 2010, p.407.)

One could hardly ask for a more effective endorsement of the need to record this most chimerical of music, and I would add recordings such as *One Four and Two Twos, Ericle of Dolphi* (Evan Parker, Paul Rutherford, Dave Holland and Paul Lovens from 1976) and *Endgame* to these 'musical moments', some of the best to emerge from Gen One's later 70s small-group work.

▶ *Dynamics of the Impromptu*, which had a great title if nothing else, was recorded in the dying days of the Little Theatre Club, at the cusp of 1973/4. The Watts/Stevens SME asked Derek Bailey to join them for these historic recordings (so it was, essentially, an SME session). It was an important release for Trevor Watts, at least: "I ended up with the tape with Derek, John and I which became *Dynamics of the Impromptu,* but only years later got it issued...This same recording [that] John Corbett, the writer in Chicago, said was the finest example of that music he'd heard." (Watts, *op. cit.*)

▶ *No Fear* and *Mining the Seam* (presumably from the coal face of free improvisation) were both made in 1977, and have the same line-up as the above title, only with the substitution of Bailey by yet another world-class bassist, Barry Guy. These two records are more properly Free Jazz, with themes and

No Fear by Trevor Watts, Barry Guy and John Stevens, May 23rd 1977 solos, but their sheer pungency and derring-do compel me to add it to this list. Similarities with Amalgam's epochal *Prayer for Peace* are obvious in these two recordings, especially Watts' shredding, angle-grinding tone, keen enough to wake the dead. The title track of the former "is one of the best recorded moments in British free jazz" (Cook/Morton, *op. cit.*, p.1504), with a great riff and subsequently no holds barred free interplay. Guy once again demonstrates what a great asset to any playing situation he is. "His constant configuration of harmony and his brilliant grasp of long pulse define many of these tracks." (Cook/Morton, *op. cit.*, p.1504.) In this, he is like the late Lol Coxhill, being a boon to any group he may be invited to join, however temporarily.

▶ Two further 'supergroup music' studio gigs need mentioning: *One Four and Two Twos*, aka *4,4,4,4* (Emanem 5027), already cited in Evan Parker's section previously, was Stevens' session, five improvisations from August 1978 (this was the 'one four' section of the CD, which ended somewhat prematurely when they all found themselves mired in a nearby boozer, ending up somehow

Endgame by Trevor Watts, Howard Riley, Barry Guy and John Stevens, April 1979

unable to return to the studio, for some unearthly reason!) in the company of the saxophonist himself, Guy, and trombonist Paul Rutherford; and *Endgame*, a recording made for the ECM subsidiary, JAPO Records (JAPO 60028) in April 1979, with Stevens, Watts and Guy again, and pianist Howard Riley, one of the few group sessions that the latter played on where he wasn't the nominal leader. This appears to have been part of a brief *rapprochement* with the English free scene by Manfred Eicher, who had put out a few related records on his ECM imprint in the early 70s. He also provided the studio for the recording of AMM's final album of the 70s (see p.113), which also appeared on JAPO. Unfortunately, Stevens' drunken behaviour so appalled the immaculately mannered Eicher that he refused to work with him from then on, thus shutting down that particular European avenue of possibility, for a while at least. Eicher, of course, had the good sense to keep the door ajar and the label produced several Evan Parker-related records in subsequent years (The Electro-Acoustic Ensemble).

Just like Parker, Stevens was a polyandrous performer. As Peter Riley sourly noted above, Stevens had affairs with jazz-rock (Away) and even (metaphorically crosses himself) folk (John Martyn on both *Live at Leeds* and *One World*) and Ralph McTell. He played on some of these albums with polystylistic bassist Danny Thompson, another player who appeared to be not at all bothered by generic strictures and who, in my inner address book, is a slightly more populist next-door neighbour to the mighty Dave Holland.

It is worth concluding this section by mentioning one of Stevens' last recordings from this period, *Live at The Plough*, with Mike Osborne on alto and bassist Paul Rogers (on Ayler Records) from 1979, at the eponymous pub in Stockwell, south London, where he held a very influential weekly workshop for many years, and from where, for example, Nigel Coombes, Roger Smith and Colin Woods all emerged. Stevens' pedagogic side was to the fore on these occasions and he remains, along with Eddie Prevost and Maggie Nicols, one of the great educators that the music has produced. His Search and Reflect approach even became part of the Open University syllabus, which started in January 1973, conveniently for my thesis.

Thanks here to Martin Davidson's 'Appreciation of John Stevens' on the European Free Improvisation website (1996), and the 'Tribute to John Stevens' booklet, put out by Community Music Ltd. in November 1994, both lent to me by Richard Leigh.

AMM

AMM approached the end of 1972 as one of the featured 'acts' of the International Carnival of Experimental Sound (or ICES) event at The Roundhouse in August 1972. By then, they were down to a duo of percussionist Eddie Prevost and tenorist Lou Gare, both members of the original group that had formed in 1965. Cornelius Cardew, the best known member, and 'tabletop' guitar innovator Keith Rowe, had left by 1972, to pursue Maoist musical aims with, initially, the Scratch Orchestra. The profound political, and perhaps personal, differences between Prevost and Rowe emerged within the pages of the short-lived *Microphone*, as David Toop opined in the much later LMC magazine *Resonance* (Vol.2, No.1, p.34): "If the Musicians Cooperative had a regular magazine, it was *Microphone*…although the content…was not restricted to improvisation."

Without going into too much detail, Rowe published a letter, regarding the work of composer John Cage, in Edition 5: "The outlook for Cage and the Imperialist Class reeling from one defeat to another both economically and politically is very dark," (p.11).

This should give the reader an idea of the thrust of the letter. In the following edition, Prevost retorted: "I suggest that if 'service to the people' is so important to Keith and his musical colleagues (namely Cornelius Cardew and the Scratch Orchestra) then they really must make their own musical actions louder than their words," (p.6).

Thus (temporarily) ended the partnership that formed the backbone to *AMMusic* and *The Crypt*. I've heard it described, reductively, as "Taoism verses Maoism". The Prevost/Gare duo now produced a very different AMMusic to the Cardew-era incarnation. Quiet, reflective, with a burnished tenor tone from Gare who, at times, sounds uncannily like Sonny Rollins, this AMM produced a retro-referential sound that would have been unthinkable with the earlier group. This was quiescent music mostly, going nowhere at its own pace, with silent sections disturbed only by environmental noises (like the footsteps walking across the floor on *Live At The Roundhouse*, which was recorded at ICES itself). The music did, however, retain the mysterious quality of the earlier phase and, as all 60s survivors know, 'that which can be described is not the Tao' (with apologies here to Lao Tse, who died 531 BC, and who still appears to have something to say).

The full story of ICES was featured in *Wire* 336 (pp.36-43). A rag-bag of avant garderie, the most famous performance was probably Charlotte Moorman's 'ice cello', which was gradually melted by heaters over

Moorman's naked body ("I was quite bored," revealed Steve Beresford), its 'organiser' being the late Harvey Matusow, "American ex-Communist and McCarthy collaborator turned avant garde impresario", according to writer Julian Cowley. Whatever, it sounds quite a chaotic or fluxic happening. Most artists weren't paid, and hence it fizzled out rather quickly, which was a shame as the final two editions of *Microphone* had been advertising it enthusiastically: "I.C.E.S. 72 Intermodulation/Gentle Fire/AMM/Come to The Edge/B and C/Electro Music Ensemble/and hundreds more at the Roundhouse, Place, Channel Ferry, German Institute and hundreds others from Aug.15th-26th. More info – Ingatestone 2552." (From 'live music dates', *Microphone* 6, p.8.)

Microphone 7 featured only a front page and an apologetic insert from editor Nigel Rollings telling readers that the magazine had 'collapsed', but it gamely said on the front that the intention had been to feature an article on ICES. A shame, it would have no doubt made an informative read.

The reason for mentioning this event, which is, after all, just outside our time frame, is that it both symbolises a more innocent time and provides a very rare glimpse of AMM at that point in time, the only other available recording, apart from the live AMM album from that event, being *To Hear and Back Again* (Matchless MRCD03) by the same duo that played ICES, from 1974/5. The latter starts off a little bit like *Sonny Rollins at the Village Vanguard* and features many interactions that sound more like Free Jazz than Free Improvisation.

The 'straight' composer/musicians (Cornelius Cardew, Christian Wolff, Christopher Hobbs) had left AMM (it had only been a way station for them, after all), so the previous wall of sound, most quintessentially presented in *The Crypt* recordings, was replaced by a soundfield where it was fairly easy to distinguish who was playing what (unlike the previous multi-laminated field of the late 60s). In *Unity First* (a very Free Jazz title), the first track of *To Hear and Back Again,* the *Village Vanguard* apophthegm is particularly appropriate, with Prevost channelling Max Roach on this occasion. This bare acoustic duo, minus any electronics, made it sound somewhat more like 'mainstream' Free Jazz. However, this was still 'total improvisation without a net', and the unpredictability shines through. The use of silences was still prevalent as a structural feature. Gare also would play bowed gong occasionally (which Prevost still does) and assorted 'little instruments'. The return of Rowe would change all this for a time, in an appropriately unpredicted way.

It seems that in 1976, both the dialectical materialists (as opposed to the zen spiritualists), Rowe and Cardew, returned to the 'imperialist' AMM. The resulting sessions were unsuccessful, for reasons that can only be guessed at. However, and perhaps surprisingly, Cardew and Gare (who apparently felt that the duo had offered a degree of freedom that he felt couldn't be bettered, which is an interesting perspective to say the least) were the ones to depart, leaving the newly reunited Prevost and Rowe to work out how things were going to go from then on. Perhaps the others felt excluded by the Prevost/Rowe matrix?

Lou Gare did, in fact, return to the family bosom a few years later (1989-91). However, pianist John Tilbury, whose overall improvisational style was much sparser than that of Cornelius Cardew, joined the duo in 1981 to make the duo a trio (Prevost, Rowe, Tilbury), a curious triangular reflection of Barry Guy joining Lytton/Parker at around the same time. Both of these threesomes proved to last a very long time thereafter, but Rowe eventually bailed out of AMM after 20 years or so, the old antagonisms with Prevost having re-emerged, as these things tend to do. Happily, Parker/Lytton/Guy still remain an item, and usually turn up every year or two to play on these shores. Family therapists would have a field day with this material, no doubt.

It was an Ordinary Day in Pueblo Colorado is a typically oblique AMM title chosen, no doubt, for its aggressively banal and faintly sinister feel. Like a Magritte picture. It is unique in the AMM output, emerging on JAPO in 1980, but recorded in December 1979, so it is just within our remit, and must surely be AMM's 'rock' album, with Rowe's guitar

It Was An Ordinary Day in Pueblo, California by AMM, December 1979 to the fore and in ascendance (just as it was with his contemporary stay in Amalgam). He sounds somewhat like Sonny Sharrock in his Last Exit days, or perhaps even James 'Blood' Ulmer? Looking at the CD pictures, he has turned into A.N. Other Hairy Bloke, so it is rather apposite that he partially sounds like another Hendrix disciple here. But all this emerges, inevitably, from the inevitable AMMusic matrix, which bypasses analysis, ultimately.

What interests me here, among other things, is one of the aspects of the record that is discussed in producer (and previously rock journalist) Steve Lake's notes which accompany the CD, i.e. the non-spontaneous ordering and intention of the 'radio mixes', the latter device being one so beloved of early AMM recordings and their followers: "A first take had to be abandoned when a disco troupe piped up with something too banal even for comic deployment…and on the second take, Carly Simon began warbling. She's still in there, actually, but we smeared her contribution beyond recognition in the mix."

Now call me an old politically correct worry-wart, but doesn't this smack of possible sexism? And, more germane to this book, it's hardly 'free' is it? Had the intention of this technique always been to provide some sort of 'comic relief'? Surely the whole point is the juxtaposition of the banal and the intense, and the tension produced by this? How can you be *too* banal? It's like being *too* outrageous? This smacks of the old Peking Radio snatches, so beloved of Rowe and Cardew, in the early 70s AMM, as opposed to the unmediated synchronicity of the radio samples of earlier years, which produced no end of oddly apt collisions. The 1979 recording could perhaps be seen as a precursor to hip hop samples, which are self-conscious inserts into the soundfield, rather than an aleatoric device in unpredictable service to the overall tapestry.

Did Rowe and Prevost agree with Lake's stereotypy and pigeon-holing? The Bridey Murphy trope seems to me to be rather forced in its 'edgy' counterpoint. It is, as Lake says, that these recordings "keep indeterminacy on a leash…blurring distinctions between composition and improvisation". It sounds like it, but not in a good way, in this instance.

This is a most curious album, unique in the AMM annals, and

sui generis in the output of this most *sui generis* of groups. Prevost's drumming is tremendously powerful throughout all this, and his work on *Spittlefields'* (*sic*) *Slide* is a model of controlled power, reminding me, at the risk of Prevost's ire, of Ginger Baker at his best. *For A* is also a *tour de force* for Rowe and, if one shuts one's eyes, one can almost hear the strains of Hendrix's *Foxy Lady*.

This period of AMMusic (1972-81) was perhaps the most curious and dichotomous of its lengthy history, two distinct periods, with two distinct duos and two distinct recordings. By the start of the next decade, it had settled into a period of ongoing stability, which, thankfully, has been marked by an accompanying plethora of recordings, mostly through Prevost's Matchless label. This was the band that I saw on a number of occasions.

BARRY GUY

At this stage, I am impelled to again quote Cook and Morton, in this instance writing about Alexander von Schlippenbach's Trio: "Searching for new things to 'say' about such music can often be nearly as frustrating and demanding as the playing of it." (Cook/Morton, *op. cit.*, p.1425.) However, I seriously doubt that this comparison is really the case.

Having got this off my chest, it is time to turn to one of the music's most inspiring, technically gifted and emotionally replete improvisers, bassist Barry Guy, a veteran of the 60s 'wars' who has produced a tremendous bulk of both small and large group improvisational, as well as solo, works. Unfortunately, at this stage of the book, much of the itemisation of his work in this period consists of recordings that have already been alluded to. Given that we have already covered the work of Derek Bailey, Evan Parker, John Stevens and Trevor Watts, this is inevitable. However, Guy demands a section of his own. His immense talent and live presence, his immaculate work in the trio and duo format, his innovative solo work and, of course his long-form work with the London Jazz Composers' Orchestra, deserves a book in itself, and I truly hope someone will eventually undertake a biography of Guy, a musician whose interests and skills cross so many boundaries. It goes without saying that Guy also enjoys a very successful career playing baroque music to the highest standard, which cannot help but inform his playing in the free environment.

▶ Guy released *Statements V-XI for Double Bass and Violone*, recorded on October 30th 1976, in 1977 as Incus 22. The violone is a pre-18th century bass with frets. This was a hugely challenging album for those of us who were used to bass playing by rock musicians (however skilled the Jacks' Bruce and Casady were). The record demonstrated the entirety of Guy's *armamentarium*, from his ability to 'walk' the bass, as did the past jazz masters, to the production of 'inauthentic/false' notes and tones, through to violent percussive assaults on the instrument (popular today with bassists like John Edwards), 'transgressive intrusions' such as inserting implements (the bow, drum sticks) between the strings, at times several at once, producing 'inappropriate noises', banging the body of the bass with mallets, literally 'slapping' the instrument, and what not. Seen live, this all made sense, a use/abuse of the instrument which was much more immersive than the sounds produced by the likes of Jimmy Page, with his violin intrusions: these bored me bum-less one evening in 1971, at the Belfry Club near Birmingham (on their 'small gigs' tour), when I was expecting to be genuflecting at the feet of the Led Zeppelin guitarist with his 'extended' solos. The fact that I didn't find myself doing this was a key moment in consciousness shifting for me. As was the snore-inducing drum solo by 'Bonzo' Bonham (30 minutes or so, presumably while the others 'refreshed themselves' offstage). There must be more to live improvisation than this, my younger self thought.

More positively, and in an allied field, some 15 years later, I would like to think that Thurston Moore and Lee Renaldo might have been influenced by Guy's techniques, with Sonic Youth's similar improvised

Statements by Barry Guy (solo), October 30th 1976

guitar adaptations and extensions, as well as by Glenn Branca's guitar orchestrations. If not, they should have been! Sonic Youth remain one of the most exciting bands I have seen, Led Zeppelin one of the most tedious.

It is interesting to note the similarity of Incus 22 to contemporary ECM record covers, in its spartan exactitude. ECM producer Manfred Eicher was also a bassist, which may or may not be relevant here. (Incus Records artwork had a general sparseness, which recalled ECM, but which was rinsed of any bright colour.) Barry Guy's small group work at this time can be broken down into:

▶ Howard Riley's Trio with Guy and Tony Oxley, which produced several recordings of the 'free improvisation piano trio' prototype, which format the three had made their own in the late 60s/early 70s. An adjunct to this trio (which was a working one that regularly appeared on the live circuit) was a one-off session with violinist Phillip Wachsmann, on *Improvisations are Forever Now*, with Wachsmann replacing Oxley. This was another percussion-less trio, like Iskra 1903, which also featured Guy, who admitted to me that he was intrigued by this combination of instruments. These groups' (now antiquated) pedal-controlled amplification add a serrated corona to the sounds of the instruments, somewhat like phasing did for 60s rock acts, a device that now sounds rather dated and quaint. I do wonder whether the design (by Martin Davidson) of the cover of their *Underground* (a circuit board), by the Riley/Guy/Oxley incarnation from 1974/5, was meant to reflect this notion of contemporary progressive electronics?

▶ Group work, usually trios or quartets, with other first generation peers from the SME/LTC factory, which have been cited earlier in the text – *No Fear*, *Mining the Seam*, *Applications*, *Interaction and...* (all three with Guy, Watts and Stevens), *4444* (aka *One Four and Two Twos*, under Stevens' name on Emanem), *Endgame*, *Ericle of Dolphi*, all of them outstanding examples of 'group music'.

▶ Add to these, a late 70s trio with Riley and John Stevens, *Facets* and *Organic*.

▶ Incus 18, *February Papers*, with Tony Oxley leading. This was, like the contemporary (1977) SME, a very string-driven thing, with Ian Brighton (guitar), Wachsmann again on violin and also David Bourne on violin.

▶ Guy even found time to record with the Rolling Stones, on *Angie*, according to Duncan Heining. (Heining, 2012, p.341.)

Guy was never a musical snob, playing in a Dixieland band when young, and his totally assured playing, and his genial nature, made him an asset for any grouping he chose to involve himself in. Like Evan Parker, he is a true polymath.

HOWARD RILEY

Another classically trained musician, Howard Riley has followed an individual path throughout the years, developing a true solo voice in the 70s (as did Bailey, Parker and Guy, as we have seen). He taught at the Guildhall School of Music and, latterly, at the Goldsmiths University of London site, where he has held a continuous post since the 70s. That a musician so eminently designed to head for the pastures of classical music has devoted so much of his career to free improvisation (as have Barry Guy and Phil Wachsmann, to name but two others) is something for us all to be truly grateful for.

Riley's Trio at the time, with Guy and (latterly) Oxley (who emigrated to Germany in the mid 70s), had become a fearsome live act by the cusp of the decades, but Riley released *Singleness* (Jazzprint110CD) in 1974, a solo recording that gave notice of his future intentions. This was at the time when solo piano was coming back into fashion, through Keith Jarrett and Chick Corea, for example, on their ECM recordings of the time. Riley's work was more dissonant, uncomfortable to some ears perhaps, percussive and wayward, with dark hues, echoes and rumblings, but executed with precision and *elan*. He produced a few solo albums at this time, and many since. The times I have seen Riley are usually as a solo player, and what a fascinating player he always is. Almost certainly, now Stan Tracey has passed, he is our greatest talent on the keys, along with Keith Tippett, with Alexander Hawkins (b.1981) coming along nicely, representing the younger improvisers.

Riley's trio produced challenging works, in the guise of *Synopsis* (Emanem 4044, 1973) and *Overground* (Emanem 4054, 1974/5). He then decided to return to America, where he had spent his postgraduate years, to obtain a Bicentennial Arts Fellowship in September 1976, giving him one year's tenure as Creative Assistant at the Centre for the Creative and Performing Arts at

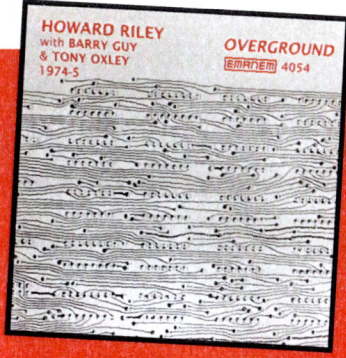

Overground by Howard Riley, Barry Guy and Tony Oxley, November 1st 1975

Buffalo, New York State. (Wickes, *op. cit.,* p.255.) This was very much in accord with the times, where modernists like Anthony Braxton and Cecil Taylor were obtaining fellowships at educational institutions, a more secure source of funding than ratty venues where every penny had to be fought for. (Taylor finished up dishwashing in one such venue, in the hard-times 60s – something one could never envisage Duke Ellington doing.) Riley began to give solo recitals across the States, and has continued giving them over the subsequent decades. He released several solo recordings to reflect this new focus.

Riley's career seems to have developed in parallel to the main stream of British improvisation.

PAUL RUTHERFORD

This most underestimated, and neglected, of the early improvisers was another virtuoso, from that era that produced so many. He had taught, as had Riley, at the Guildhall, and had earned his chops in the Forces (like Stevens and Watts, whom he met there). Like Guy, he played Dixieland in his early years. His subsequent work with the SME and with Iskra 1903 has

The Gentle Harm of the Bourgeoisie by Paul Rutherford (solo), July 2nd 1974, August 20th 1974, December 17th 1974

been discussed in *Beyond Jazz*. Like his peers, Bailey, Parker, Guy and Riley, he began to play live solo gigs, where his true virtuosity could shine out. 1974's *The Gentle Harm of the Bourgeoisie* (another great title, recorded live at the Unity Theatre), Emanem 4019, is a tough proposition for the neophyte to this kind of music, and lays itself open to all the usual criticisms of musical incompetence and lack of seriousness. He certainly pioneered an original use of mutes and of his voice to create multiphonics. Derek Bailey, for example, considered it a *sine qua non* of free improvisation, and said as much in an article in *Wire*, No.36, in February 1987, praising the re-release of *Gentle Harm* in 1986. Its sheer ingenuity, humour, cheekiness, lyricism and subversive quality tend to downplay the sheer skill at work here; just don't look for tunes and consecutiveness. Of course, this is one of those records that invites wiseacres to comment that Rutherford 'couldn't play' his instrument, just as the cynical berated Thelonious Monk 20 years previously, and rappers/hip-hoppers 20 years subsequently. Some things just never change.

He went on to produce several other solo recordings over the next few years, as well as a duo with Paul Lovens on Po Torch, and many appearances with the Globe Unity Orchestra, the London Jazz Composers' Orchestra, Tony Oxley's sextet and Charlie Watts' Big Band, among many others.

Trombonist and humorist Alan Tomlinson best continues Rutherford's legacy, an equally delightful sprite of the long horn (as the beginning of Prum's film demonstrates). Like many humorists, however, Rutherford's story had its dark side, with depression and drink his regular companions, and he ultimately paid a price for his passionately held communist views. Seek out the *Guardian*'s obituary by Richard Williams (August 10th 2007) and the appreciation by Steve Beresford in the e-magazine *Point of Departure* (Issue 13, September 2007), for accurate and sensitive reflections on this pioneer of free improv.

CHAPTER 3

Some Thoughts about Jazz in the 1970s

"*J*azz *is constantly undergoing change, in a dynamic pattern that includes regression and retrenchment as well as progress.*" (Ira Gitler, in the notes on the sleeve of *Looking Ahead*, by Eric Dolphy and Ken McIntyre, 1960.)

I was trying to think of a different, 'sexier', name for the so-called 'second generation' of English free improvisation, and came up with a Duchamp-ian conceit, *John Rex* (or even *Jean Rex)*, standing in for 'Genre X', as the French surrealist did with *Rrose Selavy*, i.e *'eros, c'est la vie'*. Somehow, this seems to fit in with the English improvisers' wit. I can't see it catching on, however.

Leaving my fripperies behind, I'd like to quote from Coda (September 1974) to orientate us to the challenges that faced free improvisers by the mid 70s: "It is not necessary…to swing [which had been the *sine qua non* of jazz up to this point in time, *author*], to play effectively, as long as… solos have good ideas. It is possible that the music we know as jazz may eschew swing as it evolves…It is not valid to condemn music simply because it does not swing." (Pekar, p.10.)

Despite the rather schoolmarm-y tone, this comment had a fair point. How far could this music go before it got so beyond jazz that it barely qualified as such?

Pekar goes on to delineate: "A buoyant rhythm feeling that jazz musicians project…by using syncopation and by alternatively building and releasing tension." (*Op. cit.,* p.10.)

These few words very concisely describe the music's allegedly quintessential features.

This, however, later became a rather moot point. Thelonious Monk, with his astringent piano technique, didn't 'swing' in this conventional way (early commentators going as far as to claim that this very technique concealed an inability to play 'properly'), nor did Cecil Taylor or Albert Ayler, although surely nobody can deny that all these three musicians 'had rhythm'. But, in the final analysis, the tide was slowly turning against the avant garde's particular version of swing: "As an art form evolves, it can sometimes lose some of its most important characteristics." (Pekar, *op. cit.*, p.10.)

Neo-classical jazz history tends to discount, and/or patronise, both Free Jazz and Fusion (as is amply demonstrated by their neglect in Ken Burns' monumental film documentary about jazz music, simply entitled *Jazz*). Jazz 'Top Ten' lists are usually as predictable as their rock music equivalents: *Kind of Blue* and *A Love Supreme* usually at the top (fantastic recordings that they are, obviously), but they remain as stolid and unmovable as *Sergeant Peppers/Revolver*, *Astral Weeks* and *Pet Sounds*, the Mount Rushmores of jazz/rock music 'product'. The period of 1973-9, with the aid of the retroscope, appears to be the last one of serious modernist development in both these genres, especially after post-punk imploded in around 1981, and the Marsalis School (in America) and the Jazz Revival (in this country) gained prominence. After that, the backward glance became the main determinant of quality, or so it appeared.

In the world of literature, the three Bs – Ballard, Burgess and Burroughs, all an enormous influence on so many 70s musicians – seemed to be a last flowering of modernism in that particular realm, before the likes of Martin Amis, Brett Easton Ellis and Jay McInerney, who were very informed by and associated with the 1980s, rose to public attention.

The 'neo-classicists' in jazz focused on a pre-70s, notionally pre-lapsarian 'golden age', much like UKIP do nowadays with their notional 'Land of Cockayne that is forever England'. Poor old 1960s, constantly being demonised by traditionalists. Yet in many ways the 70s were even worse, in real terms, for 'sex, drugs and rock 'n roll', but somehow the

60s have also, paradoxically, at the same time, managed to become, bizarrely, a mythic land of pre-immigrant 'sovereignty'. Or was that the 50s? No one seems to know, not even Nigel Farage.

What is clear, however, is that neo-classicism in jazz and rock, like neo-conservatism in politics, triumphed in the long run. Even Miles Davis mellowed out. The culture slowly, but surely, turned away from the avowedly experimental. Our own English 'Jazz Revival' of the mid 80s furthered the process of ancestor worship, with its Holy Writ of Blue Note and Hard Bop. The 1970s could, then, be seen as the last gasp of modernism before a more conservative era began to establish itself. 1980 saw the return to active duty of several 1950s giants: Davis himself, Dexter Gordon, Frank Morgan and Johnny Griffin all emerging from retirement to a new generation of admirers, a case of *déjà entendu*, perhaps. By this time, Al Foster was the only member of Miles' group that had grown up with, and been directly influenced by, 60s Free Jazz. (Nisenson, 1997, p.216.) The latter genre (as opposed to Free Improvisation) did manage to obtain an allotted place on the 'jazz family tree' history – after Hard Bop and before Fusion – but by 1980 it was increasingly seen by taste-makers to be an ossified form, ineluctably tied to its time and circumstance, Vietnam, civil rights battles, black power, etc, etc.

So, whither the 'Sound of Surprise', to use Whitney Balliett's famous description of jazz? Who kept the modernist flag flying in these years, when events were conspiring to turn the clock back? Witness the rise, and rise, of Wynton Marsalis and Stanley Crouch, two sides of the same conservative coin: the opening of the 'Jazz Museum' i.e. the Lincoln Centre; the systematic academicisation of jazz, starting with the *Smithsonian Collection of Classic Jazz* in 1973, and the gradual replacing of the 'on the road' generation, exemplified by the big band era, where younger musicians had the chance to play with more experienced guys in a live situation (Charlie Parker's early years in Jay McShann's band being a famous example), by learning in educational institutions. From now on, jazz education centres focused on theory, technique and the 'canon'. All of these factors contributed to a set series of ideas of what constituted jazz (and what didn't), and free improvisation almost certainly *didn't*. At least many of these institutions featured prominent advanced musician-teachers: Anthony Braxton, Cecil Taylor, Roscoe Mitchell, who are examples from across the pond; Keith Tippett, Steve Beresford, David Toop and Howard Riley are examples from this side. Certainly, teaching tenures offered more security for the teachers, in terms of work and pay, than their typically precarious former reliance on live bookings.

Jazz was newly re-cast as 'America's classical music'. On the one hand, and as a counterpoint, there were the groups and individuals who followed styles and notions that were antithetical to these new idea of 'purity' or 'authenticity': Ornette Coleman and his opaque Harmolodics theory; the members of the Association for the Advancement of Creative Musicians (AACM) including the Art Ensemble of Chicago, Anthony Braxton, George Lewis, Leo Smith and Henry Threadgill; John Zorn and the Lower East Side improvisers; bassist William Parker's work; the old master Cecil Taylor, among many others, all of whom were notable for their hybridity and healthy pluralism. (See Lewis, 2008, pp.384-8.) In this country, we had the musicians discussed in this book. What these improvisers in both countries faced was the 'regression and retrenchment' described by Ira Gitler in the quote at the beginning of this chapter.

This process does seem to have started around 1973: "In 1973, the Smithsonian Institution released the *Smithsonian Collection of Classic Jazz*, assembled by critic-turned-curator Martin Williams. An unprecedented attempt to bring jazz music's 'masterpieces' from all eras and various record labels together in one place, the boxed, six-record set exerted enormous influence over the artistic pantheon." (Anderson, 2007, p.182.)

Needless to say, the collection didn't feature any free improvisation, the nearest it got being the inclusion of *Crosscurrents* by the same Lenny Tristano band that made two of the very first totally freely improvised tracks, in 1948.

At around the same time, synchronously, a four-record compilation performed a similar act of canonisation for folk-rock – *Electric Muse: the Story of Folk into Rock*, released in 1975 as a combined Island/Transatlantic Records release. This, in turn, was a development from the famous Harry Smith *Anthology of American Folk Music* collection from 1952 (and re-released in 1997 to a new generation), which had proved to be such a huge influence on the 60s folk scene.

Reggae eventually had its own Alexandrian Library moment with *Tougher than Tough: the Story of Jamaican Music*, an essential overview, released in 1993. Gradually, all these 'minority' genres were being preserved in their own vinyl/digital boxed aspic.

GENERATION TWO AND ITS LINKS

"I regard the punk thing with a bit of amusement and a certain amount of affinity." (Lol Coxhill, alluding to his time with The Damned.)

Curiously, the phenomena described in the jazz world above, i.e. the repulsing of the avant garde, was replicated in the world of rock/pop music at around the same time. The second generation's links with punk and post-punk have been much commented on. I would say that the latter sub-genre ended in about 1981, as many of the various individuals and groups associated with it turned to more populist strains, including the trappings of dance and funk.

This transmogrification was best exemplified perhaps by the mutation of Scritti Politti from a scratchy, cod-reggae Marxist collective from squat-land into singer and writer Green's reincarnation, in the early 80s, as a blue-eyed soul crooner presented with a high production sheen and record sleeves which mimicked conspicuous consumption memes (look at the sleeves of their mid/late 80s singles for confirmation of this). This approach met with not inconsiderable success after their 1981 makeover, while Green claimed that the songs and sleeves were 'deconstructions' of pop music's 'signatures'. Having cakes and eating same springs to mind. The story of post-punk, and its links with free improvisation, is best told by Simon Reynolds in his peerless *Rip It Up and Start Again* (pp.198-221), the title, ironically, being a hit from one of the bands, Orange Juice, that helped dig the post-punk grave.

Sticking with Scritti for just a while longer (I think that their story is a cynosure of the times, hence my dwelling on it for so long), Reynolds tells of these post-punk ideologues' encounters with their fellow Camden-

The Engineer – "a refurbished canalside gastropub and garden" (Googlemaps). In 2000, the cartoonist 'speedwell' predicted, in *Resonance* magazine, that "this pub will become a posh eaterie in 11 years time"... Before that, it provided a service as the LMC's toilet of choice

ites, the London Musicians Collective, who, by 1978, were well settled into their new location at 42 Gloucester Avenue, with Scritti living in a famously chaotic squat in nearby Carol Street, which was a few yards away from Camden Town tube station. There were, retrospectively, hilarious 'pissing competitions' between the two: "Typical of Scritti's interactions with 'opponents' was their encounter with the genial improvisers of the London Musicians Collective...Its headquarters were over the road from the Engineer [which were notoriously where the nearest toilets were; coincidentally Carol Street also had no bathroom, *author*], a pub whose back room had become 'the court of Scritti' [a kangaroo court, by the sound of it, *author*], according to Steve Beresford, one of the co-founders of the LMC.

"One evening the entire Scritti collective attended an LMC performance. Afterwards everybody retired to the Engineer where, says

Penman [Ian, a *New Musical Express* journalist of the time, controversial himself because of his own 'deconstruction' of pop journalism, *author*], there was a 'big ideological Rob Roy squaring off between the two sides'." Beresford recalls Green "...denouncing the bourgeois imperialist improvisers...and claiming that *he* was playing '*people's* music'". (Reynolds, *op. cit.*, p.207.)

Unfortunately for Green, most of the LMC had heard it all before several years earlier, from the likes of Keith Rowe and Cornelius Cardew. This sort of thing was *de rigeur* at this time, in both free improvisation *and* rock. *Musics* was apparently known as 'The Squabblezine', so named by Nick Kimberley of the much missed immortal Camden Town bookshop Compendium, and the *NME* saw itself as the scourge of the sexist, racist and, worst of all 'rockist', tradition of post-Elvis pop/rock. So, plenty of room for self-righteousness on all sides then, all taken *terribly* seriously by many, so some humour was needed to offset the hegemonic homilies.

Green, however, seems to have had the last laugh, when *the* Miles Davis played on Scritti's 1988 45, *Oh Patti (Don't Feel Sorry For Loverboy)*, having previously covered their track *Perfect Way* from Scritti's 1985 LP *Cupid & Psyche* on his own *Tutu* recording of the following year and, what's more, began featuring *Perfect Way* regularly in his own concerts during his 80s 'comeback'.

Way to go, Green, engineering a generic crossover that many jazz buffs found hard to stomach (which was a tad disingenuous, given Miles' undoubted ear for a good tune when he heard one).

Apart from Miles' unforgettable contribution, as a 'sideman', to hard bop alto saxophonist Cannonball Adderley's *Somethin' Else* as far back as 1958 (Adderley paid back the compliment by featuring on the Davis album of the following year, *Kind of Blue*, which I gather is fairly well regarded in jazz annals), the trumpeter almost never, ever, played second fiddle, so Scritti's *coup* was a considerable achievement although, sadly, Miles never got to appear on *Top Of The Pops*.

Luckily, the first generation did have a well-developed sense of humour, which Gen Two inherited. The Clash were offset by The Flying Lizards (which included Toop and Beresford) and, in the free improv sphere, AMM had Alterations. It is interesting to note, however, that the second generation, as alluded to earlier, tended to avoid fixed 'groups'. There were a few, the Recedents (named after their hairlines, apparently), Alterations, the Promenaders, 3/4 Pullovers, but this tended not to be the norm. Such a concept as a long-term group (like the Coltrane Quartet and the Davis Quintets) was perhaps considered as faintly 'jazzist', just as The Clash were seen, in their particular arena, as 'rockist'.

As laughable as all this sounds from the safe vantage point of 40 years later, these issues were argued about with considerably "scary outpourings of vitriol" at the time, as Clive Bell (*op. cit.*) put it. The British improv scene had some definite affinities with the post-punk scene, as we can see, so all this must have been 'in the air' at the time, a culture turned in on itself, as marginal cultures are prone to do.

One of the post-punk bands mentioned by Clive Bell at the time were the long-forgotten (if they even registered at the time, which is doubtful), Reptile Ranch from Cardiff, a trendily off-putting name to suit the times, who were cited by Bell in his delightful summary of the LMC. To be frank, the one track of theirs that I have heard, on a *Messthetics* (in turn, the name of a Scritti Politti composition) compilation of very obscure post-punkers from 1978-81 (on the Hyped2Death label if you can, or indeed want to, find it), sounds like standard stop-start, Farfisa-dominated, punk, in thrall to the early Fall. No bad thing in itself, but hardly something to make one reconsider the history books. The similarly Bell-cited Dislocation Dance is probably more significant for its nomenclature than for pure musical merit, which was another sign of those times.

Dislocation Dance, a Manchester band, also get a mention in Reynolds (*op. cit.*, p.192) as one of a series of 'funny little groups', including a band that, beyond parody, decided to call themselves The Hamsters. What interests me here is the choice of names. 'Dislocation Dance' is a near relative of 'mutant disco' (many examples of this meta-genre soon appeared on the Ze label, another very hip reference point at that time). 'Fractured' was the verb to be seen with in 1979 (it was the name of Joy Division's publishing arm, so enough said). It all implied something a wee bit sinister, hinting at illness, deformity, breakage, something 'wrong' somehow, in the state of Camden, or Salford. Just take a look at the groups who were at the notional cutting edge in the late 70s, which, almost certainly, many of the second generation improvisers were aware of, and were probably listening to.

▶ From England, we had The Pop Group (which was surely the most arch name of all?); A Certain Ratio (a definite rival for that particular distinction, which, for added *frisson*, alluded to the Nazis, as did the soon-come New Order); Rip, Rig and Panic, named after a Roland Kirk LP (another arch yawn, but with whom future free master drummer Steve Noble played); Pigbag; Maximum Joy ('joy' was a buzzword in those times); 23 Skidoo (who knows?). And, going back to the earlier part of the decade, we had Gong (who did have the honour of appearing, very early, on the BYG Actuel label, the late 60s avant gardists label of choice, on a couple of occasions before Pot-Head-Pixiedom completely took over command of the ship), Henry Cow, Robert Wyatt and, indeed, the Virgin label crew generally.

▶ From America, we had James Chance; Bill Laswell's Material, 'punk-funk' as it was called, and which also included ex-Ornette guitarist James 'Blood' Ulmer (who released a shreddingly good album on Rough Trade in 1980, that is probably the best of this whole genre); Defunkt (with Lester Bowie's brother, Joe, and Lester himself); WasNotWas ('neurotic Jewish funksters' is my wife's description); even a trend-surfing Frank Zappa, with his own mid 70s George Duke/Ruth Underwood Mothers: "1973 was the year that post-Bitches Brew jazz-rock fusion gained momentum." (Wills, 2015, p.90.)

This was a real stew, gumbo or brew, or whatever, but Zappa deserves special mention here, if only for his genuinely genre-busting *Hot Rats*, *Uncle Meat* and *Burnt Weenie Sandwich* albums. He was never the most modest of men, and considered himself a humorist as well as a musical genius, and his albums did (sometimes, but not so much on these particular albums) have a *drollerie* that the free improvisers shared. Unfortunately, his wit lost its edge very quickly around 1970, with its obsession with un-reconstructed sexism and tedious 'on the road' anecdotes, usually a prurient, Lord Longford-type, fascination with groupies (curiously enough an interest he shared with Robert Fripp, another intellectual musician obsessed with technique, and who also recorded absolutely everything he played for posterity). Both guitarist/band leaders represent one validation of Freud's theories of repression and creative genius, outlined in *Civilisation and Its Discontents* (1930).

If these affinities between the worlds of rock/punk and free improv seem rather tenuous, just consider these situations where the two converged:

Steve Beresford spoke very fondly of The Slits (and Viv Albertine of him, in her outstanding autobiography of 2014). Albertine started attending the LMC, and Beresford appeared on the band's final album, 1981's *Return of the Giant Slits*, providing "'daft noises', on flugelhorn, keyboard and toy instruments during their American tour". (Reynolds, *op. cit.*, p.208.) Just take a quick scan of Reynolds' 'post-punk timeline' at the end of his book (*op. cit.,* pp.545-549), to see what a plethora of genre-crossing recordings came out in the late 1970s, even in, or maybe especially in, the pop/rock field.

"One of the LMC's articles of faith was the idea that a true heaven-made musical marriage would consist of ultra-virtuoso improvisers and non-skilled naifs getting together and getting it on…all this polymorphously perverse shifting and drifting, the fluid line-ups and one-off collaborations, represented an attempt to deconstruct the conventional rock band." (Reynolds, *op. cit.*, pp.208-9.) So we got, against all the odds, a UK Top 5 hit from The Flying Lizards' cover of *Money* in Autumn 1979, featuring both Toop and Beresford, a Dada-ist version of Berry Gordon's classic paean to capitalist principles.

Punk spokesman Mark Perry also attended the LMC and was involved in two experimental outfits, The Door and the Window, and The Lemon Kittens. The latter at times approached performance art, and featured the goth beauty Danielle Dax and the rather less gorgeous Karl Blake, who was later associated with Current 93.

The Manchester Music Collective (MMC) was very active in and around 1978, and released several singles by crossover acts like Steve

Miro and The Eyes and Spherical Objects (all on the Object Music label). The MMC was formed by improvisers Trevor Wishart and Dick Witts (of The Passage, a briefly much lauded post-punk band). Much of this stuff could be described as 'post-rock/punk', a designation that Reynolds himself came up with 15 or so years later (but I'm still not sure what it means, as with Ornette Coleman's Harmolodic theory). Some classifications don't bear too close scrutiny, but they do sound very seductive and decisive, so it's worth running with them.

It is also worth mentioning that any study of the nationwide increase in musician collectives and co-ops, in these years, will reveal some similarities with the rock music DIY 'movement' of the time, in terms of the presentation of the genre in both cassette and vinyl compilation form. The Bristol, Manchester and Liverpool groups (*Street to Street* by the latter, and *A Manchester Collection*, are good recording examples) all used these formats – admittedly fairly primitive by modern standards, but effective in communicating across regional networks. Many of the *Messthetix* bands were only ever recorded in these forms, as were their free improv peers. Certainly, for example, the 3/4 Pullovers recordings were only available in cassette format, until Martin Davidson rescued them in 2000 for his Emanem label.

The examples cited above represented the first stirrings of multiple cross-referencing between free improv and more popular experimental forms (avant-rock, electronic) that has continued to this day. To take us out of our time frame for a short while, and to illustrate the point more fully, the following are examples of some later creative liaisons of interest, however brief, which built on the early *rapprochement* between the forms:

Evan Parker, ever the polymath, has recorded with artists from the rock field as varied as David Sylvian, Scott Walker, Robert Wyatt and Jah Wobble, each contribution being marked by his usual empathy towards other artists' ideas and objectives. He has also worked very productively, both live and in the studio, with drum and bass-ists Spring Heel Jack.

Derek Bailey, in turn, played with younger players, including DJ Ninj, and The Ruins from Japan, and TH Drenching, a real mixture to be getting one's head around.

Clive Bell has also played with Jah Wobble's band, which I witnessed at a WOMAD gig a few years ago and was hugely impressed by.

This Heat were a post-punk band of considerable musical maturity and range, whose drummer was free player Charles Hayward, and who I also saw drumming for Keiji Heino's Japan-oise trio Fushitsuscha in May 2000 at London's Garage, never a gig for the faint-hearted.

One of the improvisers from the third (?) generation, and one of its most popular, is percussionist Mark Sanders, who was the "'bank-clerk type', a teenager who seemed to be more than a little overwhelmed by the presence of (John) Lydon". The band in question that Sanders was auditioning for was the first Public Image Limited. It would be a more than interesting counter-factual to hear what Sanders would have sounded like on *Metal Box*. Ironically, he did end up, many years later, collaborating with Wobble on a few of the latter's albums. (All this from Strongman, 2007, pp.45-6.)

Terry Day, who has his own section later on in this book, played in the original Kilburn & the High Roads, the pub rock legends, along with George Khan and Russell Hardy.

I'm sure that informed readers can come up with other examples but it is, again, instructive to consider how few of this second wave of British improvisers, apart from Lol Coxhill, feature in the Cook/Morton *Guide...* or, indeed, in Richard Cook's solo encyclopedia. No Toop, no Beresford, no Bell, no Russell, no Day. This is not a criticism of these books, by the way, both of which are more than fair to Free Improvisation, but it does demonstrate how even further beyond jazz these players had moved, in the eyes of the 'history makers' and the encyclopedists.

'NEW/REDISCOVERED MUSICAL INSTRUMENTS'

A book that is perhaps the literary correlation of the extended techniques, instrumentation and instrumentalism of those years, is David Toop's first book, *New/Rediscovered Musical Instruments*, published in 1974. It is more of a monograph, in actual fact, and features contributions from Hugh Davies (formerly of the Music Improvisation Company), the

LMC's Paul Burwell, percussionist and pyrotechnician, Evan Parker, Paul Lytton, Max Eastley and Toop himself. Long out of print, there are apparently moves to have it re-published, which would be a service to fans of the arcane and outlandish, or even just of Harry Partch, the modern day progenitor of this sort of activity.

Toop, in his preface to the book, describes how his subject has affinities with many of the musical preoccupations of the likes of John Stevens and Evan Parker: "Some instruments can immediately be related to the instruments of the Western Symphony orchestra. Some can be traced with more difficulty to the instruments of Medieval Western music, Oriental classical or religious music, or aboriginal peoples of Africa."

He alludes, in an ironic way, to free improvisation, a music in which many of these instruments were featured: "It should be borne in mind though that these instruments are contemporary with much music that is, to a large number of people, 'not music at all'."

Toop also describes the progression (as it seemed then) of jazz, before neo-conservatism got its foot in the door a few years later: "The progress of jazz has often been charted by extremely rapid discovery with regard to playing techniques – the appearance and role of the drum kit has become almost unrecognisable when placed alongside that of just 15 years ago."

Of course, since 1980, electronic technology had produced the ability to make sounds that were undreamed of in 1974, but it is a moot point whether this would count as jazz in the minds of the likes of Ken Burns, who had more sympathy with the sentiments of Ira Gitler's quote at the beginning of this chapter.

One of the dangers of the lionisation of 'proper' jazz (*a la* Marsalis/ Crouch) is pointed out: "The continued use of conventional instruments in the face of the technical demands of new music has, in some circles, engendered a cult of almost grotesque virtuosity." (Toop, *op. cit.*)

So, if I am interpreting Toop correctly, he suggests that the 'cult' of virtuosity is replacing genuinely creative or progressive music. Today, one increasingly notices that there is a plethora of university educated musicians who can basically play any score put in front of them and are technically extremely proficient. But where is the new Coltrane or Davis?

Or Evan Parker or Wheeler? Have they had any originality trained out of them, like so many 'classical' musicians (remember that jazz is the new classical music!) who find it difficult, if not impossible, to improvise with any confidence? This is an oversimplification, of course, and there are many talented young improvisers that one can catch at The Vortex and Café Oto most evenings (in north London), but the overall trend in most forms of music seems increasingly conservative and nostalgic.

At the same time that the punk/post-punk/second generation of free improvisation was extolling the virtues of 'difference' and 'surprise', another school was extolling those of 'the tradition' and 'continuity'.

In the introduction to the Toop book, Madeau Stewart also questions the conditions that we traditionally listen to live music in, at least in most urban situations: "Nightly emerging from concrete block houses – commonly known as concert halls – large audiences all over Europe accept the sounds they have been subjected to as right and proper. Right and proper also are considered their ritual bursts of handclapping – a strange form of punctuation to the music indeed, but the only form of participation tolerated."

It is good to subject to scrutiny the stereotypical behavior that most of us exhibit in the live situation. Clapping after solos and at the end of numbers is seen as traditionally 'appropriate' and 'polite', but not all musicians are agreed as to its suitability. Some see it as distracting and even demeaning. The LMC, certainly, questioned the norms of performance (the duration, the role of boredom, etc), as we will see.

Toop's little book is well worth seeking out, as it reifies the sense of explorative thought (as did *Musics*) that surrounded free improvisation in those days.

THE LONDON MUSICIANS COLLECTIVE (LMC)

A whole book could, and should, be written on the subject of the LMC, as could and should be many of these subjects, isolated here in their single chapters.

Without wishing to come across as all *Daily Mail* anti-PC, I feel that I have to quote from the second page of *Musics* 21, if only to give a historical context, and because it gives a *madeleine*-like (not Davidson) flavour of those far-off times. *Musics* and the LMC were so inter-connected that it is futile to make an absolute separation of the two, although they were, in fact, as I have stressed on several occasions, completely separate entities (who just happened to share the same premises, but hey, these things happen). The following is inserted into the contents page of this edition of the magazine, one of its last: 'SEXISM/ LANGUAGE/MUSIC'.

"The typesetting and paste-up team are very unhappy about the sexism inherent in parts of this magazine [and possibly in the music itself? *author*]. In particular the assumptions made by Peter Riley that all musicians are male, the remark made by Gunther Christmann regarding his 'girlfriend', and Trevor Wishart's use of the term 'grabs you by the balls'. We feel unhappy enough to refuse to set and paste up anything like that starting with the next issue."

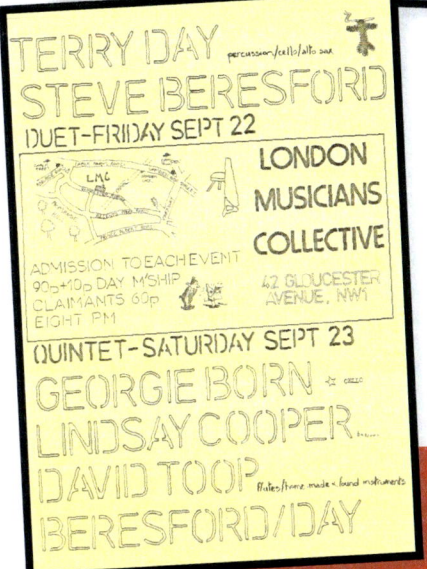

Two LMC fliers from the early 80s

Sadly, there were only two editions left before the magazine went 'tits up' (sorry, really couldn't resist that). The comment does, however, have a further resonance in these days when a self-confirmed 'pussy-grabber' is the President of the United States. I am genuinely not trying to trivialise this issue, though. Around this time, the American radical feminist philosopher Mary Daly (Daly, 1978) was highlighting the many ways in which our society suppresses women, and one of these ways is an androcentric use of language.

The slow acceptance of female improvisers into this male bastion had been a long time coming, and is still not satisfactorily resolved (if it ever can be). I will discuss this issue in slightly more depth later, but a book, or many books, are needed, before sexism/misogyny in music generally can even be discussed non-defensively, and without fear of recrimination from all of the parties concerned. Particularly as we seem to be going backwards in this age of cyber stalking and other forms of digital abuse. I would recommend two works that have very interestingly addressed the topic of female improvisation and its implications: the Fischlin/Heble compilation, *The Other Side of Nowhere: Jazz, Improvisation and Communities in Dialogue* (2004), and Ian McKay's book *Circular Breathing: The Cultural Politics of Jazz in Britain* (2005).

It does, in retrospect, seem a bit of a shame to berate the magazine about its insipient sexism at this point, as *Musics* 20 prominently featured an article about the Feminist Improvising Group (FIG), followed by a discussion between several leading female improvisers, and two pieces by film maker Annabel Nicolson.

However, these were the times that they were, and previously sidelined issues were gradually brought to the fore, to the discomfort of some. For example, consider these rather odd comments by Clive Bell in his otherwise exemplary *History of the LMC*: "I recall one musician warning me that after a John Stevens workshop he had observed that most of the male musicians had erections. I couldn't really see what was so wrong with this – maybe the music wasn't so cerebral and abstract as some people made out?"

It's really difficult to know where to start with this comment, so bizarrely disingenuous as it is. Lindsay Cooper, late of Henry Cow and at that time a founder member of FIG, puts it more bluntly (*Musics* 14, October 1977, p17): "The sexist extremes of 'cock rock' are a triumph for music's power to spread dominant and oppressive ideology in an easily marketable form."

Sorry, Clive.

And here it was, squarely in the world of free improvisation. My wife, ever ready with the *bon mot*, said about Bell's observation, "there's no accounting for taste", a somewhat gnomic observation in itself, I do realise. But what to make of this 'erection section'? Did these guys have a medical problem with priapism? (Not a disorder to make light of, in actual fact, if one looks it up in medical dictionaries.) It does, though, say a lot about the sexual needs of the attendant workshop 'members', to be frank, and I wonder what the views of the FIG might have been about this phallocentrism? Not at all surprised, I would surmise. Or especially flattered, if they had been the recipients of this sort of attention. Unfortunately, their views were not recorded, if they were sought at all.

I'm making fun of all this, but it does put into some sort of perspective the paste-up team's reaction in *Musics* 21, quoted previously.

TEMPORARY AUTONOMOUS ZONES (TAZ)

Cultural theorist George McKay has written one of the more interesting books on English free improvisation, including chapters on gender and racial issues (2005), which are very welcome additions to the literature. His earlier work (1996), on modern counterculture, discusses the advantages and disadvantages of collective liberationist, anti-hierarchical, organisations. McKay quotes Hakim Bey's idea of the Temporary Autonomous Zone (TAZ) (*op. cit.*, p.8 & p.156), being the idea of a space, physical, psychological or metaphorical, in and around which a culture of resistance can be formed. This puts me in mind, however fancifully, of the LMC and, in particular, their HQ, from early 1978, at 42 Gloucester Avenue (Camden Town, north-west London) and some of the 'events' both in the premises, and around them.

"The 60s-style 'tribal gathering' [the most famous of which occurred in Golden Gate Park in San Francisco in January, 1967, *author*], the forest conclaves of eco-saboteurs [the M11 campaign, for example, *author*], the idyllic Beltane of the neo-pagans, anarchist conferences, gay faery circles…Harlem rent parties of the 20s, nightclubs, banquets, old-time libertarian picnics…we should realise that these all are already 'liberated zones' of a sort, or at least potential TAZs." (Bey, quoted in McKay, 1996, p.8.)

Auxiliary sub-TAZs can be re-formed, elsewhere, at some other time. The LMC did this with Toop's Festival of Environmental Music, and Company took its 'zone' all over the world. Nowadays we have Café Oto (and its various projects) in Dalston, north-east London, and a huge choice every year of festivals like All Tomorrow's Parties. Back then, the LMC's Camden Town address became the zone (at a time when free improv was suffering from its usual lack of decent medium/long term venues) for many of the music's manifestations, and also for various associated media: "A flexible performance space," as Bell puts it (*op. cit.*) The site had what might nowadays be sold to interested parties as having a 'distressed ambience' (the lack of a toilet, bar or any disabled access of any kind certainly distressed some punters, I would imagine).

London did, indeed, also have a distressed vibe at that time: the war had ended 30-odd years before, but the effects of German bombing were still there for all to see. Jonathan Romney had his own perspective on this: "Improv as a good night out? Traditionally, that's only been imaginable for participating players; for non-initiates, listening to the form has always been on the list of pursuits that were supposedly painful and, therefore, *jolly good for you*. There was an element of that in the LMC's old Gloucester Avenue premises, tucked away in Camden Town's sprawling British Rail outhouse-zone – a warehouse building up a fire escape, *sans* toilet, *sans* bar, *sans* comfy seats and with the notoriously un-funloving London Film-Makers Co-op as neighbours." (*Wire*, No.99, May 1992, p.37.)

While typing this out, I was suddenly aware of the affinity of those premises with that of the Little Theatre Club, up several flights of stairs, a rudimentary bar, hard seats, neighbours from another discipline, the audience almost considered as an afterthought. At least the LTC had a toilet though.

The same article (Romney, *op. cit.*) describes the LMC's auxiliary TAZ in the University of London's swimming pool, called 'Fiume' for the day, which is well out of our time period (1992), but a demonstration that the LMC still had the eye for a good concept when it saw one.

THE INTERREGNUM: THE MC MORPHS INTO THE LMC (OR MAYBE IT WASN'T THAT SIMPLE?)

In some ways, the LMC added to free improv's negative image as being austere, humourless, po-faced and passive-aggressive politically correct. Just as post-punk and its house organ, the *NME*, put many off with its finger-pointing, 'experimental' journalism. However, the second free improv generation had several jokers in the pack, who we will be looking at in the next chapter, making it appear perhaps less 'hair shirt' than the pioneer improvisers.

What we can do now is to look at that brief period between the running down of the MC and the beginning of the next phase, in 1976. In some ways, the transition across what I have called the 'interregnum' or caesura of 1975/6 appears relatively smooth, at least to the outsider, bearing in mind though, that there were already some convergences and affinities between the two organisations (the MC and the LMC) that encourage us to see them as, essentially, one and the same thing.

David Toop is straightforward in his letter, addressed to the LMC's 1990s magazine, *Resonance*, about the inter-relationship of the two bodies, the MC and the LMC: "There was…an overlap in the mid 70s, as various Musicians Cooperative members were invited in by the new boys or worked with them…The LMC was not a name change and re-staffing of the Musicians Cooperative. The LMC was formed by the slightly newer lot of musicians, simply because everybody was fed up with playing in bad rooms above pubs or nowhere at all." (Toop, *op. cit.*, 1993, p.34.)

Please note the reference to 'new boys', not girls. This is presumably one example of what got the goat of person/persons unknown in *Musics* 21? There did not appear to have been that much change in the intervening 14 years, then, between 1979 and 1993, when Toop made his observations?

In the following edition of *Resonance* (Vol.2, No.2, p.46), Richard Leigh points out another forgivable mistake regarding linkage, that between the LMC and *Musics*, which actually started in April/May 1975, over two years before the first LMC Festival in September 1977 (at

Battersea Arts Centre). The LMC itself emerged from meetings between various stakeholders in 1975/6 (many of whom had also been founder members of *Musics*), and it sent out its first newsletter in August 1976, but despite sharing many co-members (and also with the now moribund MC), the two entities were separate.

"My memory of the Musicians Cooperative is that it was set up as a reaction to the Jazz Centre Society had clearly no intention (*sic*) of doing anything for improvised music…It's easy to see why the mistake [of their direct causal link, *author*] was made, though: if you have a bunch of people producing a magazine at the premises of the LMC, and you notice that almost the same bunch of people seem to run the LMC. It's easy to make assumptions about a link. Clearly the overlap of interests and attitudes was considerable – it's just that there was no formal connection." (Leigh, *op. cit.*, p.34.)

As I have mentioned on a few occasions, I was 'blooded' (as it were) at the Musicians Cooperative's first-ever International Festival of Improvised Music in early 1974, a TAZ that moved between Ronnie Scott's and the Collegiate Theatre. To my utter surprise, a friend burned me a very lo-fi recording (that is, not fit for official release) of some of the playing from those nights of late January 1974, and which I had no reason to think I would ever hear again – a combination of old and new recording technology! What, of course, I couldn't have been aware of at the time, at the age of 18, was that the MC had just lost its use of Ronnie's, which had been a haven for a considerable time, and that it had moved to the Unity Theatre, in Mornington Crescent just down the road from Camden Town, a left-wing and left-field venue (as was the LMC in years to come), which became the music's nominal epicentre through 1974/5. The Cooperative began to hold regular Tuesday nights at the Unity from March 12th 1974, changing to Thursdays in May. Over the summer, a policy was introduced to pair an MC grouping with one from the 'provinces', which rather belies any image of the MC as being stuck-up, snobbish or separatist. At this time, in fact, various free improv collectives were being established across the country, as we will discuss later.

The Unity Theatre burned down in November 1975. Evan Parker suggested to me that this event might have marked if not the official end of the MC (Stevens and Watts had already opted out, and Derek Bailey's position appears to have been ambiguous, with Company perhaps uppermost in his mind by that point), then probably the practical reason for cessation of its formal activities. The whole Company concept is slightly controversial here, when talking about 'collectives': undoubtedly a tremendous concept, if not an original one (multiple *ad hoc* combinations had, after all, been a feature of free improv since its start), Company seems to have relied on Bailey's "strong personality" (Bell, *op. cit.*), ultimately a jazz 'conceit' originating in the 'strong leader type', e.g. Duke Ellington, Count Basie, Miles Davis, or also Frank Zappa, Bob Fripp, etc., which is a divergent methodology to 'collectivity'?

Bell (*op. cit.*) further describes the LMC thus: "For many years the LMC was a large collective (200 members), supposedly running itself in an authentically collective manner. Open monthly meetings enabled the entire membership to participate in a lively criticism of any member who had actually done any work. The problems of collectivity are well known. These days we shake our heads and think we know better, but the LMC's factional struggles were a simple result of a large number of musicians all passionately involved and trying to get a hand on the steering wheel."

The 2016 film *The Commune* shows that the power of these idea(l)s are far from spent.

Large groups tend to inevitably produce 'anti-task' behaviour, i.e. action designed to meet the needs of its individual members rather than the stated group task. (Ohholzer/Roberts, 1994, pp.30-8.) This usually puts a stop to collective productivity, as Bell more than suggests.

The LMC, however, despite these reservations, left us a legacy of free improv TAZs, whether Company or LMC Festivals or beyond these, and which saw us through a couple of decades at least, so it is a powerful bequest, for which thanks should be given to those concerned. The last LMC Festival was in 2006, so not so bad (30 years) for a group of embattled improvisers playing sounds that many did not consider music at all. The fact that these players have stuck to their guns throughout is a tribute to sheer bull-headed perseverance and faith in the form.

Before finding the old British Rail workers canteen in Gloucester Avenue, the LMC had organised events all over London. Its emergence through a mysterious series of meetings make it difficult to completely and accurately establish all of the original LMC members, but they were undoubtedly fairly co-terminous with the *Musics* originators (whose founder members are more clearly established, as outlined in Chapter Eight), and they put their first newsletter out in August 1976. The influence of the First Generation was obvious, in particular the educational programmes of John Stevens and Maggie Nicols, who 'taught' people *how*, not *what*, to play in an improvisational context.

The co-terminosity, also, of the first LMC Festival (September 1977) with that of the first Company Festival (four months earlier in May), gave notice of the power of the burgeoning 'movement'. It needed a *locus*, which it got from early 1978. Bell (*op. cit.*) reiterates the TAZ notion: "If we accept the liberal idea of art as an autonomous space, where other values can be considered and explored, then the LMC building was like a corporate expression of this. Established by free improvisers, one of its most distinctive features as an organisation was its openness and inclusiveness." (Bell, *op. cit.*)

Now, without going into detail, there was not a ubiquitous agreement on the 'inclusiveness' of the LMC in those years, but I feel that this is an almost inevitable side product of working over many years in relative artistic isolation. Things may well have improved in more recent years, what with 'improv international' and all that, but the music still exists as a minority interest, and a particular mindset can establish itself in such a febrile atmosphere.

1978, the year of TAZ 'events'

Lots of things happened in 1978, an important year in our story. To name just one: Alterations, perhaps the most 'representative' Gen Two grouping, consisting of Toop, Beresford, Day and Peter Cusack, made their debut on June 22nd, and will be discussed later.

February saw the performance, the participants in 'protective masks' (as evidenced in photos in *Musics* 17, pp.24-5), of 'Whirled Music', consisting of Beresford (as ever), Toop (ditto), Burwell and Max Eastley, a 'sound and vision' artist who made the essential *Buried Dreams* with Toop in the 90s. The photographs illustrating the event basically feature a bunch of blokes with what seem to be lamp shades on their heads, or something that John and Yoko would have done in their 'bag-ist' days in the late 60s. (They were actually fencing guards, I was eventually informed.) One of the features of this gig was that it started in darkness, a condition that AMM (and much later, Autechre) have explored for its disorientating effects on both band and audience, the former apparently often losing track of their identity/contribution in the mix, as can be experienced in AMM's seminal *The Crypt*. 'Whirled Music' used whirling and spun instruments, for which Toop's original book no doubt came in useful for ideas. Funnily enough, Toop *does* describe affinities with his then recent book: "That strand of improvising, the invention of new sounds for performance and installation, was at the heart of *Circadian Rhythm.*" (Toop, 2012.)

This gig is described by Annabel Nicolson, from the London Film Cooperative, and a collaborator with the LMC at the time. Little idea is given about what it all sounded like, although it looks like a lot of fun, and there is apparently a record on the Quartz label, which I have yet to hear. Disguising their identities gave a bit of Residents-like ambiguity. Guitarist 'Buckethead' can be imagined to be waiting in the wings, to play future Company Weeks with his head in, well, a bucket.

Far more important and influential was Toop's 'Festival of Environmental Music and Performance (Music/ Context)', of which the above performances (in 'Circadian') were but a part, held in and around Camden Town over several days, from July 28th through to August 5th 1978, coincidently just after the debut of Alterations. Toop (2012) dates the idea for 'Circadian Rhythm', the most conceptually pure of the events in the Festival, to Balinese temple music, "an event of such long duration that a passage of sleep was necessary for both participants and witnesses".

To accentuate the notion of 'creative listening,' Toop planned an unbroken 24-hour performance by an assorted group of interested individuals. The idea came from Evan Parker who had, shortly before, witnessed a six-hour performance by Rain in the Face, the Toop/Burwell duo, at St. Katherine's Dock, which bowled him over. The influence of LaMonte Young seems evident here, as well as Balinese gamelan. The original adventurers who were up for this idea were: Parker and Toop themselves, the drummers Paul Lytton, Lovens and Burwell, Hugh Davies, Annabel Nicolson and the ever-dependable Steve Beresford (a sprite of a figure, who seemed to be everywhere at this time, a significant creative catalyst). They, in the end, eventually lasted for 13 hours, spanning July 29th and 30th.

Musics 20 (December 1978) is pretty much devoted to Toop's Festival and Circadian Rhythm, and this was clearly the LMC's Woodstock (with the same ablution problems, no doubt). The front cover, which features Lol Coxhill with his soprano, somewhere on the Regents Park Canal towpath, is very evocative of a lost time. Toop, in his 2012 unpublished article, compares it to Viennese Aktionist Hermann Nitsch (who was featured, in all his g(l)ory, in *Musics* 9, pp.24-5), which seems a tad grandiose given the excesses of Nitsch's intestine-fests, but nevertheless, this event, at least in Toop's eyes, "sank into legend – glorious or abject failure, a moment of madness, the last gasp of 60s excess before 80s pragmatism took over". (Toop, *op. cit.,* 2012.)

Toop also suggests even more influences here, from Eric Satie's 24-hour solo piano marathon, *Vexations,* to Andy Warhol's celluloid snore-athons *Sleep* and *Empire* (but not, strangely enough, the Solihull Technology College event of a year earlier, which seem to be much more apposite, to be frank). Toop (*op. cit.*), in the end, sees it as a triumph of *hubris*: "Easy to say now that our ambition was too great and our preparation was too feeble; that we were not being realistic about how much an audience can take, not being sensible about the limits of improvisation, the boundaries of human creativity."

He also experienced some of the more obvious difficulties involved in such hubristic endeavours: "Sometimes we were all playing, sometimes it broke down into small groups, but there was no planning. Sometimes a lot of us were asleep! At one point very early in the morning, Paul

Burwell and I went for a walk through the streets around the LMC. I was really struggling, hoping that the light, air and conversation got me through the wall, which they didn't." (Toop, personal communication, 2016.)

Evan Parker would certainly seem to agree about the scale of the aspirations of the time: "It was the end of a golden age of opportunities," (quoted in Toop, *op. cit.*, 2012), demonstrating that even Evan is not averse to using the 'Golden Age' trope at times.

Let us, to conclude this chapter on 70s younger improvisers, take the opportunity to explore briefly the world of female free improvisers, a topic which we alluded to very briefly earlier, and which crosses the notional barriers of time and genre that I have imposed (and one of the many topics that I would suggest for future research).

'COCK-IMPROV'?

"It was not until the early 70s, when feminism seriously started to question the extent to which women had benefited from the capsizing of old ways of thinking, relating and behaving, that attempts started to be made to redress the imbalance." (Wickes, *op. cit.*, p.238.)

By the late 70s, 'cock rock' had become an accepted, mostly affectionate and parodic, term for the phallocentric rock bands of the time (Led Zeppelin is the case for the prosecution), the sort of bands that were so accurately and fondly lambasted in *Spinal Tap*, the band who found that there was a very fine line between freedom and fatuousness. It is worth positing whether there was a similar male matrix in free jazz and free improvisation. I very briefly discuss the issue of gender in free improv in *Beyond Jazz* (*op. cit.*, pp.290-1), and would recommend McKay's more extensive essay on this topic in his *Circular Breathing*. (*Op. cit.*, pp.245-296.) It behoves me here, however, to add a few more words to contribute to the description of these few years and their challenges.

Although almost all of *Beyond Jazz* focused on male improvisers, it does mention how Maggie Nicols had quickly established herself as *la grande dame* of the music, both as a singer and as a teacher/inspiration, initially through her Oval House workshops, which started in late 1970 and built on some of John Stevens' methods and philosophies. Nicols' workshops have continued through to today and she is, along with Eddie Prevost, one of our greatest improvisation educationalists, working as much with attitudes as with techniques, and with what some would see as utopian ideals about releasing individuals' and society's unlocked potentials.

The convergence with punk again rears its pointed little head. In the period around 1976/7, several very important punk bands formed, with female musicians an integral part of their sound and image: Siouxsie and the Banshees, Penetration, X-Ray Spex with Poly Styrene and Laura Logic, the Adverts with Gaye Advert, The Slits and (slightly later) The Raincoats, Au Pairs and Delta 5. America had Talking Heads' Tina Weymouth, Blondie's Debbie Harry and the much scarier Lydia Lunch from Teenage Jesus and the Jerks, who set the pace for no-wave, a 'style' that, in some ways, was beyond criticism (in both senses of the word). There may not be an *a priori* link necessarily, but it is unlikely that the women interested in free improv would not have taken at least some interest in these developments. Certainly, one of the most important female improvising bands, the Feminist Improvising Group (FIG), formed in the autumn of 1977 at the end of the 'Summer of Punk', which may, or may not, have been an influence. In November that year, Rock against Sexism was formed, with links to the Anti-Nazi League and with the aim of encouraging women to play music. By summer 1979, Rome held an International Festival of Women in Jazz, and, in April earlier that year, the rather staid *Jazz Journal* devoted a whole edition to the issue of 'Women in Jazz'. That it was seen as an 'issue' at all says almost everything about this subject.

Although to some it may seem counterproductive to focus on gender when discussing music as a unitary entity, a form of tokenism perhaps, we should remember that, only ten or so years before this period, the pop group The Honeycombs had built a career on the fact that their drummer, Honey Lantree, was a woman, i.e. shock, horror, and that she could play a musical *instrument*. Really…? Pass the smelling salts.

Women at that pre-feminist time were, occasionally, in very important positions in the music world, but it was usually in areas where the male public didn't have to be uncomfortably reminded of that fact. One example was Delia Derbyshire, composer and musician, who successfully adapted one of the most famous tunes in 20th Century music, the *Doctor Who Theme*, originally written by Ron Grainger. Grainger wanted to obtain Derbyshire a co-composer credit to acknowledge her alchemy, but the Powers-That–Be(eb) preferred to keep the members of the BBC Radiophonic Workshop anonymous (especially, one presumes, if they were of the female persuasion). She and her colleagues worked very much 'behind the scenes', with the attendant lack of credit, although her role has surely now been recognised in these more 'enlightened' times. One wonders if the same level of *incognito* would have been maintained if she had been an ambitious young man, like George Martin had been with his 'lads', The Beatles? Somehow I doubt it.

The centrepiece of *Musics* 14 (October 1977) was a lengthy piece by Lindsay Cooper called *Women, Music, Feminism – Notes*, an early exploration of the implications that feminism had for free improvisation. Cooper noted, in the byline, how little of the reports in the previous edition, which focused on the Socialist Festival of Music held in May at Battersea Arts Centre, had mentioned the women/music sessions. It is also noteworthy how much space had been given to Cornelius Cardew's pontifications about the forthcoming revolution of the working class (half of whom were presumably women?) in *Musics* 13, whenever he was giving himself a break from criticising Rock Against Racism and the whole punk rock movement as being "the most reactionary, fascist trend in *popular culture* today" (the latter being given, for good measure, condescending italics).

One of the many problems facing women (and men) in left-wing organisations, or those who had left leanings, was the relegation of gender (and race) issues to a position well below that of the ultimate struggle against capitalism/class, the need for the 'proletarian revolution' as opposed to 'bourgeois revisionist socialism'. Looking at Cardew's comments, one is struck by his sheer anachronistic and reactive stance, in our age of globilisation and de-industrialisation, what with the traditional working class bastions so eulogised by Cardew, the coal, steel and shipbuilding industries, for example, having gone the way of the penny farthing or spinning jenny. This is as opposed to the struggle for full equal rights for women and ethnic minority peoples, which still, unfortunately, remains a huge issue in our times.

FIG was an important grouping, just as The Slits were in the punk scene. The group was started by Maggie Nicols and Lindsay Cooper, who were soon joined by Georgie Born, Cathy Williams and Corinne Liensol. Several other women participated over the years, including European improvisers, and they eventually became the European Women's Improvising Group, losing the 'feminist' tag along the way. From the beginning, there were sadly unavoidable 'issues' around being taken seriously under the 'male gaze'. The Slits were accused of being musical primitives, which they were in some ways, but was intended to be a put-down and which they, in time, easily transcended. FIG had also to establish itself in a world that, in many ways, was even more male-dominated than rock. Their first gig, on October 31st 1977 at the Almost Free theatre in London, sounds to have been a memorable one, hilarious and tense in equal measures. Arranged by Music for Socialism, it made several points about the public and the private, with the musicians enacting stereotypical domestic tasks ('women's work') throughout their performance, making a counterpoint of the *avant* and the banal, a connection which many second generation players went on to make. As we have seen in Circadian Rhythm, this could extend to the musicians having a nap in or between sets. But, this performance also put a rather different perspective on the toys, 'little instruments' and everyday domestic paraphernalia that male free improvisers felt free to use to 'express themselves' creatively, but which women might interpret differently: "The Hoover, softly whirring in endless vacuity, and the Kenwood mixer, grinding and circling, were shown for what they are not – not liberators, but enslaving accoutrements, women's assigned instruments that allow precious little room to improvise." (Hemmings & Pitfield, *Musics* 15, p.20.)

Later 'liberators', like mobile phones, the internet generally, texts and e-mails, are more of the same.

"In the late 1970s, there was a debate in feminist circles about the existence of the possibility of a 'female music'…it was *supposed* to be more flowing, less structured, lighter, warmer, softer, but beyond that there was little agreement." (McKay, quoting Mavis Bayton, *op. cit.*, 2005, p.249.)

In these days of gender fluidity, we will get nowhere near answering this question in a book of this sort. It was an interesting question, though. Whatever the answer, it was being asked in 1977. The debate extended to the types of instruments improvisers used. The hegemony of 'classical' instruments was challenged by the free improvisers, who thought water, for example, could be an instrument (see the cover of this book). Water, of course, being supposedly the ultimate female medium. But unconscious stereotypes still dominated, and it can become tempting to use cheesy, sexualised innuendo when discussing this field of endeavour.

Peter Riley totally excels himself in this instance, in this record review of Bailey/Honsinger, Incus 20: "The cello is the most sexually intimate of instruments. The player is wrapped round it and it occupies that personal space immediately in front of the body…it also forces the legs apart... The ecstatic implications of this close contact force out a vocal lyric expression [by Honsinger, one assumes, the Keith Jarrett of the cello, *author*], a dream-like metonymy of the orgasmic cry." (*Musics* 12, May 1977, p.23.) Phew, missus!

The piano, the violin, the voice are associated with female performers, but not the guitar, the double bass and the "blowing instruments" (see what I mean about innuendo?) which are usually associated with the alternative gender (although women did begin to increasingly play these instruments over the forthcoming years, both in improv and in rock). One of the problems for FIG was that their humour, however dark, was used against them, some observers decrying their not taking the music 'seriously', one more female 'fault' given, as we all know women can be, to triviality.

This was all ironic, given the reaction of the po-faced audience that I was part of, in 1982, at a Company gig, who sat spellbound (but not in a good way) as John Zorn played a discombobulated clarinet inserted into a bowl of water. (See also Chapter 5 for more of this gig.) Interestingly, one of the people who read my first book told me that, on the same tour, a (female) member of the audience 'flicked' Zorn's water over him while he was doing his piece (a nice 'female' touch, I thought, as opposed to the more likely male reaction of tipping it over his head?), which proves absolutely nothing, but still…?

Slapstick also was a frequent tool of the Dutch school of improv, for example, but somehow it became inauthentic in the hands of women.

More positively, it is encouraging to see that, on the 'events' page of *Musics* 16 (on the back page), there is a considerable amount of women musicians advertised. Even Company, on February 17th 1978, took on board Lindsay Cooper and Georgie Born for a gig, which demonstrates how 'current' Bailey was being, or at least trying to be, then. Around Bailey, women usually did the organising, not the playing, as we have seen. A Women's Workshop at the Woman's Art Alliance in London NW1 was 'for women only'. You can almost hear the lads' equivalent cry of: "It's political correctness gone mad." (The expression hadn't been coined yet.)

As a final thought, I'd like to put in a few quotes from FIG from *Musics* 20, which was mainly concerned with Toop's "Music/Context" (December, 1978). The female improvisers discuss some of the complications of labelling and of trying to play in a 'gendered' way.

Sally Potter: "One of the pitfalls of women playing collectively is that in an attempt to de-hierarchise the product there's often a sort of curiously uniform quality…because nobody wants to soar up and take on a so-called hierarchical position…sometimes people don't take the space and confidence to develop a line or idea."

Georgie Born: "Often because other people step in and don't allow things to happen…the other thing…is a general grey acceptance that for anyone to take an initiative is individualistic."

Corrine Liensol: "Who, what, solo, me? I'm feminist – after you..."

To be absolutely fair, Evan Parker recalls similar 'no, after you' *politesse* in the very early years of free improvisation, amongst the blokes, when the language was still being established.

Ego-less music for (some) ego maniacs. Go figure.

These were the sorts of deliberations that male musicians got into among themselves, and it is noteworthy that there are convergences here, I think, with some of the debates held around the Spontaneous Music Ensembles' "atomistic/*pointillistic*/group/insect music", call it what you will. In particular, the skills of listening, and of letting the other person(s) have their say. The avoidance of hierarchy, and not playing from the ego to the detriment of others, mirror the challenges of the music all the way back to 1966, and the formation of Stevens/Watts/Rutherford's group and of the Cardew-era AMM. (Barre, *op. cit.*)

Without dwelling much further on the more ideological or doctrinal aspects of free improvisation, and bearing in mind Steve Beresford's quote in the foreword of this book regarding the codification of terms and taboos in the music, I am at this point somewhat reminded of certain studies into the possible unconscious motivations in group behaviour: "The unconscious aim of the group became to obliterate all differences between individuals…and hierarchies…nor could decisions be made except by consensus, lest some members appear to be more powerful than others…Intended to be liberating, this state of affairs proved to be very constraining. Since one cannot oppose rules that do not exist, (group) members felt oppressed without knowing why." (Obholzer & Roberts, *op. cit.*, p.163.)

As we have seen previously, and will see later in Chapter Eight on the *Musics* magazine, the issues of rules and leadership could provoke considerable divergences within the scene. I was advised by Steve Beresford to be specific when describing any references to rules and regulations, whether formal or informal, and to be precise as to where these came from. This is, however, sometimes difficult, but is undoubtedly a theme which is prominent when studying these times and this music. From John Stevens' advice/instructions as to how to play creative atomistic 'group' music, to AMM's stated intention to completely ignore any imposed boundaries when paying AMMusic, the very notion of fundamental axioms, guidelines and/or shibboleths become a slippery one: "*God help us! Help us loose our minds. These slippery people help us understand,*" as Talking Heads put it in 1983.

And now that we are talking of playing that resists easy categorisation, let's look at three improvisers who are very much individualists, to the point of my calling them 'mavericks'.

CHAPTER 4

Three Mavericks

"A genuinely non-categorisable original, whose open-minded attitude to musics of all kinds heralded a prominent tendency within improvised music in the seventies." (Wickes, *op. cit.*, p.88.)

The above was written by John Wickes to describe Lol Coxhill, but the sentiments could equally apply to any of the three improvisers that I have chosen to discuss in this chapter. There are clearly other musicians from these adventurous years that I could have chosen and, as Clive Bell points out in his LMC history: "If you want to make enemies in a history like this, all you have to do is leave out someone's name." (Bell, *op. cit.*)

Whatever the truth in this assertion, I have decided to spotlight Lol Coxhill, Steve Beresford and Terry Day, as particularly 'non-categorisable', but who are still players who could claim to originate from the influence of jazz, however 'beyond jazz' they strayed over the years. This is why, for example, I have excluded David Toop, a clear and obvious contender, and another large presence in this book.

All three of these improvisers are generally acknowledged to be masters in the scene, and yet there is very little written about any of them in the jazz/improv lexicon. Only Coxhill features in Cook/Morton, for example. Perhaps this is because they are all 'ants in their pants' performers, polymorphous and genre-hopping, which makes truly representative 'best of' compilations very difficult to assemble. The 'prominent tendency' mentioned by John Wickes, above, was, I assume, the 'channel-changing' restlessness that started to emerge by the mid 70s, and that probably reached its apotheosis in John Zorn's work in the 80s, which brought the concept of 'attention-deficit' playing and listening (the equivalent of constant channel-hopping on the television) to the fore.

All three men could, chronologically, be considered to be part of Gen One. Day was born in 1940, and Coxhill as far back as 1932, making him very much a contemporary of Derek Bailey, who is usually seen as the grand old man of free improvisation, but who was born only two years earlier than Coxhill. Beresford came into this world on March 6th 1950, a relative youngster, but who was still old enough to have a Janus-like relationship to Gens One and Two. Their recording careers only really started in earnest in the 70s, which is a key point for a book of this nature, based as it is in the study of recorded material and which relies heavily on this type of evidence. Although Day (born in 1940), in particular, had been recorded in the Gen One 'early days' of 1968, in The People Band, and Coxhill as far back as 1954.

None of the three, with the exception of Coxhill, could be called solo specialists or virtuosos, but all were very much group players in the collective realm, 'first among equals'. Nick Couldry (1995, p.5) pointed out how this could affect the music: "If the group's playing is not successfully unified, there are no virtuosic individual contributions on which to focus. In this respect, it differs radically from much jazz."

All three are/were, to various degrees, humourists, or, at least, don't appear to take themselves excessively seriously, although this could also lead to them being taken, to a degree, as 'clowns', which they certainly were not (on the whole!). Lol Coxhill's problems with this labelling will be demonstrated below.

To sum up, they have never received the attention they deserve, and I hope that this chapter is a small contribution towards correcting this omission.

LOL COXHILL

Coxhill's dry, acidulous verbal style, which is replicated in his music, is best represented, and also fairly easily available, in Antoine Prum's film/DVD (2013, released shortly after Coxhill's death) about British free

Lol Coxhill at the Little Theatre Club Festival in January 1972, making it all look suspiciously easy

CREDIT: © JAK KILBY
WWW.JAKKILBY.CO.UK

improvisers: "The trouble is…I'm being told that I'm an entertainer as well as an improviser, but most of what they think of as the entertaining stopped about 20 years ago, so if I just say something that's vaguely amusing [as he gently does to and about Eddie Prevost, in the film, *author*], it's seen as being part of the act."

This is a succinct summary of the position that Coxhill found himself in, as a sort of Alexei Sayle of the free improv scene. In fact, he was a tremendously serious free improviser who happened to have a very English sense of self-deprecating fun, whose solo work should be taken with exactly the sort of seriousness that his fellow solo-*maestros* such as Evan Parker and John Butcher have received.

Coxhill was a master of the soprano saxophone who ran the gamut from sweet melodicism, channelling Lee Konitz, through to fractured multiphonics, often within a few moments of each other. He was annoyed (again, in Prum) by Stewart Lee's question about his assumed links, during an improvisation, with more 'conventional' styles (which usually grounded listeners): "I don't usually decide that I'm going to start off playing bebop licks…it goes off anywhere, at any point, I don't turn up to an improvising session thinking I'm going to play Charlie Parker tunes."

This is as good a comment as any that I've heard, about the tyranny of influences that improvisers have to deal with in the minds of observers (including myself, I would add). John Butcher, also in Prum's film, talks about "fast and attentive listening" and "virtuoso listening", which, although potentially flattering the non-participant, also alludes to the effort we listeners often make, within musical passages, to avoid 'the moment', in favour of reductive comparisons to other musicians/musical genres. Coxhill's solos often consisted of both the euphonious and the more *outre*, but then again, he had been playing unaccompanied since the 60s, which must make him the one of the earliest of his kind (in fact, he was *sui generis*).

Perhaps Coxhill's 'comedic' persona was an attempt to downplay, or react against, the image of free improv as being overly serious? Whatever, he was often a quiet presence as an audience member at so many gigs that I have attended, as Beresford still is. Usually alone and completely unobtrusive, despite his (relative) fame, he was clearly a listening fan as well as a practitioner-musician (as is Beresford), a modest attendee at a music he was so much a part of creating.

I was at the memorial gig for Coxhill at Cecil Sharp House on September 19th 2012, an unforgettable evening, which featured, very appropriately, an eclectic group of players, from the Mike Westbrook Group through to the concluding duo of an emotional Evan Parker and Eddie Prevost (at least that's what they conveyed throughout their set).

I was also at a much smaller event, 17 years earlier, in north London's Crouch End, where I live, at the Kings Head pub, where Coxhill was the supporting soloist for the opening gig of a residency by pianist Veryan Weston's trio with bassist Olly Blanchflower

Lol Coxhill memorial flier

and drummer Stu Butterfield (who actually did the organisational work). One of the pieces from that gig, a version of Heusen/Mercer's *I Thought About You*, appears on the *Spectral Soprano* compilation (Emanem 4204). Coincidentally, the event was also briefly attended by David Toop, who lived locally, and wrote: "Elastic, emotionally direct yet harmonically and rhythmically obtuse, relaxed yet walking on a thin wire of tension, this prehistoric set-up revived my interest in jazz, which I had been coming to despise…Just when you think the unnamable future has arrived, the past can clout you around the head with a lesson, out of nowhere, or even five minutes' walk from your own doorstep." (*Wire*, Issue 138, August 1995, p.74.)

This was the effect Coxhill could have. I attended the whole set (Toop apparently only came in for the last number), and I also remember it as a live *event*, which reinforced my interest in even such a traditional entity as the piano-led quartet. Such was Lol Coxhill's power. I was with a large amount of friends at this performance, almost none of them passionate about either jazz or free improvisation, but they all seemed infused with the same enthusiasm that his playing had engendered in me.

Looking at Coxhill's contribution to free improvisation, one notes his playing with the improvisers associated with the SME, AMM and Company, i.e., 'the full pack' of early institutions, a feat which can only be matched by Evan Parker. Like Parker (and Bailey), he played with almost everyone of significance in those years, making him another *eminence* throughout these convoluted times. He even pioneered electronics, for example by modifying his sax by using an oscillator and a Gibson 'Maestro' (those of you old enough to remember might recognise the latter from Zappa's *Uncle Meat* sessions, a device which produced a reverberating vibrato and doubled notes played at the octave) used, at various times, by Ian Underwood (from Zappa's Mothers of Invention), Lee Konitz, Elton Dean and George Khan.

Life

Lol (Lowen) Coxhill was born in Portsmouth on September 19th 1932, but grew up in Aylesbury. An unusual name, he later re-christened himself Loxhorn Rondo, a most Beefheart-ian nomenclature, which was perhaps a symptom of his tendency to re-define himself throughout his career.

He bought his first saxophone in 1947 (at the height of bebop in America), completed his National Service (as many of the first generation did later), in 1950-1, and played solo saxophone from very early on. He had also become interested in bebop, bypassing trad forms entirely, and had in his possession a 78rpm record of Tristano's *Intuition*, one of the very few in the country, one would have thought, and almost certainly the first on his block. His first official recordings were not made until 1971, however, which explains his inclusion in Gen Two. He had actually been playing for two decades before *Ear of the Beholder,* his first release. He also began busking (to raise money to get to gigs), something he pursued with alacrity for many years, and which almost certainly must have helped in developing his free playing (and in helping to diminish the extent to which he was taken seriously by taste-makers?).

The sheer scale and variety of Coxhill's discography, released on a myriad of labels and most of uncertain availability, and discounting for the moment his live performances, cannot be adequately conveyed in a format such as this book, but I will endeavour to itemise a few highlights from his legacy.

Probably the best overview of Coxhill's work is the double CD on Emanem records, which covers a 45-year period, from 1954-1999, entitled *Spectral Soprano* (Emanem 4204). The breadth of its contents is suggested by the sub-title, *R&B, Jazz, Electronics, Spontaneous Music, an Open Rendition of an Old Play and the Odd Bit of Singing*. This is the place to start. It also has the bonus of a photo of the great man himself, reclining on a deckchair-strewn English beach somewhere, with a gold medallion round his neck and a bright red shirt which is unbuttoned to the lower chest, and with his right hand very fetchingly cupping his balls. Obviously, this was a side of Lol Coxhill, a 'medallion man' side, that the public was rarely given access to. But one of the great things about the man was that he could always surprise you.

By the early 60s, he had begun to play with such pre-free modernists as Joe Harriott and Tubby Hayes, both at the top of their game at the time, as well as R&B musicians such as Rufus Thomas, Lowell Fulson and Champion Jack Dupree, so his portfolio was already extensive by the early 70s. He played with Delivery (1969-70), who had developed from Bruno's Blues Band into a group that backed visiting USA bluespersons (including Carol Grimes, who eventually took on the band name), and Kevin Ayers' Whole World, from the Canterbury scene, and with composer David Bedford, when the latter first came to prominence (on Bedford's *Garden of Love,* for example, which had its premiere at the Queen Elizabeth Hall in 1970). Like Steve Beresford, he later played with the Dedication Orchestra, which celebrated the work of the 60s South African *emigres*.

At the relatively late age of 32, Coxhill turned professional, giving up his initial career as a book binder, and played with a young Ray Davies in the Dave Hunt R&B Band, supporting visiting soul acts like Wilson Pickett and Martha and the Vandellas, as well as performing at Count Suckle's Roaring Twenties Club with reggae superstar trombonist Rico Rodriguez, later famed for his work with The Specials. He even auditioned for The Kinks! Apparently without success, so there is another alternative history nixed!

At this time, Ronnie Scott, ever helpful to newcomers whatever his personal opinions about particular jazz styles, featured Lol as an interval-slot performer. He also appeared with the SME at the LTC at this time.

He formed a duo with pianist Steve Miller and some of their work appeared on Coxill's debut album, *Ear of the Beholder* (Dandelion 8008, 1971). Curiously, Robert Wyatt's debut, at around the same time, was called *End of an Ear* (another terrible pun, a figure of speech seemingly much beloved of free improvisers).

Ear was a very eclectic album for its time, with what would now be called a post-modern agenda. A whimsical mix of jazz, cabaret, parlour tunes, ska, free skronk, solos (low-fi recordings on Hungerford Bridge), it also included contributions from Bedford, Wyatt and a pre-*Tubular Bells* Mike Oldfield. It sounds somewhat like a Gen Two recording from a few years later – a version of *I am the Walrus* (which Oasis in turn covered 24 years later) performed with schoolchildren (eight years before *The Wall*), tenor sax solo improvisations (several years before David Murray) and a free exchange with Dutch colleagues, all mixed into an experimental stew. I remember this record as being one of a few that one could always find at the back of an 'adventurous' record collection, usually next to *An Evening with Wildman Fischer* on Straight Records, *The Faust Tapes* and *Trout Mask Replica* (make your own list, it's fun, except that the exercise somewhat loses its point in the digital age). Whatever, it was often there with the rest of the vinyl 'losers' of the time (originals of which are now quite expensive, as is the way of things). Coxhill outlined that one of the album's purposes was "to establish the fact that it is possible for a person to work within quite diverse areas of music whilst still maintaining a positive identity as an improvising musician" (in the notes accompanying *Spectral Soprano*). 'Diverse' was clearly an important word for Coxhill, as he used it to name a later album.

Ear was released in 1971, on John Peel's Dandelion label (its only double album, record collectors!!), apparently commissioned by the DJ after he saw Coxhill busking in Piccadilly Circus. The deliberate 'low-fi' sound and smorgasbord quality of this disc belongs more to the vogue for this sort of thing some years later. Hence it tanked at the time.

At this point, it is apposite to present the comical conversation between two of our chosen improvisers from this chapter, recorded on a broiling summer day on Brighton Beach (the interchange begins at 1 hour 16 minutes into the film):

Lol Coxhill (LC): "Well, what's wrong with it?" [Steve Beresford's stage outfit]

Steve Beresford (SB): "Well, just look at it, it's the wrong design and everything!"

LC: "It looks alright, it's not as if people are going to come up and pick around [sic?] *your gear or anything."*

SB: "Yeah, but, you know, this is my projection of myself, on the street."

LC: "We're all there together, there's this collective image, all right? I know you don't wanna go about looking like that all the time, but…"

SB: "We're all individuals here."

LC: "I know we're all individuals, I'm as individual as you are, mate, you know that."

SB: "Well, I'm not so sure, actually."

LC: "Well, I am, I tell you I am."

One has to see the film to truly appreciate this interchange, worthy of *Spinal Tap* as it is, enacted in front of the tourists in Brighton, with Beresford in a bizarre 'onesie', versus the old campaigner, in a wonderfully idiosyncratic jacket in pink and black squares, which he inhabits with his usual aplomb. Beresford is obviously irritable, young, callow, and very thin and vulnerable looking, and who can blame him after a long, hot, cramped Campervan journey from London (and with it being his idea in the first place!). As his colleagues disembark from the van, one can see just how trying the journey must have been.

The particular group involved in the subsequent gig, which occurred on the famous beach, was called The Promenaders, one of many groups that Coxhill was part of over the years, including The Recedents, with guitarist Mike Cooper and percussionist Roget Turner, and the Melody Four, another trio (of course!), with clarinetist Tony Coe and Steve Beresford. Both Coxhill and Beresford (and Terry Day) band-hopped in those years, which makes a study of the era complicated and somewhat confusing, as band membership was shared across several of the same individuals, the groups were often co-existing and were often short-lasting. It was all very different to the traditional security offered by rock and conventional jazz line-ups, many of these musicians being polyandrous in the extreme.

Sartorially, Coxhill differed from the informal image of the younger improvisers, just as Bailey did, both being from an earlier generation. Lol was bald by choice (in a time where most blokes were like Samson), wore tiny glasses, and did bear a slight resemblance to Alexei Sayle, so his looks and style made him stand out in the Free crowd. John Wickes recognised his 'difference': "Something of Lol's demeanour – the stocky build, the tiny-lensed spectacles, his oddly juxtaposed sense of sartoriality, the voluntary baldness, his askance take on life and dry sense of humour – conspired to bolster an image that was at odds with the austere T-shirted and jeaned post-hippie hairiness adopted by his younger avant garde colleagues, something of a send-up of himself." (Wickes, *op. cit.*, p.261.)

By 1972, he had been the subject of a TV documentary (*Coxhill*) made by the film producer Mick Audesley, and his name was becoming recognised by the progressive rock crowd who had heard him, and about him, through his associations with the 'Canterbury scene' and with the bands/individuals from the Virgin Records roster (one of the few reliable sources of English *avant*-rock in the mid 70s): Henry Cow (featuring Lindsay Cooper and Fred Frith), Robert Wyatt, Gong, and Hatfield and the North, for example. That is certainly how I first heard his name.

Another kindred spirit was Jeff Nuttall, the author of the well known early counter-cultural tract, *Bomb Culture* (Nuttall, 1971), who wrote an appreciation of Coxhill in 1989 and was another link with the 60s generation.

In a duo with Steve Miller, Coxhill made a couple of albums for Virgin's subsidiary Caroline label, and he joined Mike Westbrook's Brass Band. One of the more memorable performances at the tribute gig after his death, in September 2012, was by a small Westbrook band. Westbrook was just the sort of 'progressive traditionalist' that Coxhill loved to play with. He also recorded with the group Welfare State on Caroline.

Coxhill found a pedagogic role for himself in 1975, by initiating an improvisation course for youngsters in Bradford.

Steve Beresford, to be discussed next, also found an educative career to complement that of live playing and recording, at the University of Westminster.

The Ogun label's *Lol Coxhill on Ogun* pairs two albums, *The Joy of Paranoia* (released in 1978) and the half solo *Diverse* (with a visual pun this time, on the cover, which features a very camp picture of a deep sea diver being attended to by a group of sailor boys). This is another good starting point at which to investigate Coxhill's considerable recorded output. John Wickes considered *Diverse* to be his best recording up to that point. (Wickes, *op. cit.*, p.264.)

The former record is, as expected by now, a variety of group sounds, with a superlative version of Juan Tizol's *Perdido*, a staple of the Ellington Orchestra, that contains a tremendously evocative solo from Coxhill. Michael Garrick's stabbing introduction on electric piano sets up a swinging, tuneful improvisation that encapsulates most of the sopranist's strengths and virtues within just the first few minutes. The latter record is partly a solo exercise, which also reminds us what a superlative player Coxhill was over a continuous period of time (this was still when solo soprano discs were a rarity). I would also recommend the solo excursion on *Lid* (Ictus 11, if you can find it), recorded in Italy in July 1978.

1977 found our man playing in the Company sessions that were released on CD as *Company 6 & 7* (Incus CD07). These recordings were not without controversy, as we will see in the next section of this chapter.

Coxhill, however, fitted in seamlessly, as he always seemed to be able to do, even in the company of fellow soprano giants like Evan Parker and visiting Americans Steve Lacy and Anthony Braxton. The gigs seemed to symbolise the acceptance, by the American modernists, of an equal footing with their English colleagues, a position that would have seemed inconceivable in the previous decades. Leo Smith, the AACM trumpeter and composer, and fairly unknown at the time on these shores, was also on hand to lend even further *gravitas* to the events.

Lid by Lol Coxhill (solo), July 1978

The Johnny Rondo Trio featured Loxhorn Rondo himself, with the SME's Colin Wood and pianist Dave Holland (no relation to the bassist), who played whatever instruments they felt like in the spirit of The Amazing Band, and toured the north of England with Steve Beresford and Tristan Honsinger, the ebullient cellist who had also appeared on *Company 6 & 7*. Further absurdities were achieved when Loxhorn toured with The Damned, one of the very first punk bands, which introduced him to another fan base entirely. Hippies and punks, Rondo played with them all.

Unfortunately, he was hit by a car in January 1979, while undertaking solo work in New York as part of a tour of the States and Canada (as Evan Parker had done a couple of months earlier). Serious dental damage was sustained and a benefit was held at Oxford Polytechnic on March 16th, a token of the regard in which he was held, which involved Steve Miller, Paul Rutherford, Stan Tracey and Ivor Cutler, an appropriately eclectic bunch of well-wishers. By May, he was back in action.

It is worth mentioning, although it is a couple of months outside our time frame, another split album, *Digswell Duets*. One side had the Johnny Rondo Duo (Colin Wood was absent) and a pairing with pianist Veryon Weston (who Coxhill had worked closely with since 1976, initially from the Digswell Arts Centre in Welwyn Garden City, hence the album title). The other featured an electronically manipulated solo saxophone improvisation. This was ten years before Evan Parker's experiments with that form on *Hall of Mirrors* (1990).

Lol Coxhill had 33 more years of playing left to him, and there are so many who will miss his presence, both on the stage and in the audience. I will leave the last words to our next great maverick: "Add Lol Coxhill to a reasonably good group and it became a brilliant group…Fairy dust or something, from his soprano saxophone would transform everything and everyone, and the music would become thrilling and coherent." (Steve Beresford, *Wire* 343, September 2012, p.14.)

I witnessed this in Crouch End, of all places (and why not?) in 1995. Beresford is spot on in his analysis.

STEVE BERESFORD

Steve Beresford emerged onto the London scene in around 1974, arriving from York, where he had experienced an epiphany of sorts seeing Derek Bailey at the university, a gig that he had helped organise. He studied music there and apparently hated the course, but stayed around for three years after finishing (funnily enough, just as I did at Warwick University, my excuse being that I was running the university record shop), playing organ in a local soul group and performing in a theatre troupe. He had visited London, however, in 1972, playing in a trio called Bread & Cheese, with American guitarist Neil Lamb and a New Yorker called Dave Herzfield, at a gig at Ronnie Scott's (on one of the Musicians Cooperative nights there), which was arranged through Bailey himself, who was returning the earlier favour.

Bread & Cheese also found themselves at the ICES bash, which Beresford was tremendously enthused by. (*Wire* 336, p.38.) However, he evidently found Charlotte Moorman's 'ice cello', which was performed at that event, somewhat less than enthralling: "It was quite obvious that the idea was that it would melt. But it was going to take all night to melt: it was a solid piece of ice in the shape of a cello. Plus, it made no noise at all. So, it's like, 'Jesus, what am I doing here?'. You know that kind of art." (Corbett, 1994, p.195.)

Both Bailey and Parker encouraged his move to London, and he

Steve Beresford, playing with Alterations for Actuel Music at the Almeida Theatre in Islington on November 22nd 1982. "An Improviser Thinks", perhaps (after Rodin)? The detritus is truly impressive

CREDIT: © JAK KILBY WWW.JAKKILBY.CO.UK

quickly became a major mover and shaker on the free improv circuit, a role that he still retains today.

Another reason I can relate to Beresford is because of comments he made to John Corbett (Corbett, *op. cit.*, pp.197-8), that oddly echo my own first experiences of free improvisation: "I just expanded out: I wanted to hear the weirdest music in the world. I was trying to find out about Sun Ra [who first played in England in 1970, *author*], just picking up information in a tiny market town in the Midlands [also the author's place of origin]...the local library...had things like *Witches and Devils* by Albert Ayler, *Rip, Rig and Panic* by Roland Kirk. Also the popular press was writing about these people. You could read perfectly intelligent reviews of Albert Ayler in *Melody Maker*. I mean, that stuff's pretty frightening even now – we all remember the first time we heard Ayler, I think…Then I heard the Spontaneous Music Ensemble on the radio. It was weirder than anything I'd heard and I thought, I'll have to find out about these people."

This correlates precisely with my late adolescent feelings and findings about the music (although I'm five years younger than Beresford), especially the bits about Ayler, *Melody Maker* and the SME. I used the Birmingham Central Library, which at the time was well stocked with modern jazz LPs, to track down some of these challenging sounds.

Corbett, in his chapter on Beresford (*op. cit.,* pp.192-208), points out the uncategorisable nature of Beresford's music, even though, as the above quote makes clear, free jazz was a large formative influence, as it was with many of the first generation of players. He is clearly an omnivorous consumer of all types of music, including jazz, MOR, ska, pop, rock, dub to name only a few. In the 80s, he concentrated on commercial music, TV soundtracks, etc. and correspondingly played much less free improvisation throughout that period. He was a co-founder of *Musics* and of the LMC, and played in many loose conglomerates (3/4 Pullovers, The Promenaders, Alterations), but, due to the tendency of Gen Two musicians to avoid 'jazz-type' groups (i.e. those with fixed, long-term membership), he is less well known than he should be. It is very hard to 'fix' Steve Beresford, and this tendency has maybe been to his detriment, in terms of his historic profile.

I think of the times that I have seen The London Improvisers Orchestra (formed in the 1990s, motivated by a visit to this country from ur-'comproviser' Butch Morris). This large-group improvising scenario features several different 'conduction-ers', each one also being a member of the orchestra itself, who take it in turns to guide and give form, from the front, to his or her colleagues' musical matrix. The 'conduction' itself is an improvisation, and the conductor tends to improvise blocks of sound through solo/small groupings, as well as the orchestra itself, that are themselves creations of the moment. I have found that often the conductions that have seemed the most coherent and fun, for both musicians and audience, were those directed by Steve Beresford, who seemed to inspire the improvisers both individually and as a group to give their best. There is an example of a Beresford 'conduction' on *Spectral Soprano*.

Beresford is nominally a pianist, just as Terry Day is nominally a drummer. But take a look at the instruments he plays on *The Bath of Surprise* (his 1980 solo album), far too many for me to enumerate here, and which make even the Art Ensemble's instrumentation look underwhelming. Look it up on YouTube. The toys and trumpets were in evidence even in the early days, influenced by John Cage and possibly by the AEC themselves. He says that this grew out of playing places that didn't have pianos (Corbett, *op. cit.*, p.198): "I'd just have toy pianos and stuff. The music (the Four Pullovers, with Roger Smith, Coombes and Day) was very, very stridulatory – scraping noise, unvoiced noise. I always liked that band. Pullovers had a real direction to it, a special sound." (Corbett, *op. cit.*, p.198.)

A late 70s flyer for a Manchester Musicians Collective gig at the Band On The Wall venue, in Manchester itself, featured, third on the bill amongst the post-punk detritus: "Steve Beresford (from London) and The Toy Town Symphony Orchestra." (From the notes to *Messthetics* #106.)

In fact, he started to play the full-grown adult piano when he was seven years old. Born on March 6th 1950 in Wellington, Shropshire, music was an integral part of his extended family. He was thus brought up, unsurprisingly, in a musical environment, taking up classical piano lessons and the trumpet at 15. However, rather than sticking to one, or even two, instruments, he decided to branch out, thinking perhaps, by his early 20s, of the virtuosi of the first generation: "Evan and Derek had such worked-out approaches to their instruments. Either of those is like a whole world, *you could do that your whole life* [author's emphasis]. It was almost a deliberate policy, saying, 'I'm not going into it deeply in that way – they've done it so well'." (Corbett, *op. cit.*, p.199.)

Evan Parker, in fact, once described his own playing to me as :my life's work".

This, helpfully, goes some way to understanding the divergences between Gens One and Two, the 'virtuosi' and the 'musical incontinents'.

The latter (Gen Two) were making a definite choice in playing the way they did. This might also go some way towards explaining the seeming lack of 'classic recordings' from the later players, as I suggested earlier. Their recordings seem, to me at least, to lack the *quiddity* of the (slightly) earlier improvisers, possibly because their 'fragmented' (an overused word, I know) recordings sound more like 'works in progress' than completed items. Then again, completed 'works' are usually not the objective of free improvisers, so the whole concept of a 'finished product' can be essentially contested. *Caveat emptor*.

Couldry (*op. cit.*, p.10) suggests that Beresford's 'anti-virtuosic' approach is one in which "the listener is *denied* the opportunity to trace a consistent line of thought or expression", which is compounded by (as on *The Bath Of Surprise*) the use of toys and other anti-virtuoso devices (random voice interjections, primitive electronics, whistles, etc., etc.). Technical skill is thus countenanced by inventiveness, individuality and the role of re-adapted or newly invented instruments (Max Eastley and Hugh Davies, for example).

In terms of 'finished product', Beresford found that some of his seemed to have unsettled many of his peers in 1979: "The fact that I was in the Flying Lizards [with the Davids Cunningham and Toop, *author*], on *Top of the Pops* one night and at the LMC playing to three men and a dog the next night, certain people didn't like that. They thought it was somehow betraying improvised music. I thought it was great that I got to play in front of ten million people and then in front of three people. That's interesting to me, it's exciting." (Corbett, *op. cit.*, p.196.)

The 'dog' trope became quite a popular one, and gave rise to the title of Antoine Prum's film on free improvisation, called *Taking the Dog for a Walk*. The defence mechanisms at play here are complex, and I'm reminded of the Morrissey song, *We Hate it When Our Friends Become Successful*. Some improvisers have become quite popular and successful at melding free improv/jazz/rock: individuals like John Zorn (a favourite of Beresford's, and who had considerable success with the group Naked City, his soundtrack music and the Masada projects, among many other works) and Thurston Moore (with Sonic Youth), both of whom have become banner carriers for cross-genre music. Beresford and others were perhaps "dragging the self-enclosed world of free improvisation back, seeking to make its concerns relevant in a world dominated by popular culture". (Wickes, *op. cit.*, p.315.)

The *Top of the Pops* appearance was with the Flying Lizards, playing their hit version of *Money*. Beresford's work with The Slits may have rankled too, with his more 'purist' colleagues. There is a very good, and very funny, example of Beresford's self-deprecating humour: "Cecil Taylor sounded great but I didn't know how to do it, I thought he just banged the piano with his fists, but it didn't sound the same when I did it." (Interview conducted by Richard Scott (www.richard-scott/steve-beresford-interview.) The Scott interview in 1988, a period when he wasn't playing a lot of free improvisation, goes into some detail about some of the conflicts his approach could engender. It is ironic that such a seemingly affable, gently amusing individual could create bad feeling, but Beresford managed to do it with three separate improviser groupings in the 70s.

With his peers/contemporaries from the younger group of musicians
As well as the Lizards farrago, he cited to Scott another example: "I got involved with Music for Socialism, but I gave it up because it was the hegemony of the sixth form intellectual. Chris Cutler stood up and said, 'I don't have any interest in any music that isn't supported by the proletariat', which is ridiculous, I don't know any proletarians who liked Henry Cow and it seemed such a stupid thing to say. Because he is someone who despises popular music, he hates it. I was also involved in this anti-sexist music movement for a very short while until I discovered they hated soul music. It was just around punk time and everybody was making moral judgements on the basis of genre."

We have heard this sort of thing before, when talking about Scritti Politti and Cardew/Rowe, and the deadly sin of 'bourgeois individualism'.

To be fair, Beresford seems to have always been anti-elitist and, as mentioned, played in a soul band as a teenager. He even played for Roogalator for a very short time, a now forgotten group who I vaguely remember being lumped into the whole English 'pub rock'

R&B sub-genre of the mid 70s.

With his Gen One elders

"We never thought about technique. I think this is what caused some of the conflicts." (Beresford, quoted in Scott, *op cit*.) Alterations, and other configurations, would play music that has been variously described as Cut-Up/Jump-Cut, Genre-Hopping or even Sampladelic. This was as opposed to more linear, longitudinal constructs, which the first generation innovators, in their relatively long-lasting groups, tended to produce, and that were perhaps easier (relatively) on the ear, at least in the domestic listening environment. The Howard Riley Trio, for example, was a working band that was used to playing together over several years of live gigging.

The cut-up mode also makes much more sense when it is experienced live, in my experience: "But what they hated about it was that we took jazz and juxtaposed it, like we would just drop a jazz piece and drop out. And I think that was one of the things that caused the hatred in the 70s, it was like we were devaluating Derek's flattened ninths by saying, 'Ah well, let's have two minutes of flattened ninths and then do a Marlene Dietrich tune, or something'." (Beresford, in Scott, *op. cit*.)

Vaudeville and Music Hall, for example, relied on quick-change artistes, so why couldn't free improvisation benefit from their examples?

Couldry (*op. cit*., p.16) describes this approach well: "Any intuitions of form are constantly disrupted...one development succeeds another without obvious connections, indeed sometimes the impression is given that music is designed to *efface* [my italics] what precedes it, so absolute is the break."

Perhaps it is the passive-aggressive nature of the 'effacement' that Couldry describes that leads, in turn, to the vehement reactions that this music can elicit from those that dislike this form of expression?

John Zorn was a particular influence (Beresford conducted a lengthy interview with him in an early edition of *Musics*), but it should be remembered that the musicians who played his music were far from anti-technicians, in fact you had to be something of a virtuoso to play his demanding, constantly changing, improvisations. But Zorn wasn't really doing anything especially groundbreaking, he was just reasserting the joy of the constantly changing, as opposed to the imposition of the 'monster jam' of unsupportable length (whether by John Coltrane or Grand Funk Railroad?).

However, some musicians felt that Beresford's approach somehow demeaned free improvisation as a serious form. An eight-page discussion that occupied much of *Musics* 19 (September 1978) was called 'Technique and Improvisation', and featured Beresford, Evan Parker, Richard Leigh, David Toop, journalist Steve Lake, Dave Solomon, John Kiefer and Charles K. Noyes, so this was clearly considered an important issue. Beresford and Parker seemed polite to each other, but that might not have been quite the case at other times: "Evan and I had quite a big falling out at certain points. I mean, I get on fine with him now [1988], I think he's brilliant, and I never suggested for one moment that he was anything less than a brilliant saxophone player, but I think he felt my music did." (Scott, *op. cit*.)

In turn, Parker reflects, in the group discussion, that Beresford's technique is not in question. It is something else that bothered him: "Can I just explain to you [Beresford] that I've watched you with some interest. You're one of the younger musicians who've come onto the scene whose work I've had to pay attention to. So this is not through lack of respect for your abilities or intellect. The questions come from not understanding. So it's a request for an explanation." (*Musics* 19, p.6.)

Throughout this lengthy discussion, taking up pages 4-11 of that edition, the father/son overtones of the Parker/Beresford dyad, exemplified in this quote, crackle like mains electricity and seem almost like a playing out of the tensions between the two 'generations'.

Beresford makes another point, again in relation to Parker, about attire, a topic that I enthusiastically discuss in *Beyond Jazz* (Barre, *op. cit.*, pp.67-70) and which I think can tell us something about what a musician wants to 'say': "Evan was talking about the 60s when he started wearing T-shirts on stage, saying 'Look, it doesn't matter what we look like, you've got to concentrate on the music'. I was surprised about Evan actually admitting that he made a decision about what he wore on stage.

This is a great step forward from the time when nobody would even dream of talking about clothes, this would have seemed like a bourgeois deviation of the highest order; purism was something that was in the air at the time." (Scott, *op. cit.*)

One is reminded, at this point, of the Beresford/Coxhill sartorial interchange on Brighton beach described earlier, another cross-generational 'difference in opinion'. To see Beresford's own 'bourgeois deviation', look no further than his loons on the cover of *Teatime* (Emanem 5009).

Further along in the topic of 'anti-virtuosity', it's worth remembering the use, by Beresford and Day *inter alia*, of a multitude of instruments, as another pretention-buster: "The musicians may each play a variety of instruments, and these are often chosen for their comic implications." (Couldry, *op. cit.*, p.17.)

This was another disrupter of virtuosic displays and one thinks, in this instance, of Terry Day's balloons and Steve Beresford's miniature pianos and guitars.

With visiting American modernists

This rather disagreeable divergence of philosophies is described more fully in Ben Watson's biography of Derek Bailey (*Derek Bailey and the Story of Free Improvisation*). Beresford's approach to free improvisation appears to have alienated Anthony Braxton and Leo Smith, both from the AACM, who had come over the water, most encouragingly,

Company 6 & 7 by Company, May 25th-27th, 1977

to participate in the 1977 Company Week (the first one), recorded evidence of which is available on *Company 6 & 7* (Incus CD07). The Americans' musical origins were very much in classic free jazz and they, like Evan Parker, seemed to find Beresford's antics both baffling and anti-jazz: "Steve Beresford's interpretation of freedom…didn't suit the high seriousness of the AACM delegates. On the first night…Beresford poured water from a hot water bottle into his trumpet, and paddled in the resulting puddle. He then set fire to a piece of paper." (Watson, 2004, p.215.)

Fire and water appear to be two of the four classical elements that the LMC later found conducive (see Annabel Nicolson/Paul Burwell and John Zorn/David Toop). Earth and Air had to wait.

Watson tends to revel in this type of dismissal of 'conservative' reactions to his heroic iconoclasts, which include, especially, Frank Zappa, the arch radical-conservative himself, and one has to sympathise with the Chicagoans to some extent. Eugene Chadbourne describes their point of view: "This was at a time when I was talking to a lot of these guys, so I get this report: 'Well there was this one guy who was a *complete* lunatic, don't ever play with him,' I remember Leo saying. 'He doesn't have his musicianship together.' That was Steve Beresford... He'd gone through this experience where people had rejected him." (Watson, *op. cit.*, p.216.)

This was manifest in the May 1977 gigs where, basically, Braxton and Smith avoided playing with Beresford, as did Evan Parker, although in Watson's view "he'd raised a banner for a certain species of improviser". (Watson, *op. cit.*, p.216.) On Company 6 & 7 he only plays on two tracks, probably the most anarchic of the lot (particularly Track 6), with mostly the string players, Maarten van Regteren Altena, Tristan Honsinger, Bailey himself and drummer Han Bennink. Make of that what you will. No sign of Braxton, Smith or, indeed, fellow American Steve Lacy. Take a look at the body language on the group photo of the cover of *Company 6 & 7*, with Braxton leaning away from the adjacent Beresford, with his head also turned away from him. Smith and Lacy seek each other's company at the extreme right end of the row, leaving Braxton stuck in the middle with two of the 'humourists', Beresford and Honsinger, on either side of him.

Thereafter, Beresford maintained long associations with both Honsinger and Bennink, and toured Canada with the latter in 1995. Interestingly enough, by October 1979 he was performing in Amsterdam with Evan Parker, Anthony Braxton and AACM trombonist George Lewis, so he must have been seen to be doing something right in the long term.

Steve Beresford is a most vital and catalytic figure in our story of these

Terry Day at 'March Hare', for Actuel Music at the ICA on March 1st 1981. With a mischievous grin and fag in mouth, Terry Day wields a shaker/rattler, with his trusty 'extended' kit by his side, replete with beer cans (including the less-than-Dionysian Colt 45?)

CREDIT: © JAK KILBY WWW.JAKKILBY.CO.UK

years, as musician, journalist, teacher, *agent provocateur* and mischief-maker-in-chief. That he continues to be all these things is something that fans of the music should be grateful for.

TERRY DAY

Whilst reading Terry Day's own description of his life in music on his website, www.terryday.co.uk, I was reminded, as much as anything else, of an exhaustive Curriculum Vitae, providing supporting information to accompany an application for an imaginary job, such as a 'Free Improvisation Music Executive' or some such unlikely title. Such is the reach of his extensive list of musical endeavours, over what is now a 57-year career (he was born in 1940), which started in the early 60s. Just like Steve Beresford and Lol Coxhill, he is a polymath who resists easy commodification.

Like Beresford, Day is a multi-instrumentalist, a real one-man band, even in the old sense of the word. Or an English Don Cherry, perhaps, a musical nomad performing with a multitude of musicians across the globe. Even his balloon playing, demonstrated in Antoine Prum's film, made me think of alto saxophonist Marshall Allen's more extreme registers. The interested reader should certainly visit Day's website, which fully delineates both the extent of his musical *armamentarium* and of his dizzying playing environments. Just as Beresford could be said to be essentially, or even quintessentially, a piano player, so Day is fundamentally a percussionist, who also happens to play the cello, mandolin, alto/soprano/sopranino saxophones, bamboo reed flutes, recorder, balloons and no doubt many other instruments that I'm not even aware of. He, in fact, started off on piano before the influence of one of his older brothers, Pat, led him to the world of the big beat.

His solo album, *Interruptions* (Emanem 4125), recorded at the cusp of the 70s/80s, itemises in full his instrumentation, one that is as full as that described in Steve Beresford's section (whose *The Bath Of Surprise* was a similar solo exploration at around the same time).

Interruptions by Terry Day, 1978-81

Ill health kept Day away from live music throughout the 90s in particular, but, at the turn of the millennium, he gradually returned to the live situation, starting, with Steve Beresford's encouragement, with his wooden pipes and flutes, and ultimately a return to the full drum kit, which he now plays with his customary power and passion – a remarkable story of recovery and will power.

Microphone No. 5 (June 1972) presented drum kits and their occupants as the principal feature of that edition, with interviews with Paul Lytton, Tony Oxley (whose only comment was, "The most important activity for me is the enlargement of my vocabulary," a contribution that was as aggressively minimal as his playing is aggressively maximal), Frank Perry, Jamie Muir and Peter Britton. Unfortunately, Terry Day was not included, which seems par for the course (although, to be fair to the magazine, he was possibly abroad at the time). However, Paul Lytton's comment (page 3) could be equally applicable to Day:

"The sources have remained the same:

skin	wire
wood	rubber
plastic	liquid
metal	gas"

Day is both a master of the small kit (as was John Stevens) and also the large/extended one (as were, at various times Oxley, Lytton, Frank Perry, Eddie Prevost and Jamie Muir). Perry's description of his kit (*Microphone* 5, p.2), too lengthy to enumerate here, gives some idea of its size and contents, with representatives of the various materials, described above by Lytton, well in evidence. A good visual indicator of the larger kit is the photograph by Jak Kilby on the booklet provided with Day's *Interruptions* CD, with his kit adorned with beer cans and tubes of varying provenance.

Life

Terry Day was born on October 17th 1940, into a musical family – like Steve Beresford. Terry's father was a drummer and pianist. One of his elder brothers, Pat, a child prodigy on drums, had formed his own band at the age of 11 and went on to play with the blind pianist Eddie Thompson, who was Ronnie Scott's house pianist from 1959-72. (Day, personal communication, 2017.) By the age of 17, Terry was drumming in dance bands and received some tutoring from George Scott, who lived in rooms opposite skiffle-*meister* Lonny Donegan, funnily enough. When he was young, he actually wanted to major in the alto, but initially had piano lessons for about a year, having at that point no desire to play the drums, only learning them to support himself as an art student.

His first reed was actually the clarinet, in a duo with Ian Dury in 1963, when they were both students at the Royal Academy of Art and sharing a flat in Elgin Avenue. Terry's age places him well within the first generation of free players (which he very much sees himself to be a part of) but, apart from an album with The People Band (and apparently some poor quality tapes that remain in his personal archives), he went unrecorded before the 70s, with the result that he tends to be seen as part of the second generation. This is unfortunate, to some extent, as Day says that he was playing free improvisation as far back as 1960, in a trio with pianist Russell Hardy, who later became a composer with Kilburn & The High Roads. Terry Holman played bass and trumpeter Henry Lowther would sometimes sit in, and Day claims to have pioneered 'non-tempo pulse' at this time in this country.

He has a very extensive archive, recording his work from the late 60s, in individual and group situations, to the current day, and hopes to ultimately release material from this source, which may go some way to correcting the imbalance of his live/recorded history. These include recordings with George Khan/ Peter Lemer (from the infamous Hornsey College of Art sit-ins in 1968); the Ommu band with Davey Payne and Charlie Hart, Dutch recordings from the late 60s; and early Kilburn & The High Roads material (basically The People Band with Ian Dury).

The Kilburns connection is an interesting one, as Day was also an early member, as was People Band saxophonist George Khan. Best known as pub rockers and as Ian Dury's first band, they clearly fitted in with those eclectic times: "Such a motley crew: two of them disabled, one black, another perhaps psychotic, all shapes and sizes, dressed like an explosion at a jumble sale." (Du Noyer, *op. cit.*, p.200.)

This, not exactly politically correct, description, could certainly also apply to the Promenaders (minus the psychosis), who participated in the Brighton Beach gig (Day was a part-time member of this band as well), which has been described earlier in this chapter. Day's art school background was significant, and he had taught fine art for several years, from 1966-72. He attended The Royal College of Art, through which he met Shirley Watts, wife of Charlie Watts, who ultimately financed the first People Band record on Transatlantic Records. The Continuous Music Ensemble, which he was part of from 1965, had evolved from a merger of the Hardy/Holman/Day trio with a group of musicians playing at the Starting Gate pub in north London (an upstairs gig on Friday nights, which ended in 1967). Eventually they felt it necessary to morph into The People Band, to avoid confusion with the Spontaneous Music Ensemble. The two bands overlapped, however, and Day drummed at the LTC (where he formed a band with John Stevens called Free Space), and he scaled down his kit accordingly, and began to use other instruments: "By this time I had figured out that enough was enough, the best thing for the Little Theatre (and all those stairs!!) was one bag over the shoulder, one cymbal, one tambourine and that's it. So I used a very tiny set and from there went into just very, very small sounds." (Wickes, *op. cit.*, p.307.)

As Wickes (*op. cit.*, p.307) explains: "Day would add impromptu blasts on the numerous bamboo flutes he had fashioned, as part of his performance. As in the case of the Art Ensemble of Chicago, being able to play several instruments rather than proficiency on only one (if at all) was almost to become *de rigueur* among second generation improvisers."

There were perhaps some similarities here with Toop and Burwell's Rain in the Face duo, with the former on guitar and homemade decorated flutes, who were playing at the LTC from as early as 1972, at the Gen One/Two cusp.

Multi-instrumentalism and its use as a humorous adjunct to the soundfield has been alluded to earlier, as has its anti-virtuosic disruptive function. Day's balloons and bamboo flutes (also one of Toop's resources) were a significant contribution to this narrative.

Day formed close links with Holland (the country) around this time, and was semi-resident there as more work presented itself on the continent, as it did for the Chicagoan improvisers of the AACM at the time (see Lewis, *op. cit.*). In the early 70s, he undertook tours with People Band splinter groups, and participated in mixed media events with the Abstract Theatre Group involving various painters, actors, poets, dancers, mime artists, film and 'environmental' artists, i.e. the full gamut of multi-disciplinary activity. He was still playing extensively in Holland by the late 70s, with Peter Cusack, Maarten Altena (*The Fairly Young Bean* being a good example of this period) and some of the Dutch free improvisers.

By the mid 70s, he was playing with the London Musicians Collective, and appeared at the Second Generation 'Young Improvisers' (somewhat of a euphemism, as he was 34 at the time) showpiece at the Wigmore Hall, mentioned in Chapter One, which may be another reason why he is associated with this particular group. He also appeared with Company and with Derek Bailey in combinations and duos throughout the 70s.

As well as solo performances in England and Europe, he played in many other combinations throughout the 70s. Among the most interesting are:

▶ An unrecorded SME with Stevens, Watts and bassist Marc Meggido.
▶ The Four Pullovers, with Beresford, guitarist Roger Smith and violinist Nigel Coombes, which can be heard on Eminem 4038.
▶ In 'The People Show' tour of England, Holland and Belgium, but in an acting role only.
▶ The Promenaders, with both Beresford and Coxhill, as well as Peter Cusack, Toop, Burwell and Max Eastley.
▶ In 1977/8, a member of the Peter Cusack Group, which toured the above countries, in a band that included John Tchicai.
▶ Finally, perhaps *the* ur-Gen Two group, Alterations, again with Beresford, Toop and Cusack. A most incestuous group of improvisers were this lot!

As we can see, Day was one of the earliest free improvisers "to bring new thinking about performance, from another perspective to jazz" (Wickes, *op. cit.*, p.307), an approach which many of the Gen Two musicians actively encouraged and promoted. He brought a new visual element into the music, one of which was the flitting from instrument to instrument (as did all the members of Alterations). He incorporated on-stage instrument construction (his huge drum kit) and worked in other contexts, with dancers and sound poets, writing and reading his own poetry. He wasn't afraid to look potentially silly (just as Beresford did with his Toy Orchestra), demonstrating that it wasn't all po-faced attitude-striking in this music.

Frank Zappa named one of his albums *Does Humor Belong in Music?* This is a moot question, especially from someone who took himself so incredibly seriously. As the old adage goes, "If you have to ask…" However, several of the free players/groups did manage to inject humour into their music, which didn't always make them popular, as we have seen with Beresford and the Americans. *It Ain't My Cup Of Tea*, on *Interruptions*, is very Patrick Fitzgerald (of *Safety Pin Stuck in my Heart* near-fame from 1977), out-punking the punks, and which makes me laugh every time I hear it.

This seems as good a place as any to mention the 'Crackle Box', an oddity which Day plays on two tracks on *Interruptions*: "One of the instruments he used is a Crackle Box, a raw electronic device made by STEIM-based improviser Michel Waiswicz. 'It was hard to control,' Day recalls. 'After a while the sweat on your fingertips would make it cut out. It was totally random – the most random instrument ever'." (From an interview with Julian Cowley, in *Wire* 268, June 2006, p.12.)

This obscure instrument sounds and looks like some kind of sound generator designed by the Italian Futurists, and Waiswicz himself describes "The Cracklebox Project" in *Musics* 7 (page 7). This seemed to be exactly the sort of thing that *Musics* was born to feature, among its various other antiques and curiosities from the musical highways and byways. Lol Coxhill was also known to play it on several occasions.

Interruptions, a CD of 1978-81 recordings, is Day writ large, restless and constantly shape-shifting, with 32 short tracks, that sums up, in 77 minutes, the Terry Day *modus operandi*. Basic drums, bamboo pipes, 'homemade instruments', balloons, toys ('blowers, whackers and pluckers', as the cover notes describe them), plastic trumpet and the Crackle Box give *some* idea of the sounds to expect. Plink, Plonk and Scratch, even. At one point, forgetting what I was listening to, I could have sworn that it was Anthony Braxton's classic *For Alto*. That's how good he can be (and, even more impressively, on a subsidiary instrument). Plus, as mentioned, a couple of punk-ish songs with guitarist Cusack. It is very much in the realm of *Ear of the Beholder* and *The Bath of Surprise*. This is the record to get if you want to see just how much of a polymath Terry Day can be. It has its inevitable *longueurs*, but also has a real sense of musical energy and sheer fun, however inappropriate the latter may seem to some. Again, his website is exhaustive (and exhausting) and will tell you all you need to know about this most variegated and idiosyncratic of performers.

Lol Coxhill, Steve Beresford and Terry Day converge at many points in our story, one being in the considerable amount of groups that they shared membership of, and another being the sheer breadth and quality of the contribution they made to 70s improvisation.

To conclude this chapter about these truly individual musicians, I'd like to quote a paragraph from a 1979 *Melody Maker* article by Brian Case (September 29th, p.28), which, conveniently, links all three men together: "Playing with him (Beresford) presents problems for some, bonuses to others. Lol Coxhill: 'You can take it two ways – go into the humourous hit, or go across it. The funnier he gets, the more serious I get. You can hardly not be aware of him.' Percussionist Terry Day sees him as being 'in the line of descent from The People Band'."

All three improvisers clearly appreciated the considerable skill sets of their peers.

CHAPTER 5

Company and Gen Two Groups

▶ "Company Week was a significant step towards *monumentalising* and *institutionalising* free improvisation as an idiom…Bailey's *idealisation* of the semi-ad hoc ironically yielded one of free improvisation's most venerated institutions." [Italics are by this author.] (Bill Shoemaker, e-zine *Point of Departure*, Issue 54, March 2016.)

▶ "Derek Bailey, when he first formed Company, wrote: "For some time it has seemed that the most interesting results in free improvisation come from the semi *ad-hoc* groupings of musicians. The tendency among improvising groups previously has been to form regular groups, play together as often as possible, and attempt to develop a personal identifiable group music. This still happens, but there is a growing pool of musicians, drawn from many countries, who work together regularly but not continuously, and not on the basis of being members of a set, permanent, group. Company is an attempt to exploit these possibilities and perhaps to provide further opportunities for this kind of relationship to take place." (Ben Watson, in notes accompanying *Company 6 & 7*, 1991.)

▶ "I walked into the dressing room and thought, 'How are these people going to play together? They can barely hold a conversation among themselves!' Derek brought them together, but on their own they didn't have that much in common." (Eugene Chabourne, in Watson, *op. cit.*, p.215.)

Bill Shoemaker notes the irony of the avowedly non-idiomatic becoming unpredictably predictable, or predictably unpredictable. The

Alterations at the Almeida Theatre, Islington on October 22nd 1982, their armamentaria promiscuously displayed! Steve Beresford, Peter Cusack, David Toop and Terry Day. As Beresford admitted, "Cecil Taylor sounded great...it didn't sound the same when I did it" (banging fists on the keyboard)

CREDIT: © JAK KILBY WWW.JAKKILBY.CO.UK

defence mechanisms that I have highlighted in the first quote are ones that guard against the fear of extinction, perhaps? They might be a defence against the impossible task of the fixing of the transient in aspic (which was an oft-stated concern regarding the recording medium, in the early days of the music). I am, at this point, reminded of my own earlier comments, about monumentalisation and idealisation (with regards to neo-conservatism, to Marsalis/Crouch, the Smithsonian collection and Lincoln Hall). Could the TAZ of Company be free improv's own pop-up Lincoln Hall? 'Free improvisation at the Philharmonic', even?

My own Company experience? I attended one evening of the late '81/ early '82 Company Tour, which took place at the University of Warwick Arts Centre (a brand new building at the time, as I remember), on February 1st 1982. The tour members at that point were Bailey, Parker, John Zorn (on duck calls, clarinet and alto), Steve Lacy, Dutch pianist Misha Mengelberg and Scottish percussionist Jamie Muir. The most memorable part of the whole evening probably belonged to Zorn, almost unknown in this country at the time and who apparently hated the tour (Watson, *op. cit.*, p.231), playing through a clarinet mouth piece which was dipped into a bowl of water.

Needless to say, not everyone was appreciative of this innovation, as we saw back in Chapter 3. Most of us just sat there in baffled silence, having never had the chance to see David Toop doing a similar thing some four years earlier at the LMC (as portrayed on the cover of this very book). I still find this sort of 'water music' an underwhelming technique, to be absolutely frank, as did a certain Meredy Benson, 'The Public House Bookshop [in Brighton, *author*] Cleaning Lady', in a letter published in *Musics* 13, p.32: "John Kiefer organised a concert to be held in our basement…a while ago, with David Toop and Paul Burwell – I thoroughly enjoyed it but for one small part. I couldn't really appreciate the beautiful sound of water being poured on water while watching one jug full overflow onto the floor. While I truly appreciate these natural sounds, I don't feel that 'water soaking into the carpet' really adds much to the overall experience."

Perhaps this is one of the reasons why the robust flooring of the LMC

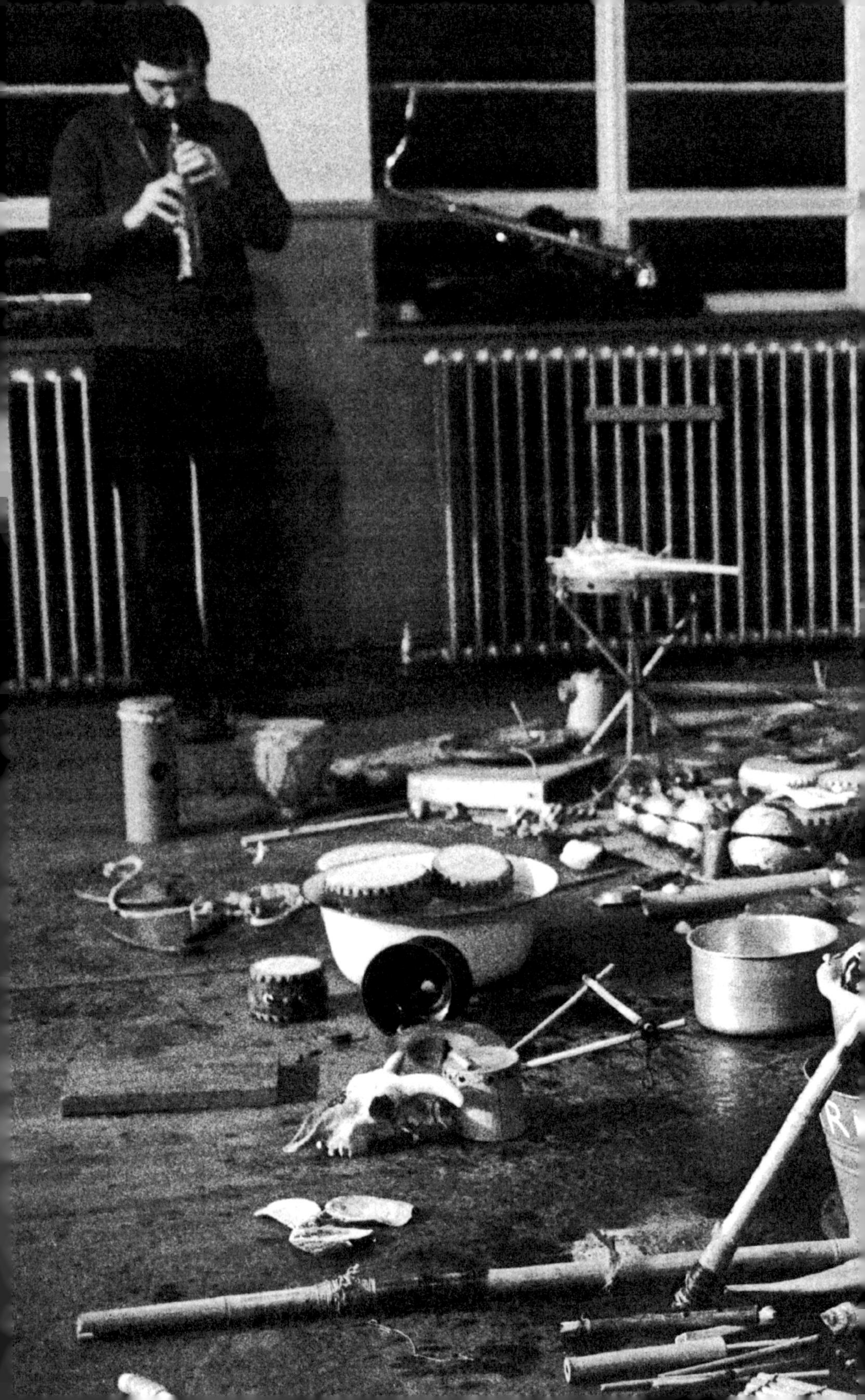

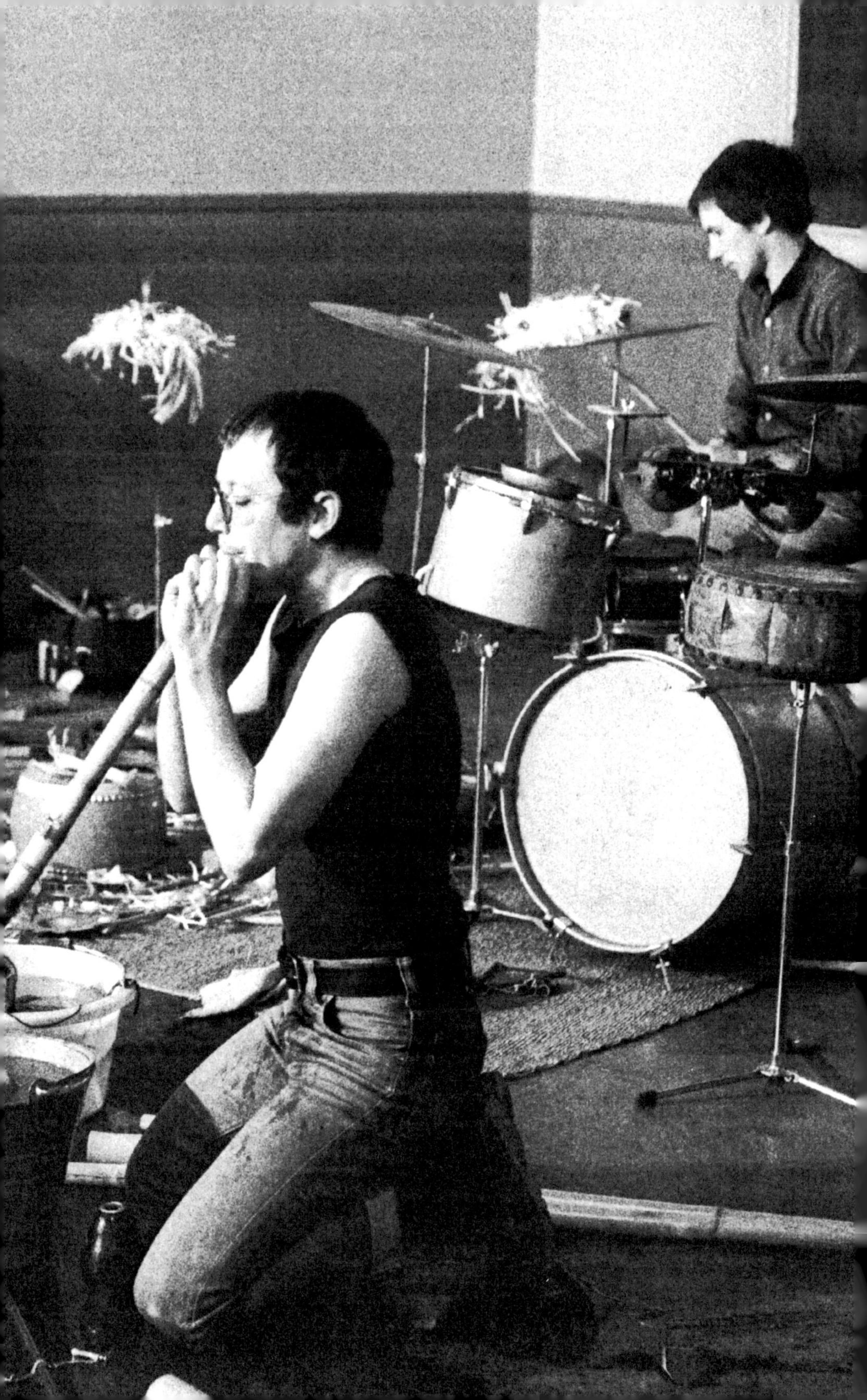

HQ at Gloucester Avenue was so celebrated in free improv lore? Lol Coxhill, on the other hand, made a bigger splash, as it were, but had the courtesy to use a slightly larger body of water (on a YouTube clip from a Copenhagen swimming pool in 1996, called *Underwater Sax*).

Company was a shape-shifting aggregation of improvisers (and occasional performers from other disciplines), across various artistic modalities, as contra-distinguished from the 'fixed' groups such as AMM, SME, Parker/Lytton, the Howard Riley Trio and Tony Oxley's Angular Apron, from the free improv Golden Age. As discussed in Chapter Six of *Beyond Jazz* (Barre, *op. cit.*, pp.253-275) however, it is evident that the Gen One players played across several semi-fixed groups, and quite a few of them were members of more than one configuration within the same time period. The working life of several of these early groups appears to have been around three or four years (Music Improvisation Company, the original Iskra 1903 and the original Howard Riley Trio and Tony Oxley Groups). Some lasted considerably longer (Parker/Lytton/ Guy; the Schlippenbach Trio, with Parker; the various incarnations of AMM, under Eddie Prevost; the SME, until John Stevens' untimely death in 1994). There was a creative tension between fixity and freedom, as we will see later in this chapter when we look at second generation 'fixed groups'. Were Gen Two 'proto-punk' in their rejection of 'rockist'/'jazzist' conventions around what constituted a 'group'? This included the 'corporate' notions also put forward at the time, by the likes of the original Public Image Limited, some of the contemporary Sheffield *avant electronicists* like Heaven 17 (with the British Electric Foundation), and COUM Transmissions, out of which emerged Throbbing Gristle and the whole school of 'industrial music'. It was a very busy time.

Or were the later generation merely an attention-deficit extension of Gen One, but with the sheer virtuosity of the latter rinsed out?

THE EARLY COMPANY YEARS

Derek Bailey, as we have seen, focused on solo guitar improvisation in the mid 70s, and recorded a trio of absolute classics of the form, in 1973 (*Incus Taps*), 1974 (*Lot 74*) and 1975 (*Improvisation*).

'Improv International' (Chicago, Holland, Clapton) in action: Anthony Braxton (sopranino sax), Steve Lacy (soprano sax), Maarten van Regtena Altena (double bass), Leo Smith (trumpet), Derek Bailey (guitar) at the ICA on March 4th 1979
CREDIT: © JAK KILBY WWW.JAKKILBY.CO.UK

He eventually felt limited by this focus and started calling his playing with other improvisers 'Company', around early 1976, as a corollary to his solo work. It transmogrified from one-off gigs, to 'Company Weeks', to 'Company Tours' and, inevitably, recordings, the latter of which were, in the final analysis, fairly traditional in format, especially in the early years, and which featured, basically, a rotating programme of the same few players. By the very early 80s "the more theatrical tendencies apparent in improvising circles at that time turned up in Company...a clown, a dancer, performers 'into performance', were sometimes included," (Bailey, 1992, p.135) as well as non-improvisers such as pianist Ursula Oppens.

The 'more theatrical' aspects were obviously not going to translate onto vinyl (as it was then, being the only way to experience a previous event, apart from the very occasional VHS recording). One of my very favorite Company recordings, as well as one of my favorite records, period, is *Fables* (Incus 36), which featured a dream quartet of Bailey, Parker, George Lewis and Dave Holland. This was basically a fairly old-fashioned recording, by May 1980, when it was recorded, a studio group free improvisation, and the Company imprint seemed somehow incidental. Company 'live', on the other hand, was a definite event, wherein "players from any part of the spectrum" (Bailey, *op. cit.*, p.134) made it a visual, as well as an aural, experience.

Bailey called these collective playing situations, with the combination of the performers involved changing constantly, "*ad hoc* groupings", which can basically be translated as "*improvised* groupings", and he compared them to a theatrical repertory company, which he saw as the nearest approximation to Company in terms of the working methodology of both entities.

Company One (Incus 21) was recorded on May 9th 1976 (the day after its first formal live gig at the Purcell Room) at Riverside Studios, with Bailey, Parker, Tristan Honsinger and Maarten van Regteren Altena, which made it a very strings-dominated affair. *Company Two* (Incus 23) followed fast on its heels, with Bailey, Parker and Anthony Braxton, on August 22nd, essentially a horn-fest, and *Company Three* (Incus 25), with a duo of Bailey and Han Bennink, just one month later. It was an impressive start, with three albums in just five months, featuring a truly international cast, and Incus Records was on a roll. *Company Four* (Incus 26) featured a duet with another American modernist, Steve Lacy, again made in 1976. After this, Company recordings tended to feature somewhat larger conglomerations, and started to look and sound different to the previous small-group free improvisations.

The backgrounds of almost all of the players in the early Company years were from modern jazz. This approach slowly began to change with the introduction of classically trained string players like Honsinger, Altena and violinist Phil Wachsmann. These 'conservatory drop-outs' had no allegiance to jazz, in the same way that many English second generation players, like David Toop, Max Eastley, Steve Beresford and Clive Bell, were not 'jazzers' by background.

Around the same time, July 1977, punk rock was establishing anti-elitist credentials, as with Ed Banger and The Nosebleed's topical *Ain't Been To No Music School* (on Rabid Records) which, somewhat ironically, featured the highly skilled guitarist Vini Reilly, who shot to fame shortly afterwards, in 1979, with his Durutti Column on the eponymous debut on Factory Records (FAC 14).

What the English and Dutch free improvisers both shared was a fondness for *bricolage* in their playing, an orientation that Company participants increasingly chose and that bands like Alterations, The Promenaders and The Recedents developed in the latter half of the decade, and thereafter.

The first Company Week, eventually released as *Company 6 & 7*, was a taste of the highs and the lows of these sorts of events. The last Company Week of the 70s was held, just short of a year later, again at the ICA (back in the days when this venue featured adventurous music such as Throbbing Gristle's debut in 1976, as part of the *Transgressions* installation) between March 30th and April 6th 1978, and which featured a grab-bag of talent – Bailey himself of course, Leo Smith (still game, despite Beresford's subversive antics the year before), Maurice Horsthuis on viola, South African Blue Note Johnny Dyani, Dutch pianist Misha Mengelberg and Terry Day. This was a real *smorgasbord* of AACM, classical, *kwela*, Dutch swing and aboriginal English free improv.

It is interesting that Bailey chose to 'branch out' in the early 80s, as he felt that Company gigs were becoming too 'cosy' (Bailey, *op. cit.*, p.135), which was the same way he felt just before he left both the Music Improvisation Company and Iskra 1903 in the early 70s. His biographer, Ben Watson, however, opined that "in the 80s, Company Weeks were certainly interesting events, but they did not have the messianic fervour… of Free Improvisation in its classic period…Company Weeks became flagships events for Free Improvisation, and hence prone to preciousness, competitive exhibitionism and lame jokes." (Watson, *op. cit.*, p.226.)

Watson goes on to consider the 'classic period' (i.e. the late 60s/early 70s) to be "the heroic years" (*op. cit.*, p.229), a typical Marxist conceit, but also a further collusion with the 'golden age' trope. This may just be another example of the monumentalisation mentioned at the beginning of this chapter, one of the themes of this book, but it is instructive that, by

1988, Bailey felt that further casting about was necessary, to widen the music's gene pool: "He invited musicians from Leeds, Manchester and Sheffield to Company Week and made polemical assertions about the relative strength of Free Improvisation in the provinces compared to the metropolis." (Watson, *op. cit.,* p.227.)

Bill Shoemaker (*Point of Departure*, Issue 54, March 2016) reinforced this idea: "The second generation is a measure of how the London improvised music scene had cultivated a national constituency."

This was an appropriate acknowledgement of the English free improv diaspora, which we will be looking at in more detail later.

THE SECOND GENERATION 'SUPERGROUPS'

There is an argument that I've heard, which goes something along these lines: "I can get into the early free improvisers because you can see that they can play their instruments, can play solos and suchlike, and that they came out of jazz, but the next bunch can't play anything for any length of time, don't appear to be able to concentrate, and to have attention deficit syndrome. Plus they seem to have the need to make silly noises with non-instruments. Enough already."

In actual fact, players like Steve Beresford, David Toop, Dave Solomon and John Russell, to name but four, *didn't* have a working relationship with jazz music, so there is *some* truth in the above. The second generation *did* reject some of the conventions that had crept in, even after only a few years of free improvisation practice in England. One convention, represented by the Musicians Cooperative, was that, because the music was not taken seriously by most people, instrumental competence to a highly developed degree was essential to counteract claims of charlatanism. Most musicians demonstrated this by focusing on one, or perhaps two, recognisable 'proper' instruments. Derek Bailey and Evan Parker were exemplars of this thinking. There were some exceptions to this, for example with the Parker/Lytton duo and their extended instrumental armamentarium, and with early electronic experiments by the likes of Hugh Davies (with the Music Improvisation Company) and percussionist and composer Tony Oxley.

Bill Shoemaker, in his editorial quoted above, goes on to set up an "aesthetic distance" between the generations, citing Gen Two's "absurdist high jinks", with their use of kitsch and dada routines "disrupting free improv's move towards a carefully arranged idiom". I'm not sure how 'carefully' the Gen One players did actually try to create an 'idiom' or free 'language' but, as we saw with the first Company Week, some improvisers had clear ideas as to what free improvisation was, and equally important, what it *wasn't*. I do wonder whether Shoemaker is, as his name suggests, trying to shoehorn the feet of this conveniently retrospective demarcation into a particularly recalcitrant item of categorical footwear, and that he perhaps overestimates the Oedipal nature of the (slightly) later improvisers that represented Gen Two? He also seems to be providing a convenient contra-modernist philosophy for the second generation, one that sought to disrupt the notional "carefully arranged idiom" of the first? I somehow doubt that many of the Gen One musicians would have seen their endeavours as forming part of some kind of master plan, however seductive this idea might have been.

Conveniently, for our purposes, *Teatime* (Emanem 5009) recorded across 1973/4/5, will be taken as the introductory recording of the second generation. I realise that some will put forward *Balance* (Incus 11), recorded in November 1973 with Ian Brighton (guitar), Colin Wood, Frank Perry, trombonist Rudu Malfatti and violinist Phil Wachsmann, as a more appropriate choice. *Balance*, however, has not been transferred to CD, so it is a rarity. As it doesn't have Derek Bailey on it, the decision has presumably been made by Incus not to re-release it. Julian Cowley describes *Balance*, as the title suggests, being about "sensitive interplay, nuance and close-knit subtlety...concerned with finely crafted coherence," whereas *Teatime* "is rowdy, unruly, funny and melodramatic...about performance, participation and boisterous congeniality". Rough spontaneity, as opposed

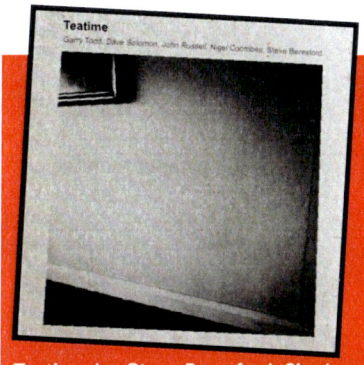

Teatime by Steve Beresford, Nigel Coombes, John Russell, Dave Solomon and Gary Todd, 1973-5

to "poised chamber improvisations" (one cod-percussive *Teatime* track is, accurately, called *Irritating Tapping*). (*Wire* 322, December 2010, p.56.)

The latter description sounds closer to the spirit of Gen Two, to be honest. *Balance* sounds closer to that of Gen One.

Teatime features Gary Todd on tenor sax, Dave Solomon on drums, John Russell on guitar and the shortly to become seemingly omnipresent Steve Beresford on 'piano and toys'. What strikes the listener on hearing it for the first time is its discontinuousness, its cut-up ordering of sound, with differing combinations of the musicians involved, solos, duos, trios and a quartet, almost like a future Company evening. The sound on *Low-Fi* is, guess what, blooming awful. The live tracks feature (Beresford's?) laconic and sarcastic comments on proceedings. Nothing here can be called smooth or slick, to put it mildly. Most of the recordings, chosen by the musicians themselves, came from the Unity Theatre, as Incus Records wanted a recording that could parallel the 'Young Improvisers' Wigmore Hall 'showcase', which had been organised by Janice Christianson's Albion Music, on May 2nd 1975, and which could be seen as yet another precursor to Company. Indeed, given that Christianson was Bailey's partner throughout most of the 70s, it would have been surprising if there hadn't been some cross-influencing by both parties.

Martin Davidson, who recorded the proceedings on *Teatime*, described its "brutal editing" by the players concerned, although he says, in his accompanying note, that Lol Coxhill had done something along those lines before (presumably *Ear of the Beholder*?). Abrupt editing is a feature on this album, a technique that eventually became institutionalised as 'jump cut', but was probably seen then as incompetent and/or unprofessional. Cowley cites the abrupt termination of *I didn't get up this morning* after 54 seconds as a good example of editorial ruthlessness (and of free improv's fondness for sarcastic titles). What is certain though, in all this, is that these were the earliest recordings of Nigel Coombes, John Russell and Dave Solomon, and one of the first by both Steve Beresford and Gary Todd.

Track 2, another of the few times that they could be bothered to put forward a title (another radical development, an indication of their unconcerned attitude to 'product'), is entitled *European improvised music sho' nuff turns me on*, a titular successor to the equally dodgy (in modern politically correct terms) earlier track by Bailey/Bennink on *Live At Verities* (Incus 9), *Shake Your Arse White Man*. Slightly funnier (to the modern ear) is, *I didn't get up this morning*, but it does show how humour changes over time, patronising references to black 'classical' music now being seen as unacceptable, rightly or wrongly. John Russell is still clearly indebted to Bailey's influence and tuition, and Beresford to – who knows, there are probably too many influences to itemise.

Even at this stage, definite markers were being laid by these relative youngsters: "The older generation embraced elements of humour, if only to differentiate their approach from the earnest sobriety of the academic avant garde. But Beresford made musical jokes, visual gags and deliberate silliness integral components of his performances." (Cowley, *op. cit.*, p.56.)

By 1979, this had become an established way of playing for several influential, relatively fixed-term combinations who, the reader will note, shared several members in a most promiscuous way. This was, to some extent, as it had been with the Gen One improvisers, one of the reasons that histories of these times can be confusing to the newcomer – it almost feels like all the groupings emerged from one large collective pot (which they mostly did, in actual fact). Some names repeatedly crop up, Steve Beresford at the front, closely followed by David Toop, Lol Coxhill and Terry Day. The only reason that Toop was left out of Chapter Four, as I have already said, is that his connections with jazz are even more tenuous (i.e. none at all) than Beresford's. He didn't have to go 'beyond jazz', he was already there. It is clear, however, that Toop's influence was considerable. In fact, *Musics* 16 (February 1978) contains a letter from Bill Hutchins claiming that Toop was far too prominent on the scene, at that time: "Recent issues of *Musics* have shown an increasing dominance by David Toop, to the extent where perhaps it might be more appropriate to call your magazine TOOPICS. Even SB (Beresford), who usually does well, is getting pushed into a corner, and PB (Burwell) seems to have been played off the field altogether." (Page 3.)

Ironically, the late PB was the musician who both started and ended the magazine, appearing in both editions, and to whom full credit must be given, even at this late stage, for his hard work.

Toop's position as a writer and critic probably didn't help to defuse accusations of his omnipresence, but (t)his perceived dominance was, most importantly, seen to be to the detriment of 'proper' musicians, i.e. those who displayed a certain virtuosity, or at least a loyalty, on one or two instruments, not the incontinence of 'little' or 'toy' instruments. John Russell promptly sprang to Toop's defence in Issue 17. These sorts of disputations began to dominate *Musics* from this time on, as we will see later on in the narrative.

ALTERATIONS

"Alterations' mash-up of genres, its emphasis on unlikely sound sources, everything from wind-up [in both senses, *author*] toys and drum machines, to kitchen utensils [these were discussed earlier, *vis-à-vis* FIG, and are probably best represented by instrument creator Hugh Davies' amplified egg slicer, *author*], and its thumb-nosing at avant garde orthodoxy [the latter description is surely an oxymoron? *author*], made it a quintessentially second generation ensemble – one whose membership remained the same throughout its improbable nine-year run." (Shoemaker, *op. cit.)*

Alterations remain the most emblematic of the Gen Two 'fixed combination' bands. Whilst researching, I found more references to it than any other contemporary free improv second generation band (articles in *Wire* 10, 297 and 338, *Musics* 23, just to start with, and which all inform this section). In *Wire* 297, the magazine's then editor, Tony Herrington, describes his 'epiphany' (page 114) on hearing "possibly the greatest group of all time", before going on to reference a hipsters retrospective of modern music *a la Wire*, so achingly trendy that one weeps for oneself for being so unfashionable, having never heard of some of these 'essentials', "the one the music weeklies wouldn't or couldn't tell you about", a conspiracy theory worthy of the old *NME* readers' most paranoid imaginings.

Alterations, from left: Peter Cusack, Steve Beresford, David Toop and Terry Day
CREDIT: GERARD ROUY

One listen to *My Favourite Animals* will show how strained this sort of *portmanteau* trendiness (which is something akin to the Smithsonian holy writ with its 'essential' list of references) can be. One particularly irritating later *Wire* strapline said, as I recall, "We are all David Toop now," and I remember thinking "Well I'm bloody not, speak for yourself!".

John Wickes put it in more straightforward terms: "Alterations...had its debut at the ICA on June 22nd 1978. Its aim, if it had one, seemed to be to overturn the po-faced image associated with improvised music by now letting intrude, or by deliberately inserting, elements of banality or cliché, then allowing them to be demolished by another member of the group." (Wickes, *op. cit.*, p.313.)

This was hardly new – the Bonzo Dog Doo Dah Band (which are the group that Alterations most remind me of) and the first Mothers of Invention had been doing exactly this in the late 60s, but it was certainly fairly new in the more rarified climes of free improv.

In particular, influences were allowed to trickle into this hermetic and heuristic world, offering 'outside' (i.e. of the free improv shibboleths of sound) contributions to a music that was already 'outside', to use the free jazz truism: "Little by little these elements from the 'outside world', imported from work in other groups [Beresford with the punk band Flying

Lizards and with reggae star Prince Far-I, for example, *author*], from awareness of pop trends, or even shamelessly acknowledged weaknesses for kinds of music not considered 'correct' in the taste canons of jazz and improvised music, started to dominate performances, with hilarious and sometimes surprisingly beautiful results." (Wickes, *op. cit.*, p.313.)

Of course, by the 1990s even the world of hip hop (which was, in itself, syncretic in nature) had made incursions into the high castle of 'classic' free improvisation, but in the mid 70s its walls still seemed fairly unbreachable. In Herrington's article, Terry Day "looked to capsize the high seriousness of improvised music by having at its core 'an attitude of irreverence'". (Herrington, *op. cit.,* page 114.) Day certainly contributed to this with his vocal stylistics, balloons and what-not, and in an interview with Richard Cook, in a much earlier edition of *Wire* (No. 10, December 1984, pp.14-5), additionally asserted that "we're interested in being entertainers, compared with other improvising groups…we're not afraid to introduce time playing. Or chord sequences or playing together." This was a stance that would have been anathema to some of the more dogmatic members of the free improv sub-culture.

Ironically, the group apparently broke up as a result of "the tensions (which) are quite subtle: they usually involve somebody preventing you from doing something you wanted to do". (Toop, in Cook, *op. cit.*, p.14.) This was something of a surprise, given the seemingly thick-skinned personalities of those involved and their apparent give-and-take attitude.

One is reminded of John Stevens' theories about 'group music' around the time of the formation of the SME, and about 'listening' to others rather than trying to blow them off the stage. "You buy a bigger amplifier," as Beresford half-joked in response to Toop's observation. (Stevens was of the opinion that if you can't hear your fellow musicians, then you're playing too loud.) None of them, however, in the end, were Black Sabbath, Led Zeppelin, Deep Purple or even Jethro Tull. The Tull, who featured Martin, my first cousin, on guitar, have the honour of playing the most agonisingly loud concert I have ever attended (in 1971), by the way, strange as it may seem (caused by the relatively primitive equipment of the time, I would surmise). My Bloody Hearing…sorry, Valentine, were a close second (in 1992). These were the real 'Amp turned up to 11' artists, not the comparably gentle free improvisers that we are discussing. Modern 'Noise' artists like Merzbow are as kittens in comparison with the skull fuckery of early 70s rock music and its attendant technology.

Richard Cook described Alterations' sound as "a continuous state of flux with no point to fix on" (1984, *op. cit.*), which goes some way to explaining the sense of discontinuity in the music, of not being able to 'get hold' of the sound in a constantly shifting environment. It is not without repeated melodies or regular rhythm, although don't expect to find a 'groove' to anchor yourself to for any length of time. Toop even described the music as a kind of TAZ ("temporary environments in which [almost] all things were possible"), in the notes to a later Alterations compilation on the Atavistic label. Richard Leigh, in what turned out to be the very last record review of the final edition of *Musics* (No.23, November 1979, p.30) suggested that "juxtaposing things that don't usually go together…are generally taken as proof of insincerity". Take from, or make of, that as you will.

At around the same time, and throughout the 70s and 80s, John Zorn was exploring similar areas, but in a more structured way, and was doing very well in both artistic and, presumably, economic, terms (Zorn, Tzadik 7316). Leigh made a jump cut himself, at one point in his article, in suggesting that the *Alterations* album bore some resemblances to *AMMusic 1966*, opining that: "In the old AMM group, there seems almost always to have been at least one musician producing a sustained tone – so that the music's change was gradual and reflective. There is little holding of notes on Alterations, though." Leigh also made positive comments on Day's alto playing which had so impressed me on *Interruptions*. In fact, he suggests that a Day solo album be produced, which, eventually, it was, with the latter recording being "subtle and vulgar at the same time" (Leigh, *op. cit.*), which just about nails its contents. However, I have to disagree with Leigh's comparison to *AMMusic*. I can't see any resemblance myself, sorry Richard. The sheer intensity of AMM is completely lacking in Alterations who, frankly, one senses, are taking the piss. Out of themselves, certainly, as much as anything. Whatever, it ultimately makes for somewhat enervating listening over 60 minutes or so of jump cuts and stylistic slalom (take a listen to the 1983 *Live at Frankfurt* recent release, and tell me if you think I'm being unreasonable).

Simon Reynolds caught the Alterations approach very alliteratively (he was actually describing the early product of musical magpies Roxy Music) as, "a fissile, fickle, flighty mode of archival pillage and collage". (Reynolds, 2016, *op. cit.*, p.346.)

Modernist linear thinking, which assumed that free improv was the next development on from free jazz, gave way to a furious stylistic scrabble, an apotheosis of disjunction, which didn't fit in neatly with any canonical interpretations. This didn't appeal to purists, who thought that art that remade and remodeled, distanced and detached itself by liberal use of quotes and pastiche, was decadent and irreverent. This was perhaps the fundamental divergence between the two free improv generations, i.e. that between modernism and post-modernism. It is worth remembering that the latter was little known at the time – for example, my 1981 edition of Pan Books' *A Dictionary of Philosophy* contains absolutely no reference to this school of ideas and practice at all.

Michael Herr, author of *Dispatches*, which proved to be a major influence on the film *Apocalypse Now* (a work which, in turn, signalled the end of the 70s in a spectacular fashion), went as far as to assert that the culture of that decade "stoned itself blind with nostalgia". (Reynolds, *op. cit.*, p.411.) This was as opposed to looking towards the future ("the only thing to look forward to... the past", as the very popular 70s TV series of the time, *Whatever Happened to the Likely Lads?*, announced in its theme tune).

I do think that Alterations played a provocative endgame for free improvisation, at this point in time (1979), as David Bowie and Roxy Music had done, with their retro-futurism, for rock music, in and around 1972. Alterations' self-consciously ironic, and even sarcastic, approach to their material can be summed up by Beresford's 'French toast' spiel (giving the audience the recipe for a *bouillabaisse* would probably have been a more appropriate culinary gesture) on *Live At Frankfurt*. This approach, which utilised their undoubted musical talents, put down a gauntlet for the earlier, technically hyper-skilled, proponents of the first generation. The music had, very cleverly, been moved on. On reflection, however, I do wonder whether the Alterations body of work was, ultimately, somewhat of a different genre to 'classic' free improv (*Jean Rex*, even?).

The 1979 *Alterations* album is the only one in our time frame, and the band produced two further releases, *Up Your Sleeve* in 1980 and *My Favourite Animals* four years after that. Several other retrospective live releases have also emerged in the wake of their reformation in 2016. An Atavistic compilation, *Voila Enough 1979-81,* saw the light of day later on. The *Animals* album is contained in its entirety on YouTube, with plenty of Toop-ian pipe work, Beresford's 'lounge-core piano' and some very Zappa-esque vocals (of the Ray Collins kind), among countless other postmodern delights to annoy Ben Watson. Unfortunately, Alterations appear to be still well under the radar as the upload of the album had, on the day of writing (August 22nd 2016), only 826 'views' since November 1st 2014, and only one comment so far (*and* that in Spanish, but, from what I can work out, it is a positive one).

On a more positive note, Alterations did reform in 2016 and played a showcase gig at Café Oto, just as did String Thing, another free band from the 70s (see Chapter Seven), later in the year. Even these free improvisers are not immune to revisiting their past, although their type of 'retromania' is very different to rock band reformations, which appear to be little more than 'greatest hits' packages most of the time, something that the Rolling Stones set the template for 30-odd years ago.

Before we bid *adieu* to Alterations, I would like to mention a great photograph of them, taken by Gerard Rouy, playing in what looks like a gymnasium (it features at the top of Tony Herrington's 'Epiphanies' piece, quoted from above, in *Wire* 297). The image captures their *quiddity* somehow, as some photos can manage to do (no wonder 'primitive' societies were so suspicious of cameras). From left to right, there is Day behind his 'beer can' kit, his face concealed by a cymbal (or should that be 'symbol'?); Beresford plays a child's guitar, in a very 'rockist' pose, legs apart, head down, no-nonsense, etc; Cusack is playing an adults' guitar in a seemingly straightforward fashion (but who knows what he was actually playing); Toop, who is the only one sitting down, bows some sort of cylindrical implement. As a foreground to their activity, the front of the stage is littered with 'stuff', from the left, bowls/cymbals/tambourines, to the right, Toop's impressive selection of wooden and metal pipes/flutes. Oh, and a fire bucket, which was apparently not merely there for Health & Safety reasons. I have used a similar picture in this book, by veteran lensman Jak Kilby, which was shot at the Almeida Theatre in Islington, in order to illustrate the band's 'look'.

Wire 10 has yet another Alterations group portrait, again taken by Jak Kilby who caught so many of the very early free improvisation gigs in action, at the same concert. With a fairly clear stage, Beresford is on the left, standing up and playing an electric piano; Cusack is again the 'straight man' on adult guitar; Toop plays what looks like a pedal steel guitar, and Day drums with mallets, with his beer cans ranged around the front of his kits. It is a completely average group presentation in the modern age, but in 1978/9 it must have seemed somehow sonically (and visually) dissonant to both hear *and* to see the transience that this band implied, with its constant metamorphoses and sheer protean nature. Only the Art Ensemble of Chicago offered a field of sound and vision like it.

In the end, unfortunately, Alterations finished in a similar way to *Musics*, if I can be allowed to make the comparison: "It did go tits up, the entire enterprise eventually wrongfooted by displays of individual brinksmanship, bruised egos, personal animosities; which was perhaps an inevitable outcome." (Herrington, *op. cit.*, p.114.)

Alterations managed to last seven years (my own personal measure of a perfect cycle, for what it's worth) and *Musics* only four. Both left behind important legacies. Alterations left a whole stew, in the future, of multi-dimensional, polystylistic groupings. *Musics* bequeathed us, indirectly: *Resonance* (in the 1990s), *Collusion* (which ran for five editions from summer 1981 to September 1983), *Avant* (the late 1990s) and, of course, *Wire*, which continues to this day, nearly 400 editions down the line.

THE THREE/FOUR PULLOVERS

Sticking with the photographic medium, let us examine a portrait, probably taken in 1978, by Andrea Tiffin, at what might have been the last performance of the Four Pullovers who were, basically, the Three Pullovers plus Terry Day (when he was available). Beresford and Day we know, from our last chapter. The other two Pullovers were Nigel Coombes on violin and electronics, and Roger Smith on guitar, another two improvisers who have never really received their due, and were both in the 'string driven' SME of that time (another example of the polyandry of the times). This photo appears on their one and only CD, released retrospectively on the Emanem label (Emanem 4038).

In the photo, Coombes, on the left, is the spitting image of Tony Iommi in his early Black Sabbath days, his nose emerging out of a huge thicket of big hair, which is worthy of New York Dolls-era Johnny Thunders (plus he is even wearing what looks like a black robe, to complete the comparison); a kneeling Beresford is dependably busy doing something unusual with the 'little instruments' that cover the floor of the LMC (?); Day is standing on this occasion, tapping on what looks like a small, modified kit, and Smith is seemingly scrabbling away, his right hand a blur, on his Spanish guitar. All in all, not a million miles away from the Alterations study described above.

Smith, as well as Ian Brighton and John Russell, had studied with the free improv guitar lodestone Derek Bailey, whose lessons sound as much like those of a zen master as of a music teacher. While Russell very clearly has the hallmarks of Bailey's playing, Roger Smith, despite using the distinctive 'scrabble' of Bailey (usually used, I feel, when the latter appeared to be 'collecting himself'/gathering ideas at the point of some sort of musical caesura), Smith usually eschewed amplification, and played acoustic guitar in a much more undemonstrative and lyrical style than Bailey, but nevertheless in an effective way that owes nothing to the Yorkshireman. He played with the SME for around 20 years, longer than Trevor Watts even, and has, nevertheless, been rather sidelined in free music history. As in any music, there are considerably gifted players who have not received the attention they deserve. Coombes and Smith are two of them.

Unfortunately for guitarists like Brighton, Russell and Smith, Bailey cast such a huge shadow over the music that it was difficult for his near peers to get themselves heard as individuals. Their recorded output is also dwarfed by the Sheffield-ian, although Smith has several released on the ever inclusive Emanem Records, and Brighton and Russell also have considerable discographies that warrant attention, but are mostly outside our time frame.

Coombes had appeared at the 1975 'Young Improvisers' event at the Wigmore Hall, alongside Smith, Day, Beresford, Dave Solomon, Peter Cusack, Garry Todd and John Russell, most of whom became participants in the various small, time-limited groups under discussion here. He extended his violin techniques with what he called "low grade electronics", as so many of his peers did in those days, but both he and Smith represented the (relatively) more melodious half, or two thirds, of the Pullovers. Coombes was also on *Teatime*, that most important early Gen Two recording.

As discussed earlier, the *Three & Four Pullovers 1975-8* CD, on Emanem 4038, released in 2000, reminds me very strongly of early AMM and SME. It remains the only available music from these two groupings, being an archival release partly (the 1978 bit) and a reissue of cassette recordings from 1975. In many ways, they were a precursor to Alterations, and were 'Plink, Plonk and Scratch' (Barre, *op. cit.*) *in excelsis*, being a combination of strings, piano and percussion. It's a great shame that there is not more of their music to listen to.

THE PROMENADERS

This most audacious of groups consisted, from what I can gather (according to Steve Beresford), of Beresford himself (euphonium/voice), Lol 'Loxhorn Rondo' Coxhill (soprano/voice), David Toop and Max Eastley (both on one-string fiddles), Peter Cusack (guitar), Paul Burwell (drums), Terry Day (cello and drums, when Burwell wasn't available), Nigel Coombes (occasional violin), Vivien Goldman and Phil Minton (guest vocalists). This was almost a collective in itself, and some of them feature briefly in Antoine Prum's film, in one of its most entertaining sequences described earlier, set on Brighton Beach. This configuration represents the incontinence of the second generation, with its most tongue-in-cheekily irreverent material. It isn't really free improvisation, being more of a logical extension of Alterations' postmodern archival pillaging, with its tongue very much in its cheek, but the band is worth referencing due to the presence of so many of the second generation improvisers, who give it its overall tone. Its collage and segue structure predates some of John Zorn's later work with projects like *Naked City*, but with the added bonus of a very English sense of humour.

They released one record, in 1982, on Y Records (Y31), which also released albums by The Pop Group, one by Sun Ra in the same year, and a one-off quartet of Beresford, Toop, Toshinori Kondo and Tristan Honsinger entitled *Imitation of Life* (Y13). The Promenaders record is described on Discogs (the online database and marketplace) and tells you all you really need to know about this bunch of lovable rogues. It is entirely apt that the 'style' that the record is placed under is 'music hall'.

Were The Promenaders named after psycho-geographical influences, or was it too early for that sort of thing? The name certainly sounds a bit like a bunch of *flaneurs*, and the way they peregrinate around famous tunes is very inspiring. Starting off with *Nellie The Elephant* (a pachyderm which had been given some slight street credibility by Syd Barrett's *Effervescing Elephant* from *Barrett*), it soon morphs into a medley of (only a few examples) *Louie Louie*, *Whistle While You Work*, *Calling All Workers*, *Dambusters March*, *Do-Re-Mi*, *Eine Kleine Nachtsmusic*, *Let's Twist Again*. Sun Ra did a similar thing with Disney tunes, with similar results. A huge parody (almost certainly, listen to the vocals, very Monty Python), or a genuine fondness for English *kitsch* (again, almost certainly)? Both (obviously).

I certainly found my toe was tapping to this medley, which usually is a give-away in my experience, with the 'West Point' drumming a joy to listen to.

An unnamed commentator on the Y31 cover had this to say, and it will suffice to pin The Promenaders to their particular time and space:

"Pot pourris of old and new favourites...unique renditions of established melodies...some insights into their own personal contributions to contemporary music...it's been skillfully recorded to capture all the flavour of a Brighton Performance...music, announcements, sun, sea, holiday makers, ATMOSPHERE."

There are two other 'supergroups' from the second generation, further *'portmanteau'* constellations, that I would like to briefly mention, although they do fall very slightly outside of our temporal remit (sorry): The Melody Four, of which Steve Beresford and Lol Coxhill were both members, and The Recedents, which featured Coxhill. Both groups crossed the 'low/high culture' straits, which had already been partially navigated by their 70s forbears.

MELODY FOUR AND THE RECEDENTS

The original Melody Four, of which there were four members, as you would expect, was, from what I can gather, a saccharine Christian a cappella quartet who released the most fervent religious material, so, of course, were targets for 70s passive-aggressive avant gardists. The fact that the avant Four were actually three (as you would also expect) only compounded the lexicological, never mind the musical, confusion. Nevertheless, what a fantastic trio they were, Lol and Steve, and virtuoso clarinetist Tony Coe who had made a superlative duo album on Incus with Derek Bailey (Incus 34) in April 1979, called *Time*. Coe was the 'straight man', and Beresford was in awe of him: "It was obvious that he was the most amazing musician *ever* and could do anything." (Beresford in Corbett, *op. cit.*, p.1994.)

Good to hear a bit of good old fashioned hero worship in these cynical times!

YouTube has a short film (there is no other live footage, as far as I know) from a church in Holland, during a 'Jazztown on Bicycles' tour (a most appropriate method of transport for the Lowlands), which features the Four/three. Vocals by Beresford and Coxhill on *Riding the Range* establishes a mood, followed by a Beresford 'intervention', which was de rigueur by then (1996), but after a Coxhill solo 'moment' of sublime brevity and beauty, this is followed by a frankly rather tedious routine around *Xmas*, in which Coxhill puts on his 'joker' hat. Coe is on tenor on this clip and Coxhill seems to be playing up to his image as humourist, despite his disclaimers. This was, in many ways, akin to a pub band, but with *virtuosi* playing "theme records, love songs, TV tunes…Latin… which exorcised our interest in middle-of-the-road music" (Beresford, in Corbett, *op. cit.,* p.199), a decade before "elevator music" became trendy (Lanza, 1995). The on-stage 'arguments' between our two mavericks, Beresford and Coxhill, became part of the performance, as can be sampled on the clip.

The Recedents, named after the direction of the musicians' hair, apparently, were a classic noisy 'insect music' improv band (judging from the section featured in the Prum film, and despite Roger Turner's rather snooty disavowal of the style, which he expresses at some length in the film itself). The band formed in 1982 and can be heard at length on the 5-CD retrospective *Wishing You Were Here 1982-2010* (Free Form Associates), released in 2014. Coxhill was joined by the equally follically challenged Turner, on percussive instruments, and Mike Cooper on guitar/electronics. The Prum clip is fascinating and sounds like music from a future era, all distortion and scraping impact, that the Japanese would make their own in the not-too-distant future. They would no doubt go down a storm nowadays at Café Oto (where they did, in fact, play, in the very early months of the venue's existence in early 2008).

These were some of the more important Gen Two semi-permanent groups. This ever-burgeoning number of bands and individuals that wanted to be recorded by the late 70s needed labels who might be interested in doing this, but the majors, after their brief flirtation with free improv in the late 60s, were no longer remotely interested. At this point, independent labels came into their own again, reflecting corresponding trends in rock/pop in the wake of punk, wherefrom this form of self-promotion and self-help had suddenly become lionised. It is these recording outlets that we turn to next.

CHAPTER 6

Labelling Theory and Practice
Free Improvisation Record Labels in the 1970s

Independent record labels played a vitally important role in punk rock culture in the late 70s, from the *Spiral Scratch* EP by The Buzzcocks on New Hormones, through to The Desperate Bicycles and *Smokescreen* on Refill Records, through to Scritti Politti's *Skank Block Bologna* 45 on their St. Pancras label. That particular independent label culture had been preceded, however, by one that had established itself in free improvisation several years before, starting off with Incus Records, the first label that focused almost exclusively on the free 'language' established from 1966 in England. In fact, there had been a culture of genuinely independent avant music labels going way back to the 50s, with Harry Partch's Gate 5 (started in 1953) and, most famously, Sun Ra/Alton Abraham and Saturn Records, and their impossibly rare and collectable self-released artifacts, also initiated in the mid 50s – 1956 to be exact. (See Barre, *op. cit.*, pp.247-8, for more on this topic.)

Several renowned jazz record labels, for example Blue Note, Impulse, Atlantic and ECM, had gained considerable *gravitas* over the years with their own particular style, artwork, photographers and textual accompaniment (see Tashen's *Jazz Covers* for examples galore). All have been the subject of individual books, and are all instantly identifiable by their spines in any record collection. Incus Records filled the void that had been created in 1966, when the genre of free improvisation first emerged, and over the next few years Emanem, Matchless, Bead, Cadillac and

Ogun, Nato and Vinyl followed suit, most of them of English origin.

These labels enabled a basic library of early English free improv and free jazz to be built, without which histories like this one would be very hard, if not impossible, to write. Their existence eventually proved very necessary because, by 1970, the major record companies had lost patience with this sort of 'product', after a brief post-*Sgt. Pepper's* interest in the weird and wonderful (the record industry was in its pomp, after all, and was not averse at this time to taking calculated risks). However, albums like *Karyobin* (Island Records) and *Oliv* (Polydor), *The Baptised Traveller* and *4 Compositions for Sextet*, *Angle* and *The Day Will Come* (all CBS), *AMMusic 1966* (Elektra) and *The People Band* (Transatlantic) were deleted shortly after release, when the sales figures eventually emerged, and the relevant acts were not asked to return to the studios, thank you very much.

It is curious how the 70s mid-term produced some very interesting convergences of the written word and recorded sound, both of which helped the music gain a further foothold on the live circuit, i.e. the formation of the LMC and Company, of *Musics* magazine and, in the recording medium, of Incus and Emanem Records, through the period of 1974-6.

I propose to briefly discuss each of the most important record labels in turn, and would acknowledge that this task has been made much easier, since 2014, by the publication of Johannes Rod's *Free Jazz and Improvisation on Vinyl 1965-85*. I am much indebted to Rod's research in this area.

INCUS RECORDS

As outlined in my earlier book, Incus was started in 1970 by Derek Bailey, Evan Parker, Tony Oxley and a financial journalist called Michael Walters. The project was mostly floated by Walters, who wanted nothing to do with the operation of the label, and with money left over from the grant that supported the Music Improvisation Company's (MIC) recent tour of English art and college establishments. (Barre, *op. cit.*, p.245-9.)

Evan Parker takes up the story: "I had money left over from the

Arts Council grant that I got to subsidise the MIC tour of art schools and galleries. I had also been playing with (Peter) Brotzmann and Han (Bennink), and seen the early work they were doing with Bro Records and ICP. I proposed to Derek that we start a similar venture. A day or two later, he told me that he'd discussed the idea with Tony Oxley and that we should get together to take it further. There was a meeting of the three of us at Derek's place in Thornhill Square. At the meeting Tony announced that he had been talking to a businessman, a regular at Ronnie Scott's, who had offered to put up the money and help with the formalities of setting up a limited company. I was persuaded that this was the way to proceed." (Personal communication, 2016.)

However, in time both Walters and Oxley subsequently bailed out, effectively leaving the guitarist and saxophonist to run the label for the next 15 years or so. Walters left after Incus 3/4, apparently concerned that he could be taking the risk of being a director of a bankrupt company (oh, he of little faith), but feeling at the same time that the others could manage well enough without him. Oxley left after ten years: "We rarely agreed with his ideas and since there were only three equal votes he had no power. Also, we were unhappy that he had only produced two records at that point, [around 1980]." (Parker, *op. cit.*)

Profits from the earlier albums helped to pay for the next ones, but eventually there were financial pressures not to reprint albums (which had been the original intention) in order to focus on releasing newer material, something that Parker says became policy after he left in 1987.

As is very well known in free improv annals, Bailey and Parker fell out irrevocably in 1986/7, for reasons that are still opaque to most of us. After Parker left, Incus became pretty much synonymous with Company, which had become Bailey's main preoccupation. But that was in the future, and in the 70s the spotlight was still definitely trained mainly on the English free scene.

Incus artwork is minimal and severe, and all the more attractive for this. One wonders whether ECM Records were influenced by the starkness of Incus artwork or *vice versa* (ECM had started a year earlier). Evan Parker says no, and that his records were more influenced by his association with graphic designer Dave Chaston, who Keith Richards, of all people, remembers as being "the hippest guy at Sidcup Art College... the arbiter of hip, hip beyond bohemian, so cool he could run the record player". (Richards, 2010, p.73.) However, Parker also reminded me that the photographer of *Saxophone Solos* and *Monocerus*, Roberto Masotti, later worked for ECM Records, so maybe the influence was mutual? Incus also used the talents of the musicians themselves in the design of the covers, as well as artists like Mal Dean (Incus 9), some who also involved themselves in production duties.

1973 started with Kenny Wheeler's *Song for Someone* (Incus 10), one of the few albums on the label that had through composition, along with the mighty *Ode* by Barry Guy's Orchestra (Incus 6/7). After *Ode* and *Iskra 1903* (Incus 3/4), Incus did not release any further double albums until 1982's *Epiphany/Epiphanies* (Incus 46/7), which was also one of its last vinyl releases. It did, however, branch out to release three reel-to-reel tapes (*Incus Taps*) and even a 7" EP (AMM's *Live at the Roundhouse*, as Incus EP1). The latter eventually saw the light of day again as part of a full-length CD on Anomalous Records, decades down the line, in 2003.

Gradually, the next few years saw releases by Howard Riley, SME, Barry Guy, Gen Two improvisers John Russell, Gary Todd and Roger Turner, and the multi-faceted *Circadian Rhythm*, which has been touched upon earlier in this book. Both the remaining two owners produced solo albums (Incus 2, 12, 19, 27, 39, 40, 48, 49) and played as a duo on two (Incus 16 and 50). Seven Company albums were put out (Incus 21, 23, 25, 26, 28, 29, 30), a title sequence only broken by Barry Guy's first solo venture, the SME and *Monocerus* by Parker. There were, in the end, very few releases by Gen Two improvisers on Incus vinyl, around about five, something that was left to Bead Records to address/improve upon. "Our priority was to document our own music." (Parker, *op. cit.*) This was, at least, an honestly pragmatic reflection on this most idealised of labels.

Incus eventually made it all the way past their half-century, to Incus 52, in fact (which was, funnily enough, a Gen Two [or even Three?] recording, with Steve Noble and Alex Maguire). "I think of the catalogue stopping at 50, a nice round number." (Parker, *op. cit.*)

However, it must be pointed out that the label finished, after a hiatus between 1982 and 1985, with three of the best English free improvising records of them all, shortly before the great Bailey/Parker schism: Bailey's *Notes: Solo Guitar Improvisations* (Incus 48); Parker's own solo offering *The Snake Decides*, which many, myself included, think is his best (Incus 49); and the duo's swan song *Compatibles* (Incus 50), a devastatingly ironic title given what was to occur shortly. One only has to look at the cover of the latter to see the signs – the glass frame containing the photo of the duo is splintered and cracked, the back cover shot has Evan Parker staring opaquely into the mid distance, with Derek Bailey sitting beside him, looking vaguely amused, with his right index finger stuck in his ear seemingly clearing out some wax (or quizzically questioning – what?). A picture of mutual personal incompatibility/antipathy, by this stage of the relationship.

These three recordings did, however, have a lot to do with my return to the world of free improvisation in 1987. Whatever the background tensions, about which I had not an inkling at the time, I assumed, knowing no better, that they were still the best of mates. Starting to listen in again, after a gap of several years, this trio of recordings accordingly holds a special place in my heart.

I also feel that I must mention Track Five of Bailey's superlative solo album, *Drop Me Off At 96th* (Scatter 02), called simply *Interlude*. This is a between-tracks rap by Bailey in which he makes a fabulously disingenuous pitch for "my record label", before going on to play *Mart of Time, Parts Two and Three*, two of the most beautiful pieces of music that this genre has produced. These tracks alone are enough to cement Bailey's legacy, and the possibilities that free improv present.

Incus was the model that the later independents followed, the directors being inspired by both European precursors (Bro, ICP) and several in America (as described in Barre, *op. cit.*, pp.247-8).

EMANEM RECORDS

I don't know how many readers remember cassette tapes, but one of the things we used to do, back in the day, was add a track or two onto the few minutes that might be remaining at the end of each cassette side's 45-minute span, usually at the conclusion of a particular album we might have just recorded onto tape (despite the 'fact' that taping was killing music, so we were told at the time).

I am reminded of this practice when buying Emanem records, as Martin Davidson seems to want to ensure that we similarly get the maximum from the available format, in this case, the 79-odd minutes that a CD can contain. This can be a mixed blessing, dependent on the extra material that is added to the main menu, but it is a sign of Davidson's generosity and wish to share as fully as possible the music that he so obviously loves. This love has been demonstrated by the sheer wealth of free improvisation that his label contains, much of it now consisting of the early recorded 'legacy', that may have been deleted and long unavailable, or never before released. For example, Emanem's 'house band', the SME, have benefited from the uncovering of previously unreleased material such as *Summer 67* and *Withdrawal*, and previously released but long unavailable material like *Challenge* and the eponymous 1969 Marmalade album. This contribution alone makes Emanem one of the most significant labels of this genre.

Martin and Madelaine Davidson, as well as being two of the three originators, along with Evan Parker, of *Musics* in 1975, and being significant gig promoters (the famous Bailey/Braxton Wigmore Hall bash in 1974 was theirs), also managed to find time to start Emanem Records in the latter year. Emanem is now almost certainly, since the passing of Derek Bailey, recognised as *the* premier English Free Improvisation label in the world. In the corner of each CD case, the 'File Under' motif proudly announces "Free Improvisation" – no ambivalence, no hedge-betting, no 'new music' or suchlike, just free improvisation, as it says on the metaphorical can. Emanem Records has steadily released a stream of archive material, not just by the SME, but also up-to-date material reflecting modern free improvisation practice. It is thus an essential database of this music, past and present.

Martin Davidson grew up in north London suburbia "too suburban to be hippy, too hippy to be suburban", as he describes himself. (Personal communication, 2016.) He listened to the emerging sounds of Free Jazz, as did most of his musician contemporaries, and spent time in America in the mid 60s, where he could listen to the music in its place of origin. His epiphany occurred, however, at an English SME gig with John Stevens, Trevor Watts, Julie Tippett and Ron Herman, and he "soon discovered that there was a music scene based in London that was unique and ahead of anywhere else".

1971 was also the year Martin Davidson met Madelaine, through a mutual interest in socialist politics. She had been a ballet dancer, before growing too tall to make a career out of this particular creative modality. "Although Incus had been around for a while and had produced some seminal records, there seemed to be room for other labels, so we decided to take the plunge, starting off with some free jazz." (Davidson, *op. cit.*)

John Stevens introduced Martin to Steve Lacy, who was having difficulty in persuading producers to take an interest in a solo album, "a concept that was too far out for just about every record label". (Davidson, *op. cit.*) Apart from the Chicago label Delmark, that is, who had released Anthony Braxton's trailblazing *For Alto*.

The initial slogan for the label was, "Unadulterated New Music For People Who Like New Music Unadulterated", a snappy enough statement of intent, but maybe the 'New Music' was too ambiguous? The Davidsons' mission, which they took on with alacrity, was to document the London scene of the mid 70s and beyond (and, eventually, before). Martin Davidson has often described his first infatuation with the music in 1971, when he saw the SME and also Derek Bailey (much as I did, a few years later). He sees the origins of the music in Free Jazz, where his original interest lay, and accepts that free improvisation varies depending on place and context.

The first Emanem record did eventually feature soprano saxophone modernist Lacy, who was one of the few Americans (with Anthony Braxton and Leo Smith) who accepted the challenge laid down by the English improvisers of the time. This was *Solo* (Emanem 301), shortly followed by the SME's epochal *Face To Face*, with Stevens and Watts, and then by the Bailey/Braxton duo at the Wigmore Hall. Further releases involving Lacy, Bailey and Braxton ensued. A notable addition to the catalogue was Paul Rutherford's influential *The Gentle Harm of the Bourgeoisie* (now Emanem 4019), a solo trombone *tour de force* that set a high bar for this kind of playing. It remains a classic. This, along with Lucy's very early (1972) solo disc, demonstrated that Emanem can lay some claim to have been among the pioneers of this rapidly evolving specialty, the solo album. And it was also, along with Incus, an early promoter of the Anglo-American free improvisation nexus.

Lack of finances meant that little further could be issued at that time, but a considerable number of albums were sold in the States. So the Davidsons tried their hand over there, with apparently negative results, although they did manage to organise the first solo tours of North America by Steve Lacy and Evan Parker, from which two solo classics by the latter emerged, *At the Finger Palace* and *Live at Western Front*. They then went to Australia, and subsequently returned to London in 1988.

Martin Davidson has subsequently used his label to provide, among many other things, a musical library for the work of the SME and John Stevens. Stevens died in 1994, and Emanem moved back (again) to London the year after, since when the label has exponentially increased its content and variety.

The Davidsons moved to Spain a couple of years ago, from where they still run Emanem Records. Their catalogue is now of considerable size, almost certainly the most impressive of its kind in the world.

Today, Emanem's position is unassailable in terms of its Alexandrian repository of early and modern English free improvisation. In addition, the notes that accompany Emanem records, often by the owner himself, are in themselves invaluable contributors to the story, informative and lighthearted, and I have frequently used them when researching the music of those times.

BEAD RECORDS

Formed in 1974 by British violinist Phil Wachsmann, Bead Records was perhaps, retrospectively, the most accommodating label for Gen Two improvisers (of which Wachsmann was, of course, one). The label released around 20 free improv recordings in the years of 1975-83, including Ian Brighton's debut album *Marsh Gas*, the first Alterations album, as well as material from Peter Cusack, Colin Wood, an early Alan Tomlinson solo album, an early John Butcher duo with pianist Chris Burn, and from Wachsmann himself. This was the new generation's alternative to Incus Records.

OGUN RECORDS

This was the label started by the late double bassist Harry Miller (1941-83), a central figure among the celebrated South African expats, who initially recorded as the Blue Notes and later gathered together in pianist Chris McGregor's Brotherhood of Breath. Miller and his wife, Hazel, established Ogun in 1974 (which is still current, as far as I can gather). As well as his fellow countrymen, the label featured British stalwarts such as saxophonists John Surman, Alan Skidmore, Elton Dean, Lol Coxhill and Mike Osborne, most of whom were not free improvisers in the strict sense (apart from Coxhill, perhaps), but could play freely, and incredibly well, when this was needed (or when they felt like it). One of the greatest examples of this is Osborne's *All Night Long*, a blistering Ogun trio with the alto player joined by Miller himself, on double bass, and South African percussionist Louis Moholo, who continues to play today with no diminution of energy or talent. It was recorded live in Willisau, Switzerland, in April 1975.

Keith and Julie Tippett are also associated with Ogun. Both have been involved with pop/rock, he with King Crimson and she with Brian Auger & the Trinity, but both are hugely talented free improvisers. I urge the reader to see either live, to see how artificial musical categories really are.

MATCHLESS RECORDS

Matchless Records was established by AMM's Eddie Prevost in 1978, from his Essex address in Matching Tye, in Essex (I'm never sure whether this is the same place that is referenced in *Matching Tye and Hankie*, the Monty Python album?). Matchless is surely the other long-term titan of English free improvisation labels, after Incus and Emanem? Just as Emanem carves in stone the SME contribution to English free improvisation, so does Matchless with its AMM catalogue. Another similarity to Emanem is the quality of the accompanying texts, usually by Prevost himself, which are inevitably enormously informative and provocative.

Prevost has taken on the role, through his label, of AMM's historian and record keeper (there are a few exceptions, such as *AMMusic* and *Live at the Roundhouse*, which are on other labels, for now at least). The first AMM album released was MR003, *To Here and Back Again*, and this was preceded by the *Eddie Prevost Band Live*, volumes 1 and 2.

NATO

Nato was a most interesting French record label, founded in 1980 and still producing music today. It specialised in conceptual and literary albums, but the reason it is featured in this book is because it features many of the Gen Two improvisers we have been discussing, including, and especially, Lol Coxhill and Steve Beresford, who put out several albums on Nato in the 1983/4 period. I only have one piece of vinyl from this label, kindly given to me by Jak Kilby, and it is a fascinating, and at times highly entertaining, take on the work of French composer Eric Satie, whose 24-hour *Vexations* may well have been an influence on *Circadian Rhythm*. The album is called *Sept Tableaux Phoniques* (there is also a Nato production called *Six Sequences pour Alfred Hitchcock*, for another example of their *metier*) and features, individually, the three Melody Four men, Beresford, Coe and Coxhill, as well as pianist Dave Holland and Phil Wachsmann, who all offer takes on Satie's lyrical and influential piano compositions. Coxhill, for example, offers us a version of *Faction de Satie* with his soprano playing against a Japanese rock trio, which seems very much a pioneer of the sort of mix-and-match ploy that John Zorn, for example, was shortly to make fashionable on his Tzadik label.

I heartily recommend this record, and would suggest that the reader snaps up any Nato recordings that he/she may come across. There are several Steve Beresford albums, if you can find them that is, on Nato, and there are even two Christmas albums that feature John Zorn and the Melody Four, individually and as a group. In 1986, Nato released a record recorded in London, *Deadly Weapons*, which features Beresford, Toop, John Zorn (who was making several groundbreaking recordings at the time) and vocalist Tonie Marshall, which would fit in easily somewhere in Zorn's *Film Music* series with its jump cuts and stylistic pin balling. In fact, Beresford himself was occupied in making television soundtracks throughout the 80s, an area of work in which many jazz musicians had traditionally participated, and which provided steadier and better paying gigs than those to be found on the live circuit.

VINYL RECORDS

A German (Berlin) label this time, but one that released several important English improvisers through 1976-80, including the SME (*Live Big Band and Quartet*), Amalgam, John Stevens, Talisker, Howard Riley (*The Toronto Concert*) and the original release of *Improvisations Are Forever Now*, later rescued from oblivion by Emanem (as Emanem 4070).

A RECORDS

Finally, at the other end of the alphabet, we find London-based A Records, founded in 1972 by John Stevens and Trevor Watts, who were at that time playing, as we have seen, as an SME duo. A Records only put out three recordings (1973-5): two in 1973 and one in 1975, two by an augmented SME (the Spontaneous Music Orchestra), which were subsequently re-released on CD by Emanem, and numbered 4023 and 4062, and the other by an Amalgam tribute to Ornette-associated drummers Edward Blackwell and Billy Higgins.

THOSE WHO ALSO SERVED

For the sake of completeness (and apologies to those labels that I have almost certainly inadvertently left out), I will mention these two labels that came out of Birmingham and Bristol, and their own local free improv scenes, which will lead us neatly on to the next chapter:

NONDO RECORDS

This Birmingham label was run single-handedly by Dave Panton. The catalogue, as of 1979, featured works by musicians based in the second city.

ZYZZLE RECORDS

This was the only label that existed specifically to serve one particular Musicians Cooperative, i.e. Bristol. By 1979, it had released two recordings.

In early 1970, there were no English independent labels that featured free improvisation. The majors' brief flirtation with the music had been short and not-so-sweet. By 1980, there were several independents that had released a great deal of high quality recorded free improv, and this would continue over the forthcoming decades. Similarly, at the beginning of the decade, if one wanted to see and hear live improvisation one almost inevitably had to travel to London for this rare treat. Ten years later, the regions had developed very many organisations/collectives, which promoted free improv live events, single gigs and festivals of all shapes and sizes. It is this phenomenon that we will turn to in our next chapter. Free improv was expanding.

CHAPTER 7

The Regional Imperative

Unlike free improvisation, regional rock-related music had no problem gaining attention in the post-punk period of 1978-80. London had the Sex Pistols and The Clash, but elsewhere in the country was where the really hip action seemed to be taking place at the time.

▶ Manchester had Factory Records, its artifacts being as unadorned in presentation as those of Incus Records (yet far artier, with the Peter Saville designs). This label had signed Joy Division, the greatest of all the rock post-punk ensembles. The Fall also emerged in 1977, a contender for the second greatest, initially on Step Forward Records, on a wobbly rail that still continues to this day.

▶ Liverpool had Zoo Records, with the neo-psychedelia of Echo & the Bunnymen, The Teardrop Explodes and Wah Heat!

▶ Leeds had the likes of The Mekons and Delta 5, which were mixed gender configurations, and The Gang of Four, all of whom were later extensively eulogised by American critic Greil Marcus, one of the most influential commentators on rock music over the past 35 or so years. (Marcus, 1999.)

▶ Bristol was developing its own scene, out of which eventually came The Wild Bunch and the Massive Attack posse (which included Tricky), and which came to dominate 90s progressive dance and 'Trip Hop'. Meanwhile, in our time frame, it generated Pigbag, Maximum Joy, The Pop Group and Rip, Rig & Panic (the latter including, at one point, both Neneh Cherry and her step dad, Don). Pigbag and Rip, Rig & Panic certainly had a significant influence in introducing post-punksters to Free Jazz, especially though the latter's 1981 *God* album (Mark Springer's piano playing definitely pointed me in the direction of Cecil Taylor at the time, before I had heard the master himself).

▶ One has to only read the *New Musical Express* supplements, in the editions of June 20th and 27th 1981, which formed a two-part guide to the jazz of the 50s through to the 80s by a young Richard Cook and Roy Carr, to appreciate how thoroughly jazz had infiltrated the rock scene at this time, as a genre to be examined and learned from, and which no doubt contributed to the English 'jazz revival' hipster-isms of a few years later. These supplements certainly helped me in reacquainting myself with the music, and I have always felt that this burgeoning of interest in avant jazz was a reaction to the closure of the very creative post-punk period at around that time (1981), and its replacement by a more 'style' obsessed rock/pop/jazz scene.

▶ Even my neck of the woods, the West Midlands, almost never thought of as a cutting-edge *milieu* (apart from generating Heavy Metal and some of Led Zeppelin), had enough *chutzpah* to enable retrospective compilations of obscurities from the era to be released to a nostalgic rock culture: *Messthetics #103: DIY 77-81 Midlands*. Go check it out, much of the material is genuinely inspiring and original.

Being regional was being cool (at least we thought so at the time). However, in the murkier waters of early free improv, things were still very London-centric, a chauvinism which led me to subtitle my first book *The Golden Age of Free Music in London*. In the period now under consideration, however, all this began to change and talented improvisers who neither hailed from London, nor wanted to live there, began establishing themselves in what was soon to become, potentially, a national network of similarly minded improvisers.

In this vein, *Microphone* magazine, the first editions of which were entitled "New Music in London", had, by its fourth edition (May 1972), changed the masthead to "New Music in Britain". In point of fact, in a letter in *Microphone* 4 (May 1972, p.2), David Mayer writing from

Devon, asked "But why only London? Selling to people outside the London scene might be a little difficult, though I expect I'm as one-viewpointed as you might be." Which is perhaps a bit of a defeatist approach to the issue.

A WELCOME RETURN

On August 14th 2016, I was lucky enough to be present at a concert held at London's Café Oto, which signalled guitarist Ian Brighton's full return to live group improvisation. Although he had been playing live occasionally before this particular gig, this was a semi-formal event celebrating his decision to return to live playing. Situated in London's free improv nexus, Dalston, Café Oto is the near neighbour to the celebrated, and much older, Vortex Club (opened in 1987), another venue which has always been very welcoming of this sort of music.

With the wonders of modern technology, the gig had been uploaded within hours and became immediately available to view on YouTube under 'String Thing', named because of the predominance of string instruments in this particular ensemble. This was basically the return of the band of the same name, from the mid 70s, with Brighton, Phillip Wachsmann, bassist Marcio Mattos and multi-instrumentalist/percussionist Trevor Taylor who, along with Brighton, was a major figure in the Southend scene, as we will see later, and in the free improv circuit generally. This configuration had not played since 1989. On this occasion, the four were joined by Evan Parker and guitarist John Russell (like Brighton, another Derek Bailey acolyte). This was a tremendous gig from beginning to end, very much in the classic 'insect music' style, which was well received by an audience of veteran listeners and younger fans alike. One thing it demonstrated to me, as if it were needed, was how well established this most recondite of forms has become, and how its practitioners have 'stuck to their guns' over the decades, despite having every reason not to.

One other point to make, however, is the sheer curiosity of configurations like String Thing and even Alterations (who also reformed and played a 'comeback' gig at Oto in 2016) coming back together after so many years, just as rock bands (the Stone Roses, Blur and Suede being only the most obvious of examples) are prone to do. Luckily, these particular reformations produced high quality group interaction (the free improvisers, that is), as would be expected, but it is at least noticeable, surely, that even the most abstruse of free improv groupings do something as traditional ('rockist' even, to use the antediluvian term) as a 'comeback gig/tour'? I'm sure the irony is not lost on the musicians themselves. I, for one, however, am grateful that they did not let notions of 'unrepeatability' prevent them from continuing conversations that started some 40-odd years ago. This idea caused no end of controversy in the late 60s/early 70s, as the music's philosophy was being debated, but hopefully we have moved on from such absolutist positions by now.

THE YEARS OF EXPANSION ACROSS THE COUNTRY
The South East

Trevor Taylor is a much neglected figure in this music. As well as being a musician, he is a recognised recorder of jazz in the written format. His book imprint, Soundworld, published John Wickes' seminal book on English jazz, which I often have recourse to quote from, and also the now deleted magazine *Avant*, which ran for several years in the late 1990s (1997-2002). He also runs a record label FMR (Future Music Records), which he formed in the late 80s.

Based in the Southend area, Taylor studied 'straight' percussion and composition at The Guildhall School of Music, founded his own studios and, contemporaneously with Oxley and Lytton, explored the electronic modification of his drum kit. No doubt if he had been in London over these years, his name would be much more familiar than it is.

Ian Brighton, who, working together with Taylor, largely as a team, introduced free improvisation into Southend and environs, is one of those musicians who has clear links with Gen One, but who also formed them with Gen Two, making him 'Janus-faced' in the playing situation. He has played with all the major figures of the early days of the music, and of the subsequent period.

Brighton began taking 'formal' lessons with Derek Bailey, but the weekly encounters became more of a *guru/chela* situation, with discussions about improvisation and the approaches connected with it, rather than studies in technique and musical theory. Through his contact with Bailey, Brighton soon met other new players like Frank Perry, Colin Wood, Rudu Malfatti and Phil Wachsmann. He encountered Trevor Taylor in Southend and, together with clarinetist Dave Long, flautist Diz Derek, vocalist Carolann Nichols and, on occasion, bassist John Mole, formed Contemporary Improvised Music (CIM), whose language was in the style of *Klangfarben*, the art of small sounds melding into one voice ('insect music', again?). He became part of Evan Parker's Prototype for an Improvisers Orchestra, which included Wachsmann, Malfatti and Wood, with whom he formed Balance, the group which arguably recorded the first Gen Two album, Incus 11. His interest in large group configurations continued with the Alternative Music Orchestra (see below) and John Stevens' ten-piece Spontaneous Music Orchestra. At the other extreme, he released *Marsh Gas* for Bead Records, a combination of solo, duets, trios and quartets with Marcio Mattos, Rudu Malfatti, Roger Smith and Phil Wachsmann. Like John Stevens, he took an interest in children's music making, and played in schools to introduce the kids to the idea of improvised music. With regard to other influences, Brighton singles out that of Lol Coxhill, discussed and celebrated earlier in this book, with whom he worked regularly in the late 70s.

CIM played for the first time on November 29th 1971, at Ronnie Scott's Club. This was, coincidently, fellow percussionist Frank Perry's first solo outing. They also played at the notorious ICES 72 Festival. By the time of *Microphone* 5 (June 1972), Perry had become recognised enough to co-feature in this 'percussion edition' with the likes of Eddie Prevost, Paul Lytton and Tony Oxley. In July that same year, the Musicians Cooperative (MC) had begun to extend the hand of friendship to out-of-towners, and a gig at the Commonwealth Institute featured CIM itself, as well as Steve Beresford's early trio, Bread and Cheese, from York.

1974 saw the MC, now installed at the Unity Theatre, offer to pair one of its groupings with one from the regions in its regular Thursday night session. This was a considerable offer of friendship by the supposedly elitist MC. Further gigs involved the Peter Beresford Trio from Plymouth (the city which was the source of several greats, including Mike Westbrook himself, John Surman and Lawrence Sheaff), Ascension from Stoke-on-Trent and Birmingham percussionist Roy Ashbury. This cross-fertilisation eventually peaked with the 'Young Improvisers' event at the Wigmore Hall of May 2nd 1975.

The scene around Trevor Taylor and the S.E. Essex improvisers is complicated, but I will endeavour to list below its main organisational developments.

▶ The Alternative Music Orchestra (AMO) began in December 1973, an initiative of both Taylor and Ian Brighton, "either grimly chaotic or fascinatingly beautiful", according to Steve Lake, after attending a rehearsal. (Wickes, p.250.) Taylor and Brighton had seen the London Jazz Composers Orchestra at Ronnie Scott's Club in that month (the live LJCO that was also an influence on the young John Russell). The AMO's first gig was at the Unity Theatre in March 1974, organised by the MC. With this initial influence, the AMO developed several offshoots, including String Thing, mentioned above, with their specifically string-dominated approach to free improv, which the SME would later mirror, by the late 70s. Brighton, in *Musics* 3 (pp.10-11), described its formation and some of the challenges of large group music, and hinted that "from some of the elder statesmen the response was less than ecstatic, though some of them did trot along to one or two of the early rehearsals". In a personal communication with myself (August 2016), Brighton explained that, "The AMO was formed to see if a large number of improvisers could play together without that framework (i.e. a written score)…and still have the discipline to improvise freely while respecting those around them." This makes them an early version of the London Improvisers Orchestra, which still plays monthly in north London.

▶ The New Music Formation, the brainchild of Ian Brighton and Phil Wachsmann operational from May 1975, had close links with both the AMO and the SMO. It consisted of the string *maestros* Brighton, Roger Smith, Wachsmann and Mattos. It gave a performance of avant garde and improvised music at St. Johns, Smith Square in London, with Arts Council backing. (Wickes, *op. cit.*, p.308.) At a much later date, they are noted to have played, with saxophonist Larry Stabbins who later came to some prominence in the 80s, at the City Lit on March 1st 1978.

One thing to note, however, is that the Southend scene never resolved itself into a 'collective/cooperative' status, with the result that its work tended not to feature in late 70s attempts to form a national network of these organisations.

The view from the South West

The Bristol Musicians Cooperative was inaugurated around 1975, at least a year before its London cousin, by Ian and Will Menter, two also neglected figures who deserve their place in the sun for sheer cussedness and willpower as much as anything. By 1979, it had 32 members (all the following information is laid out in the Bristol Musicians Cooperative booklet, 1979), of which only two were women (hardly untypical, it must be said). In 1978/9, they put on 24 concert-type events, mainly at the Bristol Arts Centre and the university. They had been in receipt of a grant from the Southwest Arts for the past four years and, as well as weekly improv workshops, had organised two festivals in Bristol: the Unpopular Music Festival of 1978 (to which the Arts Council donated £1000) and 1979's Cooperative Music Festival. "Both ventures aim to show…the breadth and the strength of the musicians' cooperatives and collectives." (Page 2.) It seemed that a robust infrastructure for the music had been established in this city by 1979.

Around this time, the Jazz Centre Society was trying to promote free music through the regional arts associations, asking for funds from the Musicians Union and the Arts Council. One has to imagine what the average regional fund administrator thought of free improvisation, given that even London struggled to provide a basic infrastructure for music of this kind. The Arts Council came up with the Contemporary Music Network (CMN) to promote the music across the land (a large Company *troupe* did tour the UK in March 1979 under the CMN banner, to be fair).

Evan Parker, in a lengthy letter in *Musics* 4 (Oct/Nov 1975, pp.3-4), outlined some of the problems involved with institutional artistic subsidy, particularly as regards the distinction between London and the 'provinces'.

It is worth quoting at length: "Take for example the Contemporary Music Network, which was ostensibly and perhaps with every good intention, instituted in order to compensate for the conservative taste of regional arts associations. This scheme centralises decision making and limits choice in the interest of bureaucratic efficiency, perhaps with the aim of making more contemporary work available at an irresistibly cheap price to regional organisers. It is not beyond possibility that many of these organisers have just as good, if not a better, overview of the spectrum of work available to them as the central policy makers and that this Network can just as easily be seen as an instrument designed to maintain a rigid central control. Clearly the greater number of persons involved in programmatic decisions, the greater is the variety of aesthetic outlooks represented likely to be, and at the same time the smaller will be the restrictive influence of any one individual's cultural and social prejudices."

Parker is decrying centralism and the corresponding shriveling up of 'localism'. He also praises the idea of local festivals, which the Menters went on to action (for example, with Bristol festivals in 1978 and 1979). He goes on to compare England to the German model, i.e. that of "a vigorous sense of small-town loyalty", which ensures the maintaining of a local infrastructure of clubs and of regular places to play. This was almost certainly a residue of Germany's particular history of independent regions that existed before unification in 1871. Parker censures the bias of arts administrators towards "theatre, dance and opera", which are considered by our cultural arbiters as the *status quo*, i.e. what is ultimately good for us. But what had prompted this outburst by our saxophonist *supremo*?

Musics 3 (August/September 1975) contained an article by the Menter brothers, which begins, tellingly, with: "If the plight of creative musicians in London is bad, the situation for their counterparts in the provinces is dire. As the national culture becomes more homogenous, the eyes and ears of more and more people are turned towards the capital city, and away from artists in their own community." (Page 14.)

Little seems, ultimately, to have changed over the years. London has always been the recipient of a considerable amount of projected envy, resentment and admiration, a fairly noxious stew, even at the best of times, from the rest of the country, and it still does. It still remains, maybe now more than ever, the perceived epicentre of all that is 'happening' in the arts (and things in general), despite the kick in the pants the regions delivered to the Great Wen in the1960s and 1970s through pop music, fashion, film and photography. But this is to ignore, as ever, what is really going on across the country now, as it was then.

The Menters' sentiments in this short, but passionate, article, sum up the experiences/feelings of generations of creative individuals who live, after all, in the major part of our island: "However, for the individual artist in a city such as Bristol [hardly a backwater, it is *the* major city in this part of England, *author*], what this situation means is a straightforward choice – either you stay where your roots are and carry on your artistic practice, in whatever restricted form you can, or you head to the big city in the hope of finding fame and fortune. Of course it would be stupid to suggest that this is to be found in any great measure even in London, but there is little doubt that considerably more opportunities can be created there." (*Musics* 3, p.14.)

This situation seemed, and still seems, to be the truth of it, unfortunately.

What sparked Parker's diatribe in the following edition of *Musics*, appears to be Menter's complaint about the South West Arts association, which had met with silence various applications from interested musicians, mainly on the grounds of 'non-professionalism'. That is, that grants would only be given to professional musicians, which meant, in practice, musicians from or based in London, "presumably to educate the natives", Menter observes acidulously. "It is assumed that provincial musicians aren't professional because they aren't good enough. If they were good enough, they'd go to London, wouldn't they?" (Menter, *op. cit.*, p.14.)

Menter then goes on to cite Marcuse, which dates the piece somewhat, but the Catch 22 ('you can't win, either way') situation is clear enough. Or, to put it in more studied terms, 'incompatible, contradictory demands', which is essentially saying the same thing in more measured terms. It was still the 'same old same old', though, however you dressed it up.

"Why should we have to move to London to pursue our music?" (Menter, *op. cit.* p.15.) Which was a very fair point.

It is for this reason that the Bristol Musicians Cooperative (BMC) was formed in that year (1975), one of the first of its kind, with the express intention of addressing this ghetto-isation of the extra-London scenes (i.e. almost all of the country). Menter makes it clear that this project was not aimed at London musicians themselves, but at the institutions, such as arts centres, councils, student unions, community centres and suchlike (the 'Establishment' generally), that musicians depend on for their livelihood, and that it would be beneficial to develop cross-country (and cross-county) dialogues with similarly minded movements. Some of the BMC's mission statement was published by the side of the article, the main tenets being:

▶ To create a dialogue within the network of Bristol's musical community.
▶ To be pluralistic, and to feature a variety of music, including that made by 'non-musicians', which was territory being explored contemporaneously by the SMO and Scratch Orchestra.
▶ To create a space for the validation of children's music making (an area which John Stevens and Ian Brighton were also interested in), as a further development of the preceding tenet.
▶ To make contact with musicians in other towns and counties, and to organise exchanges.

It is interesting to pause for a moment here and consider whether London is still, in this era, a realistically achievable port of call, in the way that it was in those initial post war decades when it was possible to find cheapish accommodation, even in Soho, if you knew the right people and weren't excessively desirous of features like a garden and hot running water. Journalist John Harris, who usually writes about rock music, wrote an article for *The Guardian*, published on February 6th 2015, called "A Lament for the Death of Bohemian London", in which he claims that "since 2010, Soho has lost 30,000 square metres of offices and studios, and acquired twice that area of residential space". And I doubt that this 'residential space' will be affordable for the likes of struggling free improvisers.

The effects of this will be catastrophic for the creative arts in time: "From the 1960s onwards, the legend of Swinging London [or should it now be 'Swingeing London'? *author*], which still partly defines the way the city is seen, was traceable to the coming together of working class talent and loose-living bohemia – precisely the elements that are now in danger of being chased out of the centre of central London altogether." (Menter, *op. cit.*)

My own experience perhaps reflects and reinforces this observation. In 1983, I finally moved permanently to London (initially in the fairly central area of NW8, very, very near to the famed Abbey Road studios), at that time on benefits, and I was easily able to afford the cost of a room in an admittedly very rundown house. Now that entire street (Blenheim Terrace, if you're interested) has been completely gentrified and that kind of opportunity is now very rare indeed. Living in other cities has never been so popular because of the huge hike-up in rents in London and of the litigation against squatting, so maybe this might be to the benefit of regional arts communities? (I'm trying to remain positive at this point.)

Will Menter had also led a big band, originally from nearby Bath, called Bullit, influenced by the large ensembles of George Russell, the Globe Unity Orchestra and the Brotherhood of Breath. They played a London gig at Seven Dials, but folded soon after due to "internal stylistic contradictions". (Wickes, *op. cit.*, p.309.) A catch-all explanation that covers all kind of evils.

In Bristol itself, the Arnolfini was one of the most important venues, but the BMC travelled the country, as per mission statement, to work with other cooperatives in a gradually expanding culture of TAZs. Sessions and workshops were held and a label, Zyzzle, was established, with each vinyl disc individually hand-painted, as were those released on Sun Ra's Saturn imprint (and hugely collectable by now, I would have thought).

Bristol musicians like altoist Ron Cairns, keyboard player Mark Langford and drummer Bob Helson all used 'extended techniques', under the influence of American Free Jazz and English Gen One Free Improvisation. Langford was himself a graduate of another SW region, a Mike Westbrook workshop in Torquay, which had as graduates several Gen One players of the calibre of John Surman, Keith Rowe and Lawrence Sheaff.

Will Menter was at it again, in *Musics* 13, in an article covering a Music For Socialism event held at Battersea Arts Centre on May 28th 1977. His contribution, one of those by several stakeholders, makes an interesting contrast to an adjacent piece by Cornelius Cardew, which was another example of the latter's Marxist polemic about the forthcoming proletarian revolution (which we still await, 40 years on, and which looks like being a right-wing rather than a left-leaning one): "It was certainly a prominent argument during our (BMC) formation two-and-a-half years ago. We had a nationalistic resentment of people coming down from the metropolis to give us our dose of Culture – 'educating the natives' I think was the phrase we used." (Menter, p.13.)

'The idiocy of rural life' was the phrase that Marx himself used in 1848, apparently, even though Bristol measured its population at around half a million at the time that Menter was writing. This sort of patronising attitude has clearly become part of 'the idiot rural' collective unconscious, and has contributed to Brexit and the election of a game show host as the President of the United States of America. Perhaps. "We can no longer define folk music as music which was created by a particular community." (Menter, *op. cit.*, p.13.) A point of view that has increasing relevance in the age of globalisation and the internet.

The BMC finished off the decade in style, with its own week-long Festival of Improvised Music, aka "Unpopular Music", as described more fully in a supplement to *Musics* 18 (July 1978). A highlight appears to have been a three-hour discussion, "Improvised Music: Where Now?", which involved the Menters, Phil Wachsmann, Anthony Barnett and Max Boucher, among several others. Unfolding in Bristol, from May 26th to 31st 1978, what is revealing, from this vantage point in time, is the other regions represented at the Festival – Essex, Devon, Cornwall, Leeds, Surrey, Bath, Luton, Warminster, Bridgewater, Nottingham, Birmingham, Connecticut (*sic*), Tamworth and, holding up the rear, good old London. If not exactly 'improv international', it was without doubt 'improv England' by this stage. The modernist trumpeter and composer, Leo Smith, held a workshop on the 27th, another positive sign that the event was being taken seriously by the American heavyweights. However, the discussion group photo on page four of the supplement does tend to reveal that the huge majority of the disputants were still bearded men (some of whom appear to be nodding off, sadly). Never mind, the festival appears to have been a success, and a very encouraging indication of the increasing confidence of the regions.

The 'News' section of *Musics* 19 (September 1978, p.13) makes enlightening reading, and gives a clear impression of a burgeoning national interest in free improvisation. It contains the following letters from the regions:

"I have recently moved into Chester, and am anxious to meet improvising musicians in the Chester/Liverpool/Manchester area, and to help with organising performances in those areas. Can anyone interested get in touch, please?"

This plea was from Martin Archer, who subsequently became a major player in the Sheffield free scene, forming Discus Records, one of the longest lasting independent labels covering creative music. It is very strange thinking of this most confident of figures (at least, that was my superficial impression of him when we briefly met at a gig) being a young hopeful, back in the day.

"Is anyone in the North East of England interested in Free Jazz/Free Improvisation? Whether you play, would like to play, or just like to listen, I'd like to hear from you. Hopefully, we could get some kind of creative music co-op or collective going in the area." From a Kevin Murray, from Sunderland.

Last, and probably most telling, a 'small ad': "Feminist Band Needs Drummer".

So, the free improv 'lonely hearts' column features a female drummer. Sacrilege!! Where would it all end?

Moving away from Bristol, there was a most revealing article in *Musics* 6 (February/March 1976), featuring a transcription of a meeting between free improv musicians and representatives of the Arts Council on May 15th 1976. Representing the musicians' perspective were: Steve Beresford, Max Boucher, Ian Brighton, Peter Cusack, Mandy Davidson, Gerry Gold, John Russell, Phil Wachsmann and Colin Wood. The AC was represented by John Cruft (Music Director), Tony Wills (Music Officer, specialising in jazz) and Annette Morreau (Music Officer, specialising in 'modern music', who was seemingly unusually sympathetic to the music).

Peter Cusack summarised for the meeting the progress free improvisation had made up to this point: "The number of people involved had recently greatly increased, the range of activities included regular venues, New Music Formation, Albion Music, Mandy's promotion, cooperatives in York, Bristol and London, Incus Records and other musicians' own labels, occasional broadcasts, *Musics* magazine and "Improgram" [an information sheet, *author*]. The time had come to put these activities on a different basis comparable with other kinds of music, for example by giving adequate publicity for concerts, and thus reach a wider public." (Page 26.)

The point was made by John Cruft that the Arts Council looked for 'professionalism' and evidence of a public need for the music: "London already had more art than the regions. They did not give money for music to be played in the streets." (Page 26.)

The last comment speaks wonders for how the Arts Council saw free improv. Clearly, the 'concert hall' was where the obvious public need lay? Hence the huge clamour for opera, evident for all to see? And for ballet?

To be fair to the Arts Council reps, such a meeting had probably never occurred before, so they were on unexplored terrain. "The difficulties of communication between performers and audiences, in concert halls and other settings, were stressed," by both parties (page 28). Maybe the difficulties of communication between the parties themselves also needed to be stressed? To be frank, looking at the current scene, opera and ballet both still seem to be receiving the usual munificence from the state, whereas, in London at least, free improvisation is reliant on small clubs like the Vortex and Café Oto. To be fair, both these venues receive small grants, but the former clearly struggles to make ends meet. From what I can gather, regional venues also have difficulties surviving a recession-dominated economy, and many small but valiant operations have been forced to close, often due to high rents as well as general disinterest.

"Good Morning Brick Wall" – Stoke-on Trent

It is worth mentioning the Potteries scene briefly, if only for the above 'woke up this morning' feeling alluded to above, which was used by Peter Riley (who appears to have been a sort of mobile *agent provocateur* at the time) as a title for a cut-and-paste 'article' on the Stoke free *milieu*. This used the Stoke Artists Action Group's publication, *History of a Band,* and various issues of the magazine *Start* (Stoke Arts Centre), plus 'specially written' statements, and appeared in *Musics* 10 (November 1976).

In particular, Riley referred to the group Ascension (not the later skronk-guitar duo with Stefan Jaworzyn, so beloved of Ben Watson), which had a line-up of Patrick Regan on saxes, Ian Winfield on piano, Clive Buttle on guitar/sitar, Jeff Walters on bass and Nigel Harvey on the traps. In the article, Ascension seem to be treated as a TAZ of its own: "It erected a transformative working area in Stoke which has operated for six years; constantly torn this way and that by conflicting pressures as to how that musical space is related to the social sphere in which it exists." (Page 8.) This makes a change from 'musical differences', I guess. This particular ensemble started in January 1970, so were clearly a long-lived local influence. They even got to play at ICES, and were described by *The Sunday Times* as "aggressive, nasty and brutishly long" (page 9), which sounds very promising, I must say.

Leeds/Manchester

Moving on in time, by February 1978 we have the following correspondence in *Musics* 16 (page 3): "Are you a musician with no place to stay, no opportunities for meeting other musicians? Have you considered starting a Musicians Collective? These already exist in both Leeds and London. During 1977, two cooperatives have been formed by musicians in the North West. The Manchester Musicians Collective meets every fortnight in central Manchester. Recently an initial meeting was held to start a musicians co-op in Bury." (From Trevor Wishart, writing from Manchester M2.)

In the previous edition (again on page 3), the Manchester Musicians Collective (MMC) announced:

Recent events:

a) Found-objects improvisation session [which sounds great fun, *author*].
b) 'The Fall' and other young punk groups [maybe less fun, *author*].
c) Tape and tape/slide meeting [so far, so Burroughs, *author*].
d) Group which improvises on tent-poles, etc. [??]

Leaving us to ponder on the last event, Trevor Wishart sums it all up as: "A good scene at present," which it certainly sounded like.

It's very amusing to see that most venerable of punk institutions, The Fall, being described as 'young'. What with Mark E. Smith, over time, having made his alcoholic creation, 'Fiery Jack', seem like Colonel William Booth compared to his own adventures in booze. Percussionist Dick Witts, who had credits in classical and experimental music, and was also a member of various ('post-rock', as it would probably be called now) pop/rock bands, was the co-founder, with Wishart, of the MMC, and was also the convener of the Northern Improvisers Circuit Association. This scene would, of course, meld into Factory Records and one of the most important avant rock scenes of all. It was a time of huge creative possibilities in this northern city, which began to break down formerly (and formally) unassailable musical boundaries. The MMC was noticeable, in particular, in that most of its members worked in new wave rock music, a form that other collectives/co-ops were sympathetic to, but not dominated by.

The Manchester Music Collective folded in 1982, the local scene having moved on with the emergence of New Order from the ashes of Joy Division, whose singer, Ian Curtis, had hanged himself in May 1980, and with the opening of The Hacienda club. Manchester slowly became 'Madchester', as the asceticism of the late 70s was erased by club-based hedonism.

Alongside the MC piece was one by the Leeds Musicians Collective (the idea was spreading like a virus), asking for "approximately 12 musicians, to go ahead immediately and produce a series of regular performances", with The Packhorse as a regular venue. From October, they intended to run workshops and rehearsals at the Swarthmore Centre, Leeds 6. (*Musics* 15, p.3.) Leeds, much later, became well known for The Termite Club, a major regional nexus for the music, where Ben Watson appears to have spent much of his youth.

The Leeds Musicians Collective had formed as early as July 1977, and had staged a Festival of Improvised Music in August by the following year (25th-28th). Their main activity was, in fact, live concerts, and they received some funds from the Northern Jazz Centre Society, most of which went on the Festival. They also were provided with some funds from the Yorkshire Arts Association. Their *credo* was a very positive one that seemed to be echoed by most regional collectives of the time: "We hope that Leeds can be looked at as another place where improvised music concerts by all committed players, recognised or not, from all over the country, are a regular occurrence." (Bristol Musicians Cooperative, *op. cit.*, p.8.)

Birmingham

This is my hometown. Our second city, so called, which was under the auspices of the West Midland Arts Association (WMAA). Jan Steele, on behalf of the Birmingham Musicians Cooperative (another one to add to the ever increasing list), along with Glyn Bush, Steve Reynolds and Dave Panton, produced a very informative and constructive article in *Musics* 17 (May 1978), in which they provided a sample Letter of Application for financial assistance to the WMAA, in order to suggest a model to help prospective supplicants when applying to various bureaucratic bodies.

The Birmingham Musicians Cooperative was formed in early 1978 and had 23 members by 1979. (Birmingham Musicians Cooperative, *op. cit.*, p.5.) Throughout 1978/9, they put on weekly workshops at Birmingham Arts Lab and 14 concert-type events. (Birmingham Musicians Cooperative, *op. cit.*, p.5.)

I was most surprised the other day, when I was checking out the contents of the *West Midlands Messthetics 1978-81* compilation of post-punk bands, to find, on one of the most obscure tracks of all among these incredibly arcane provincial bands, one by poet Paul Lester. Recording as Lester & the Brew, the saxophone accompaniment was provided by one Dave Panton, who was still sporting for-the-time most unfashionable long hair and beard. This pleased my sense of fortuitousness (and I must ask the reader to indulge my over-developed tendency to seek linkage between things) in that it provided further evidence, if any were still needed, of the inter-dependence of improvisation, *avant rock* and other allied art forms. The Brew's EP, *A Bad Day*, as well as being inspired by the British 'Jazz and Poetry' scene, an offshoot of the 1960s Beat movement, had been enthusiastically endorsed by none other than Lol Coxhill himself: "Not only do I play it, but I make other people listen to it!" Lester would give even Terry Day a run for his money in the beat *boho* poetry stakes.

In fact, the Cooperative had stated in their aims and objectives that they included new wave and experimental rock improvised music, 'ethnic' music, contemporary classical and jazz, in their orbit and, in general, "music which is not normally catered for by the normal channels heard" (*sic*). (Birmingham Musicians Cooperative, o*p. cit.,* p.5.)

In the same way, I was somewhat surprised when Evan Parker referred me to 'Keef' Richards' autobiography regarding a reference. The two worlds are not as watertight as many of us might assume.

The Birmingham Musicians Cooperative (BMCO) had been founded after discussions in the Arts Lab Improvisation Workshops of 1977/8 – relatively late for a city of such size and importance. "One of the biggest problems we had was in getting into the mentality of assuming and anticipating a loss." (*Musics* 17, p.29.) A most revealing symptom of low self-esteem, an attitude that free improvisers were seemingly expected to assume when dealing with the powers-that-be. Most charmingly, the BMCO intended to hold a 'Musical Tour' of the Second City, playing in shopping precincts. If I remember the Bull Ring at that time correctly, these were the bravest improvisers imaginable! There is no record, as far as I can find, of how this tour went.

Dave Panton's story seems typical of the average regional improviser in terms of his participation in the local scene, mutual support and communication between and with other improvisers' organisations across the country, and regular forays to the capital to network with the London musicians.

Panton was initially self-taught, but at the age of 17 (in 1963), volunteered to join the army as a bandsman and attended Kneller Hall (a Military School of Music) for a one-year course (1964-5) studying oboe and piano, and some musical theory. He later (1966-7) attended the Birmingham School of Music for piano tuition. Leaving the army in 1967, he proceeded to pursue a music career in 'civvy street', teaching himself alto saxophone under the influence of American and British Free Jazz players. (Personal communication, September 2016.) So his path included both self-tuition and formal study, with the armed forces proving to be a valuable educative setting, as they were for many of the First Generation improvisers like Watts, Stevens, Oxley and Rutherford.

Like Coxhill, Beresford and Day, Panton had no problem in playing more 'populist' forms of music, playing in a blues band as well as with some of the post-punk musicians mentioned above. He was even involved with the psych-folk band Forest, which latterly gained attention through the 'free folk revival' a few years back. (Young, 2010, pp.397-400.) Locally, he played mostly in the solo format, before venturing down south to meet players like John Stevens, Derek Bailey, Evan Parker, Maggie Nicols and David Toop, and to play with them at venues such as the Little Theatre Club, the Jazz Centre Society and Oval House. The Arts Lab in Birmingham was itself an important gig in those days.

Panton first visited London during 1970-1, years in which the London scene, such as it was, had established itself and its influence had begun to manifest itself in the regions. Ian Brighton, for example, had also begun to take lessons with Derek Bailey, as did John Russell at about the same time. Dave Panton, for his part, describes "criticism of my reliance on themes and/or structures, and, in my saxophone playing at least, a tendency noted by Derek Bailey and Evan Parker in particular, to be too 'jazzy'". (Personal communication, 2016.)

This seems to have been a big issue at the time, and the Bailey/Parker dyad did represent the most 'pure' voices of untrammeled free improv (which set up the notional 'impurity' suggested by Steve Beresford in his quote at the very beginning of this book), so it is not really surprising that Panton felt most challenged by their approach at that particular time. Having taken "time to consider my musical approaches…by early 1972, I had begun to take on the challenge of working more or less exclusively from this standpoint, and attempted to put together a cooperative group of individuals from across the arts in the West Midlands…quickly reduced to just three of us, viz. Roy Ashbury, Fred Middleton and myself". (Panton, op. cit.)

This apparent 'failure', at that time, to establish a local network was not an entirely negative experience, argues Panton (op. cit.): "It resulted in opening up opportunities in four areas, viz. Southampton, London, the West Midlands and also Stoke-on-Trent… we (Panton/Ashbury) managed to play as an improvising duo at several events in Southampton, as well as continuing to do solo and duo gigs in London, Birmingham and Wolverhampton, as well as participating in John Stevens' Entourage project – a forerunner of what became the Spontaneous Music Orchestra."

Gradually, almost imperceptibly, free improv was spreading its wings, although gaining a true foothold in the regions proved to be a decade-long process. In particular, Panton describes close links with the Stoke improvisers (through Nigel Harvey), some of whom had participated in the historically significant ICES-72 event at the Roundhouse. Panton had, by 1973, held regular workshops at La Sainte Union Teacher Training College in Southampton, as well as the Arts Gallery there, and that particular regional scene received some coverage from the local Radio Solent. The Birmingham Arts Lab, under Jolyon Laycock, continued to occasionally present the music.

These were small, but significant, contributions to spreading the word. Panton (op. cit.) describes both the pleasure and the pain of linkage with the capital city: "Links made between all of these areas and London (were) principally through John Stevens and some of the so-called second generation improvisers. Indeed, there was a Little Theatre night dedicated to improvisers from outside London, which included myself (via Birmingham and Southampton), saxophonist Jan Steele (via

Birmingham but then at York University) and others from York, plus musicians from other places which memory and lost flyers have forgotten, but which was marred by verbal outbursts from Tommy Chase (a former be-bop drummer making a comeback at the time) who gatecrashed the event just to be hostile and was apparently later banned from these club nights by John. Indeed, hostility was a common problem if gigs were put on in student union bars or local pubs opposite rock bands, etc., in order to get an audience."

Tommy Chase was indeed a be-bop purist of the most obsessive kind and, as previously noted, was a regular on London's mid 80s 'jazz revival' circuit. He was the exact opposite of everything that free improv stands for, a neo-conservative of the first order. The college scene is another matter, however, as it did offer work in those early days of the music. For example, it gave Steve Beresford his first live contact with the music (at York University, what's more) and no doubt inspired other young people, even if it was only a handful.

Dave Panton (*op. cit.*) offers a firsthand account of the very practical obstacles facing regional improvisers: "It would have been pointless to have remained in one's local area beavering away with the expectation of being 'discovered' and given a 'break', not least because audiences for this music were very small, even in London at this time, and often invisible elsewhere, but the exposure and association with London gave a sense of kudos and credibility which might be a means of getting the attention of the converted in one's local area…inevitably many of these ventures [co-ops, collectives] ended because of internal disputes, lack of local support and/or an audience [Stoke-on-Trent], people moved on and were not replaced, or simply gave up playing totally free music."

This rather dispiriting description makes the staying power and perseverance of the few who do remain totally committed to free improvisation even more admirable and deserving of special mention.

The Birmingham Arts Lab continued to present avant garde and experimental music. Jan Steele became assistant music director (and also initiated the Birmingham Musicians Collective, which presented events at several venues across the city). When the Lab moved from Tower

Street to Aston University, Steele began Saturday lunchtime sessions, which included several London improvisers (Gary Todd, Roger Turner, Dave Solomon), as well as hosting bands from Contemporary Music Network tours, such as ones by Howard Riley's Quartet, Tony Oxley and Barry Guy's Jazz Composers Orchestra. Links were being made with the Bristol and Leeds Cooperatives.

It's cool up north – The Sheffield scene

Most of the information for this section comes from Charlie Collins, the percussionist/woodwind player who, among his many other achievements, was part of the post-punk band Clock DVA, and who managed a degree of notoriety in the exciting late 70s/early 80s experimental hurly burly, which is described in some detail in Martin Lilleker's *Beats Working for a Living*, an overview of the Sheffield scene of those years, one of the most exhaustive accounts of an individual city's contribution to modern progressive music that there is (outside of those covering London and Manchester, inevitably).

Collins' description accords with some of the themes that we have established so far – the influence and draw of London, and the concomitant desire to keep a distance from it, the wariness of establishing improvisational shibboleths that might stifle creativity, the permeability of an open-minded milieu in a time of change.

Collins himself was, as with so many other improvisers, the product of a facilitative family and was playing self-made percussive instruments made in his carpenter father's workshop by the age of 11. His early influences sound familiar: "The 60s were the perfect decade in which to grow up for those of us wanting to explore music to its farthest reaches – the experimental composers of the day were regularly on the radio, and lying in bed late at night with the transistor radio, the first contacts with Indian music and Javanese gamelan could be made." (Personal communication, October 2016.)

The influence of the improvising San Francisco rock bands of the late 60s is also acknowledged by Collins, as is the influence of local record shops (which is perhaps difficult to fully appreciate in today's digital market). Violet May's shop, and Rare and Racy – which opened in 1969 and stocked "all manner of improvised and experimental music, and would go on to influence countless generations of young musicians in Sheffield" –turned him on to such gems as Roscoe Mitchell's *Sound* and the New York Art Quartet, who were also a big influence on a young Evan Parker. Rare & Racy is still going, I am pleased to report. In the absence of the live gigs that were enabled to occur in a metropolis like London, record shops were *the* key influence in smaller towns and cities in this era.

By 1970, he was travelling regularly to London: "Train connections between Sheffield and London were frequent, and ran late [the last return from London being the mail train, which left St. Pancras at 00.05, *author*]. Thus it was that I began to regularly travel to gigs and gradually get to know London musicians/promoters." (Collins, o*p. cit.)*

We have heard a similar tale from Ian Brighton and others. But by early 1973, the arrival of woodwind player Derek Saw heralded the beginnings of a new free scene in Sheffield. Now both Saw and Collins took the train to London and reported back to those who proved sufficiently interested.

Collins (*op. cit.*) describes the local scene at this juncture: "Sheffield, at this point, still had a large number of pubs completely unchanged for decades, many with upstairs rooms and outhouses that could be used for free, so long as you pulled in the punters. Together with the policy of low bus fares, this made the possibility of throwing together poetry/improv events a serious possibility – and by 1976, with the example of punk, a younger audience was beginning to be interested in what we were doing. Sheffield's relative insularity from the national music scene was becoming an advantage, as an air of experimentation began to take hold." Collins *et al* found a permanent base for their activities (at roughly about the same time as the LMC found 42 Gloucester Avenue), a converted chapel on Backfields (through his father), which became "our de-facto headquarters for the next 18 months".

There developed a small group of regular players including Collins, Saw, drummer Pete Infanti, guitarists John Hanlon and Tony Johnson (occasionally) and bassist Terry Todd. Around this time, the Mappin Art Gallery became an important space (perhaps partly because of the arresting visual aspect of Collins' self-designed percussion instruments).

A gig that was somewhat comparable to that of the Dead Kennedys at the LMC, was the Sheffield Improvised Music Group's appearance with the fledgling Def Leppard, at an open air gig in a small field in Hall Carr: "Myself, Derek Saw, John Hanlon, Terry Todd and Pete Infanti played a freely improvised set that seriously overran, so Leppard had to play with the makeshift stage illuminated with car headlights. The enthusiastic crowd really dug us though!" (Collins, *op. cit.*)

Hanlon and Todd left around 1978 to join post-punk bands and the collective was joined by a young double bassist, the Spanish singer/guitarist/poet Luz Condero-Corasco, who later ran Sheffield Jazz – "Sheffield's contribution to the usual straight jazz organisation that most cities in the UK have'." (Collins, *op. cit.*)

Other newcomers were guitarist/objects player Neil Carver who joined in 1979, with whom Collins frequently duetted in the late 70s, and guitarist John Jasnoch, who came on board in 1980 and remains an important figure in the Sheffield improv scene to this day.

By 1978-9, the crosscurrents with the burgeoning electronic post-punk scene were unavoidable in Sheffield: "Experimentalism was almost de rigueur for the young Sheffield underground. Cabaret Voltaire were using much the same techniques as we were, but to very different ends. The Human League were experimenting with synths, and Clock DVA were making their first stirrings…They were Northern Soul boys who had their minds opened by punk and experimental music of all kinds – we were kindred spirits, and we became acquainted. " (Collins, *op. cit.*)

Collins describes an increasingly friendly environment to play, and be accepted in, in those years. In particular, he describes an openness to musical influences, which "led to many of the original 70s Sheffield improvisers being subsumed into the Industrial and post-punk scenes. Within six months I was recording for Throbbing Gristle's Industrial label, playing essentially the same way I had been for the past few years."

Interestingly, Collins also notes "a newly established orthodoxy. Sheffield Improvised Music Group, and its various offshoots, had a tendency towards a more all-embracing view of free improvisation, and a willingness to create freed of self-imposed limitations". This point of view sounds similar to concerns that were being expressed in London, regarding an increasing orthodoxy concerning what did, and did not, constitute 'real' free improvisation.

"We were always of the opinion that once established the music should be allowed to flourish and expand. What was the point in investigating Japanese and Korean rhythmic practices if I was not then allowed to incorporate them because they weren't 'non-idiomatic' enough? I guess, to really simplify it, and taking (the very wonderful and influential to us) SME as an example – we were more Trevor Watts than John Stevens."

Charlie Collins concludes that "things in the provinces had improved immensely between 1973 and 1979 – more players, more contacts, more venues and vastly improved audiences (in Sheffield, at least). It was also better for contacts between local scenes, but as always tends to happen in the UK, the national scene was still London-centric."

His final comment, however, is bitterly ironic: "It would eventually be Mrs. Thatcher's wholesale destruction of the North that would lead to us being thrown a few easier-to-obtain Arts Council crumbs – but by then, of course, it was the 80s and things had changed immeasurably."

York

This culturally and geographically important city had also gained its own Musicians Collective (YMC) by 1978, although previous organisations had existed for years, as we heard before in Peter Cusack's summary of the Arts Council dialogue described earlier. The YMC "will exist to encourage interaction between various kinds of musicians and non-musicians in York and surrounding areas, and to promote and encourage experiments in music and, hopefully, performance, poetry, theatre, etc". (*Musics* 20, December 1978.)

With this aim in mind, presumably, the Yorkshire Arts Association gave the YMC one grant of £25 for a Northern Circuit tour concert.

THE OVERALL PICTURE IN THE REGIONS BY 1979

Cusack's above words were, by now, sounding very familiar, and similar mission statements had appeared across the land over the previous two years, representing a significant shift towards regional self-determination.

Will Menter's extensive article, a survey of countrywide collectives and cooperatives in the Bristol Musicians Cooperative self-published magazine of May 1979, is an invaluable resource for this topic, and I thank him for providing me with a copy of it.

By 1979 then, there were at least 11 collectives (this was by far the most popular title chosen by the particular local musicians) in England, none of which had existed, in their then current form, five or six years previously. So, over our 1973-9 timeframe, around a dozen or so of these bodies had been formed by 1979. Menter could unearth none in Scotland or Ireland, but apparently two co-ops were formed in Cardiff in 1977, one jazz-orientated and one free improv. (Bristol Musicians Cooperative, *op. cit.*, p.11.) This should surely prompt a more thorough reinvestigation of the free improvisation scene in the rest of the United Kingdom?

Musics 19 (September 1978), eight months earlier, had enclosed another useful factual supplement in which the various regional collectives were listed, which closely approximated those later identified by Menter, as well as other useful addresses, etc. Unfortunately, it was felt necessary to add that "the list...is severely biased towards London, for which I apologise" (page 15). It's not clear who is making the apology in this case, but it doesn't really seem warranted, to be absolutely honest. What is itemised is the then current collectives/co-ops, to wit:

York	Bristol
Stoke	Birmingham
The LMC	Leeds
Coventry	Manchester
Bury	The Women's Liberation Music Project, operating from Albany Street, London NW1

The Bristol Cooperative (*op. cit.*) provided further clarification about other collectives that had escaped the overview above (some of which hadn't been formed at that time). There are a few anomalies and divergences between the two lists, as is perhaps inevitable at this time of

ever-shifting configurations. Those not accounted for include:
Bretton Musicians Collective (West Yorkshire)
This collective was based at Bretton Hall College (it closed in 2007) near Wakefield, and had formed in January 1977, hoping to include newer forms of music in its remit, as did the larger collectives. In 1979, it had 12 members (ten men, two women), was college-based and received a small amount of money from the Students Union.
Coventry Musicians Collective
This formed in 1978 and was another college-based entity within the Faculty of Art and Design in Lanchester Polytechnic (now the University of Coventry). It came about through responses to improvised music workshops run by Max Eastley, who had joined the part-time lecturing staff. Its main activities were workshops, with financial contributions from other departments towards its concerts.
East Midlands Musicians Collective
Based in Ilchester, Derbyshire, and formed in September 1978, the EMMC had only played two gigs so far, but, tellingly, one had been for the Anti Nazi League and the other for the local Women's Group, so there was clearly a left-leaning political orientation. There was a core of nine members, who were mostly involved in free jazz.
North Eastern Musicians Collective
This collective was from Newcastle-upon-Tyne and had got together in October 1978, with 20 members. By 1981, it hadn't received any grant aid and membership had dwindled to three hardy individuals (Bristol Musicians Cooperative, 1981, p.59), effectively ending the North East's brief relationship with free improv at that time and place.
Southampton Musicians Cooperative
At the other end of the country from Newcastle, this co-op had started on January 1st 1979, the exact time of my wife's first and only attendance at the LMC (no link is assumed). Their comment was: "We have the nice situation of middle-aged guys who have always played 4-to-the-bar, earning bread and butter, but maintaining their interest in music through improvisation and experimentation." (Bristol Musicians Cooperative, 1979, p.10.) It is nice to see the idea of continuity

voiced here, as well as innovation.

All in all, this seemed to represent a very healthy nationwide collection of TAZs. Certainly, compared to the beginning of 1973, the self-confidence and assertiveness of what was, let's face it, most of the country outside London, had increased in leaps and bounds, and we could now begin to talk realistically of a national free improv network, supported by a new infrastructure of record labels and touring entities like Company, as opposed to one which was basically confined to the freemasonry of the capital city. This was a significant progression in just a few years.

Before we get too carried away, however, the experience of the Cleveland improvisers should be born in mind. Their co-op folded at the end of 1978, due to "total lack of public interest" (Bristol Musicians Cooperative, *op. cit.*, p.11), which is a salutary reminder of what these pioneers faced, in realistic terms.

I am also curious to know, having itemised the countrywide expansion of these pioneers, why, in particular, Brighton (despite concerts at the Poly and at the Public House bookshop in Little Preston Street) and Liverpool (despite its post-punk profile) appear not to be represented. A Merseyside Collective had apparently been formed in April 1979, but soon collapsed through lack of interest from both musicians and the general public. (Bristol Musicians Cooperative, 1981, p.57.) Both cities do not seem to have had significant input into these developments, which is an unusual situation for areas that usually seem generally to be very sympathetic to progressive arts.

THE IMPROVISERS CIRCUIT ASSOCIATION

The idea of a national network and touring circuit for improvisers (or National Free Musicians Collective) from these shores had been floated a few years earlier, but had gone nowhere fast (one of its proponents, Trevor Wishart, left for Australia shortly afterwards, for a spell). In actual fact, there does appear to have been an inaugural meeting of a National Musicians Collective at the Birmingham Arts Lab on June 12th 1976, attended by representatives from Birmingham, York, Lancaster, Newcastle, London, Bristol and Plymouth, among others (*Musics* 8, p.2), but this initiative does not appear to have been followed through, however good the intentions at the time.

By the late 70s, however, it appears to have become somewhat more of a reality and the northern collectives, at least, appeared to have organised themselves into a circuit, called the Northern Improvisers Circuit Association with, as mentioned earlier, Dick Witts, he of Manchester post-punk ensemble The Passage (*Pindrop*, 1980) as its convener.

A potential monthly series of tours were promoted, consisting of the following gigs:
- Liverpool Academy of Arts
- Manchester Musicians Collective
- New Arts Association of Hebden Bridge
- York Musicians Collective
- Spectro at Newcastle-upon-Tyne

The switches on the circuit were envisaged to be following the rough pattern of a quadrilateral across northern England: first Newcastle, then down to Cleveland (soon to be a dead end, as we saw above), down to York, then to Leeds (who opted out in 1979 for some reason, becoming a circuit-breaker, unfortunately), then to Hebden Bridge, on to Manchester, then across to Liverpool and finally back up to Newcastle.

The Southern Improvisers Circuit Association's own quadrilateral path, notional at that point but with the tireless Will Menter offering to coordinate as a contact person, had the following nodes: starting at Derby, then straight down to Coventry and Luton, the gateway to London, after which it descended to Southampton, across and up to Bristol, through Birmingham and then back to Derby.

This *schema* could be accused of potentiating a north/south divide, but this may have been less of a contentious issue in those days. All in all, many of the major regions of this country had been covered, to some extent at least, and the London monopoly effectively challenged.

Curiously, a similar discourse was being enacted in New York's 'loft jazz', a scene that was contemporaneous with that discussed in these pages: "No single group succeeded in creating a long-term musicians' coalition – though several tried…the decentralised nature of loft practices found many musicians following similar paths, but often without the need for close coordination of these activities or overt articulation of guiding philosophies…instead, communities arose in various guises that played out, in a multitude of discussions, a central yet contested aspect of the period's significance." (Heller, 2017, pp.125-6.)

How long the model of the two Associations lasted into the 80s is not clear, but Will Menter states that: "There were several small tours for a couple of years, but it was pretty precarious administratively and financially." (Personal communication, December 2016.)

This will come as no surprise to readers who have read this far. The practical difficulties involved in communication between the various collectives would also have been considerable, in those pre-internet days, with a reliance on 'snail mail'. Mobile phones, of course, were unknown at the time, and many people did not even have ready access to land lines. However, Ian Menter was able to make this reflection, writing in July 1980: "It's hard to remember the depth of cultural isolation our founding members felt five or six years ago, and hard to imagine the effects of having no-one to talk to about the music, let alone anyone to play with." (Bristol Musicians Cooperative magazine, 1980, Issue 3, p.2.)

I will leave the last words of this chapter to Dave Panton (*op. cit.*), who expressed an appropriate note of caution to accompany the celebration of the undoubted achievements that had been made by the end of the 1970s: "So by 1979 it seemed that free improvisation was as much a part of local provincial scenes as it had become in London and there were established links between them all, even though audiences were still relatively small. But the future did not bode well, a less generous attitude towards the arts was just around the corner as the Thatcher era moved government towards the right."

CHAPTER 8

Musics: 'An Impromental Experivisation Arts Magazine'
The 'Little Life' of the Free Improv Journal

Or, to stretch the metaphor to breaking point, a Temporary Autonomous 'Zine?

Musics was nothing if not autonomous, as it featured no advertising, this being a point of principle from its inception. The magazine would not accept paid advertising or grant aid, hoping that the money would come from Subscriptions (£1.80 a year at the start, £2.80 by the end, four and a half years later). It was hoped that the major retailers would prove to be 'alternative' bookshops such as the much missed Compendium, based in Camden Town, record shops (of which there were so many then) and various music venues/gigs.

Musics was the uber fanzine for this particular brand of music, and it preceded the most famous 'zine of all, *Sniffin' Glue*, by two years. In fact, a recent arts music magazine emerging from the Saatchi Gallery, called *Art & Music*, had this to say in its Autumn 2016 editorial: "It's not too much of a stretch to conclude that, without spiritual *samizdat* rags like *Sniffin' Glue*, several generations of independent-minded cultural magazines, including this one you're holding in your hands, might never have found a reason to exist."

Ignoring the pungent disingenuousness, presumably unintentional, of *Art & Music* being produced under the aegis of a powerful multi-millionaire businessman and Tory magus, whose 'independent mindedness' might therefore be questioned, I would have thought that *Musics* should have been put forward as the true '*samizdat* rag' of that era, formed as it was at least a year before Mark Perry's "stapled-together, photocopied organ". (*Art & Music, op. cit.*)

This chapter can be read as a sort of 'Best of *Musics*', as I have rummaged through all 23 editions so that you, the reader, don't have to bother (unless you want to, of course, which you should). *Musics* was a 'little life', as John Stevens once described free improv, with its own micro-climate and, once I'd finished reading the whole lot I felt an immediate sense of loss, a bit like the feeling one gets at the end of a holiday before having to return to the daily grind, or reaching the end of a weighty Victorian novel.

Some names constantly recur throughout a reading of the *Musics* collection, which can help orientate the reader to the environment, a factor that not everyone entirely approved of – David Toop, Steve Beresford, Richard Leigh, Paul Burwell, Peter Riley, Annabel Nicolson were just a few of these. I also remained aware of Clive Bell's warning, in his LMC history, that missing out a person's name from the annals could gain one instant disfavour in the 'little world', as can happen in 'little worlds' in general.

A trawl through *Musics* is one through the politics and operations of the years concerned, in both free improv and allied topics. Covering the print run from edition to edition, as I have done here, may seem overly schematic, but it does provide an alternative history of the period under examination, and of the various convergences, divergences and affinities within the scene itself, which are reified clearly in these pages and which, for the historian, provide compelling reading. Derek Bailey, who was *not* one of the regular contributors, was typically acerbic, and rather sour, about the magazine: "Something that four years of *Musics* has taught us (is it only four – seems like 400?), is that the whole business of improvisers writing about improvisation very quickly leads to delusions of grandeur, a complete disregard for any observable truth and galloping aesthetic debility. Whatever happened to the 'I just play man', man?"

(*Musics* 21, March 1979, p.12.)

This is perhaps a tad rich from an improviser who, only a few years later, felt it incumbent upon himself to write a whole book on the subject, and very much implied that it isn't merely a case of 'just playing' (or even just a case of leaving the music unrecorded or undocumented).

David Toop was, and still is, at the forefront of the troupe of writers/ musicians that Bailey was so sniffy about. Here, in one of *Musics*' putative successors, *Resonance* (Vol.8, No.2), is Toop's description of the 70s 'Rag Tag Army', a term that was originally meant to apply to the LMC, but was equally applicable to its literary cousin (Toop being a founder-member of both): "The membership [of the LMC] certainly offered a generous slice of late 1970s bohemia and activism: anarchist and feminist politics, collectivism stringently opposed to entrepreneurism, wannabe entrepreneurs, performance artists, academics, drunks, interested media persons, trained musicians and unashamed incompetents, drifters and lost souls, the famous, the infamous and the terminally obscure." (Page 15.)

But before all this was *Microphone*, the written voice of Gen One throughout 1972. After *Musics* had run its course, there emerged *Resonance* (from September 1992 through to 2005), *Avant* (1997-2002) and, most resilient of all, *Wire*, which has developed a self-preserving polymorphous editorial approach. *Wire* is the lone survivor, but it features both advertisements and non-avant music (in my view), which is fine, but a long way from its original self-remit (in 1982, as a then quarterly), which was to cover both Free Jazz and Free Improvisation, as well as more 'mainstream' jazz. I have always been a fan of *Wire* and, as a long-term subscriber, have seen it shape-shift several times over the past 30 or so years, but perhaps it *is* a distant

Microphone issues 1-7

cousin of *Musics*, but several times removed. One can, after all, still get a great deal of information about playing dates (even if many of them are outside the UK) and occasional interviews with British free musicians in the pages of *Wire*, but probably never again will we see a publication so single-heartedly devoted to *English* Free Improvisation as *Musics*.

We have mentioned *Microphone* earlier, which essentially only consisted of six editions and a stillborn seventh (of which only the front and back cover, and an insert letter, ever saw the light of day). This last 'edition', sadly, seemed all ready to devote itself to the ICES event, but the inserted letter, from editor Nigel Rollings, explained that their account was overdrawn by £40, which meant the end of the line, and which Rollins thought could "be attributed to advertising: the advertising *of Microphone* and advertising *in Microphone*", i.e. the money spent on advertising the product, and the concomitant lack of interest in advertising in it.

"It is surprising that promoters of avant garde music feel they can afford to miss the opportunity of reaching the sympathetic (even if small) audience which readers of *Microphone* potentially form, when it has been proven time and time again that advertising to the general public fails to attract large audiences." (Rollings, *op. cit.)*

Rollings also made it clear that there *was* significant interest in the music outside London as the circulation figures, such as they were, indicated. However, to be fair to the 'general public', *Microphone*, which cost seven pence from their pockets, was a stapled together, small (the biggest edition, No.5, was 12 pages, the first was only four) *samizdat* and looked like a punk fanzine five years before the main event. Glossy presentation is clearly one of the reasons that *Wire* has such longevity, but both *Microphone* and *Musics* suffered greatly in this respect. Avant was much more *Wire*-like, as was *Resonance*, glossy covers and all, but even they eventually went under, the former having had a similar lifespan to *Musics*. It is hence very impressive that *Musics* lasted as long as it did, considering its refusal to pursue advertising revenue. As a DIY product, it far exceeded the achievements of any of the more celebrated punk productions, especially when one considers the internal tensions that manifested themselves throughout the project.

Another perhaps 'tilting at windmills' production was *Anthems*, which came out of Stoke-on-Trent – a regional centre that we have heard something about earlier. *Anthems* was envisioned as a "non-metropolitan quarterly alternative to *Musics*" (Bristol Musicians Cooperative, 1979, p.12), but, in the end, only one full issue was published, and also an 'obituary issue' (No.1a) that was appended to Stoke's general arts magazine, *Start*, which apparently gave some space to free improv.

It is not clear who wrote the description of *Musics* for its Wikipedia page, which is, as is usual with Wiki, useful up to a point, but their description of its expiration somehow reflects the latent forces that always underlay the manifest content of the magazine: "Tensions and unresolved contradictions accumulated, and eventually a small faction formed within the collective and soon undemocratically added to the front cover of issue No.23 the words FINAL ISSUE."

It needs to be stated, at this point, that Richard Leigh, who was an integral part of the magazine from start to finish, completely disagrees with the content of the above quote and states that he does not recall these 'tensions', ascribing the magazine's demise to lack of funding rather than internal conflicts between its members, and that all were in agreement as to its cessation.

Archetypes of betrayal are at work here, expulsions from the Garden of Eden, etc., and I suspect that the author of the Wiki page (Leigh suspects that it *may* have been Barry Truax, a Canadian academic and writer who explores theories of sound acoustics) *may* have had his own agenda here. Leigh does admit that this is pure surmise, however. For those that haven't seen it, i.e. almost everyone, the *Musics* 23 cover has a very striking black-and-white portrayal of a spinning planet (ours, one is to presume) with objects, cars, boats, animals, people, being centrifugally spun off by its rotational force, somewhat like Cornelia Parker's famous 'exploding shed' installation, *Cold Dark Matter: An Exploded View*, which conveyed a similar sense of kinetic discharge. In the bottom left-hand corner, the words FINAL ISSUE appear, in bold. It is still not clear by whom, and how, this 'explosive' tag was put in, but what is clear is that the magazine went out with a bit of a whimper, whatever the final cover suggests.

Steve Beresford describes both a convergence and an affinity between *Musics* and the LMC, co-located as they eventually became, and sharing many of the same human and environmental resources. He identifies typical group behaviour and attitude that some 'fringe' artists and stakeholders can exhibit: "I was one of the founder members of *Musics* magazine and we started the Musicians Collective, which was after the Musicians Cooperative folded. But we had much more kind of liberationist ideas and we let anyone in [which the Co-op didn't, one had to be invited to join, *author*], we didn't really realise that a lot of people that get attracted to those types of organisations are in there because of the organisation not because of the music, know what I mean? They like having meetings basically, and endless ideological discussions which never get anywhere. It never really did what I wanted it to do, which was bring people together and sell the music, to reach out and convince people that this music was fun. [A self-imposed impossible task? *author.*] How are you going to convince the public that it's fun if the musicians don't even have a good time playing it? You wonder, well, why are they playing? They're not getting paid. I always thought it was fun." (Beresford, interviewed by Richard Scott, 1991, *op. cit.*)

What Beresford is essentially describing is the defensive, 'fight or flight' mechanisms that groups and their members can display, a tendency to focus on 'internal enemies' rather than external (just like the Labour Party is doing at this current time). This can manifest as passive-aggressive nit-picking and hair-splitting, sometimes taken to absurd lengths, as portrayed so perceptively in Monty Python's *Life of Brian* as 'The People's Front of Judea' versus the 'Judean People's Front', with both parties arguing vociferously about what is fundamentally a convergent view of events.

As we shall see, there can be both financial and philosophical divergences subsequent to the setting up of genuinely autonomous projects, which are unsupported by revenue from adverts or from publishing houses. *Musics* was a labour of love by those who created it but, over time, splits gradually crept in, some more serious than others, which are real dangers in collectives, as will become evident: the Steve Lake/Val Wilmer debate; Phil Wachsmann's criticisms of a Richard Leigh review; hostility to the perceived dominance of Toop and Beresford; the 'Evan versus Steve' 'conflict' described by Charles Noyer in Issue 20; Annabel Nicolson's attack on Jak Kilby, etc., etc. Read on and all will be revealed. Or at least outlined.

Wiki-person describes *Musics* as "arguably the most significant music publication of the 70s". A tall claim when one considers the opposition, at this time, when the counterculture was, arguably, at its most outspoken, self-empowered and creative. However, its perceived importance was validated when Café Oto held an evening to celebrate the magazine in July 2016, an event curated by Thurston Moore, formerly of New York avant rock improvisers Sonic Youth. Furthermore, Moore's Ecstatic Peace imprint has released a facsimile edition of all the *Musics* in one (admittedly very bulky) book, which has been available in selective shops since September 2016, for those of you interested enough to take the plunge into full *Musics* immersion. It's not cheap, mind you (just short of a hundred quid), but it does offer, as David Toop says in the Foreword, "a social history of the era, as reflected through improvised music and associated activities", and is an invaluable investment for those who are sufficiently interested in the subject and the times.

MUSICS BEGINNINGS

It was, ultimately, an incestuous scene, as so many 'scenes' can be, however separate *Musics* and the LMC claimed to be. *Musics* did convene and arrange the inaugural meeting of the nascent LMC, and many of the same individuals were involved, including Beresford and Toop (as is to be expected), Burwell (who featured in the first and the very last edition of the magazine), Evan Parker, Richard Leigh and John Russell, all of whom loyally wrote and reviewed across all 23 editions.

Musics resulted from a telephone conversation between Evan Parker and the Davidsons, Martin and Madelaine, "in which we bemoaned the lack of publicity and finance given to the amazing London scene" (Davidson, personal communication, 2016), sometime in late 1974/early

1975. Madelaine claims that the idea originated from her, as she had a background as a journalist and production sub. Ironically, the Davidsons left the country after the first couple of editions, to try their hand(s) in America. The name was suggested, and accepted by all, by Paul Burwell at the first tentative meeting *chez* Davidson, and Burwell proved to be a significant driving force in the forthcoming years, making a huge contribution to the magazine's content and layout.

Burwell (d.2007) is another figure in danger of being forgotten by history, but he was a vital force in those days, and beyond. Best known for his 80s Bow Gamelan Ensemble, the name of which is self-explanatory (but remembering that Bow stands for the east London area rather than the horsehair rod used in the *arco* playing of string instruments!), he became known for his outdoor performances, of considerable scale, with his monstrous junk-sculpture percussive constructs. This was a logical outcome of the more hypertrophied kits assembled by the likes of Terry Day (for whom the building of the kit was an important part of the 'act'), Paul Lytton, Frank Perry, Jamie Muir and Tony Oxley. These large kits were not the same as those played by rock bombasts like Carl Palmer of Emerson, Lake and Palmer, but 'extended' kits, parts of which were arrayed on the floor, making the percussionist abandon the customary position behind and protected by the kit, and come to the front of the stage, both exposing him to closer scrutiny and humanising his contribution. I will never forget Japanese improviser Keiji Heino's solo percussion set at the LMC Festival of 1995, at the Conway Hall, with the entire stage, including the boards themselves, acting as one of the many sources for his incantatory explorations. As can be seen in the Alterations photograph used in this very book, Heino was not the only one to adopt this methodology of multiple sound sourcing.

The *Musics* Editorial Board was: the Davidsons, Beresford, Max Boucher, Burwell, Colin Wood, Parker, Bailey (however, very little was heard from him thereafter in the pages of the magazine, preoccupied, as he presumably was, with Company), Peter Cusack, Hugh Davies, Richard Leigh, John Russell, David Toop and Phil Wachsmann. The magazine came out bi-monthly and represented the *broad* interests of both Gen

One and Gen Two. Over time, what became one of the most interesting, and telling, part of the magazine was the Letters section, where many of the conflicts of the time were acted out, as we shall see. The gradual development of the regional collectives, described in the last chapter, is also a running theme for us archivists to tease out, and this was closely documented in its pages.

Another feature to point out is the generally poor quality of the photos featured, which is not a criticism of those taking them, but an aspect of the DIY 'amateurism' that the publication may have been accused of. Economics played their part, inevitably, in terms of reproduction quality. This issue was highlighted by the Annabel Nicolson/Jak Kilby discord (Issue 17), which will be described later, when the very role of the lens person was questioned.

23 OF THE BEST, THE STORY OF THE TIMES THROUGH MUSICS (APRIL 1975 – NOVEMBER 1979)

Twenty Three is a significant number in my musical universe, being part of the name of one of my favourite bands of the time, 23 Skidoo, and also of an obscure new wave group called 23 Jewels (featuring a young Clive Gregson), who briefly caught my attention at the time (short-spanned as my attention was). Proving? Absolutely nothing, I'm afraid, but I quite like obscure digressive linkages, so I beg your indulgence at this point for a few moments. Current 93 are another minor obsession, from slightly later on, named after a notional magick 'current' posited by Aleister Crowley, who served as a poster boy for both the hippie (in the 60s) and 'industrial' (80s) underground cultures. Not forgetting Alfred 23 (being the number of saxophones he owned) Harth, the reeds player for Just Music, a German free improv band of the time (who, coincidently, have the honour of being the second ECM vinyl release, after pianist Mal Waldron on ECM 1001), and who went on to forge a modest solo career. To finish off this unlikely conceit with a *reductio ad absurdum*, there was even an obscure band called 23rd Turnoff (which is a junction off the M6, towards Liverpool, just to demystify the name), who released a hugely collectable (and very interesting) single in 1967 called *Michaelangelo*, before disappearing in a puff of psychedelic smoke and emerging in a Nuggets-style Valhalla afterlife of freakbeat obscurities. 23 Skidoo were certainly the type of band who *Musics* would probably have appreciated, had the magazine survived a few years longer, ethno-musicological poly-stylists that they were.

So, back on track, the retail cost of *Musics* was initially 30 pence, going up to 35 pence in October 1977 (Issue 14) and up to 45 pence (Issue 21) in March 1979, so it went up by 50 per cent in just over four years, which sounds par for the course. A contemporary price, for example, is the 1976 cost of the weekly *NME* – 15 pence – so *Musics* was around twice the price. But, for a specialist bi-monthly, this surely wasn't excessive? At least in those days, wages for those working in the public sector went up at the same time (*far* too much as far as the establishment was concerned, a situation which it set itself to address in the following decade and beyond).

Issue 1 (April/May 1975)

The masthead was worthy and ambitious, as was the bold, bright red description at the bottom of the front page: **"A magazine for new ideas and developments in music, performance and related arts. This forum presents new ways of regarding sound and communication and their changing social and cultural context."**

Musics issues 1-6

So, among other things, it was an early warning of the cultural studies storm about to break? And, it was something in the nature of David Toop's ambitious 'Music/Context' of three years later, perhaps?

The first edition was produced on a Gestetner printer, with stencils typed by Madelaine Davidson, and articles "mainly written by musicians, who also assembled it by running around our kitchen table". (Davidson, *op. cit.*) Derek Bailey's *caveats* regarding musician/writers can be reintroduced here, if one wishes, but it is an arresting image, that of these dedicated improvisers scurrying round a domestic kitchen table (what role did the kitchen sink have?), intent on producing a cottage industry product of significance.

Theirs was a broad, sprawling remit, trying to do several things at once, which soon became evident over the next few issues. The neological subtitle of the first two editions, "an impromental experivisation arts magazine", suggested an underlying confusion. Who were the target audience? What did they listen to? What were the 'related arts'? *The Face* magazine, to take but one example (from the early 80s), was a new production that immediately and successfully found an eager audience (among whom were readers disgruntled with the *NME*'s po-faced approach to rock/pop culture, with all the 'fun' rinsed out): but what sort of audience was *Musics* aimed at?

Musics 1 featured a very exhaustive piece by Paul Burwell on 'Music Writing', which, with any luck, Derek Bailey eventually found time to read and that might have counteracted his rather jaundiced views on musician journalists. Burwell also contributed two conceptual pages (p.8 & p.25) on 'boxes', potentially a provocative topic given many musicians' fears of being typecast or compartmentalised.

The piece on page 8 seemed to be some sort of statement of intent, although it can, unfortunately, come across as a statement of crypto-racialist patronisation and inverse class snobbery: "Jazz is mainly a geographical term – it means Afro-American group instrumental post-improvised music, and its long-standing association with the entertainment industry should be at least as alienating to us as O.E.M.'s [Old European Music, i.e. "a staple secondhand product of middle class culture" (p.3) *author*] association with aristocratic and bourgeois social structures." (Page 7.)

If Burwell is making prescient comments about neo-conservatism (which I doubt, it being too early for this, I would have thought), this isn't made clear. Otherwise, it doesn't really make any sense. Why should we find popular/"middle class culture" musical product alienating, necessarily (unless, perhaps, one has a problem with one's parental record collections)? And what, exactly, is 'post-improvisation'? I'm afraid that I have recently started to distrust 'post-' anything memes, partly because of the inverted comma deluge that has ensued from this notion, and which has been recently reduced to the bizarre idea of 'post-truth' (an example of my point exactly), whatever that means (lies, basically), that modern political figures such as Donald Trump, Nigel Farage and Boris Johnson are supposed to be adept at. Most free improvisation musicians and their audiences appear to be white, middle-class, and male (beards are now optional), but Burwell's comment appears to be partly a pontification about black musicians 'selling out' (if I'm reading it correctly) to so-called 'bourgeois structures', i.e. those that might be able to ensure them a decent standard of living. Is it any wonder that so few black musicians and listeners were interested in the music, if this is the sort of criticism they were supposed to put up with?

Under 'Special Events' we come across, on the very last page, an advert for 'Eleven Improvising Musicians', which was to be the first major concert for most of these mainly second generation players, at the Wigmore Hall, one of the signal events of the decade for the music, and another convenient historical caesura (May 2nd 1975) between Gens One and Two. It is noteworthy that the term 'second generation' was already being used, even at this relatively early stage.

Issue 2 (June/July 1975)

This edition featured a piece by Clive Bell on the *shakuhachi*, a Japanese bamboo flute, which was a hint of the sort of ethno-musicological pieces that the magazine would specialise in, with regards to exotic musical instruments from all corners of the globe and which, from then on, gradually began appearing on stages and record players near you. David Toop had already become, by then, a considerable bamboo flute pin-up boy, as had Terry Day.

Jack Cooke's review of *Face To Face* by the Stevens/Watts SME discussed the proliferation of duo recordings (as we have previously noted) in recent jazz-related recordings, and in free improv in particular:

"It now seems to be the basic format for expressing new ideas. And, indeed, once you discard traditional instrumental roles and role-relationships… the duo principle…begins to come somewhere near the ideal experimental improvisational set-up." (Page 30.)

The duo format began to increasingly fascinate Derek Bailey around this time, Evan Parker was playing extensively with Paul Lytton in their particular dyad, AMM were down to two, so were the SME and, over the next few decades, so were musicians as influential as Cecil Taylor, whose towering set of live recordings on FMP, from 1988, featured five drum/piano duos out of the total 11 recordings (one of which was a duo with Bailey himself). Both Bailey and Taylor seemed to feel an especial affinity with drummers. Cooke clearly sensed this interest very early on.

Issue 3 (August/September 1975)

This issue features the Menter brothers' article on the Bristol scene and Ian Brighton's piece on the AMO. One noticeable feature of *Musics* generally, was its increasing coverage of free improvisation across the country and this continued throughout its lifespan, starting in this edition. The "Impromental…" masthead was left out from this issue onwards, for some reason.

According to Steve Beresford, around the time that the LMC was forming in 1975 there was a large meeting in West Square, London SE1, which featured Saturday improv workshops at the time: "I remember Trevor Wishart saying he hated this London colonialism, how come we were doing everything from London. He said we've got to have a National Musicians Collective…Then the NMC was formed and didn't happen, obviously. And Trevor Wishart moved to Australia anyway." (*Resonance*, Vol.8, No.2, p.24.)

We have seen, in Chapter Seven, how this proposed mega-collective ultimately didn't really take off, although a preliminary meeting did occur in Birmingham the following year. The extra-London scene continued to quietly develop, however. In fact, Wishart returned to England by 1977, when he was instrumental, with Dick Witts, in setting up the Manchester Musicians Collective.

Issue 4 (October/November 1975)

This kicks off with a (very) long letter from Evan Parker, which is an article in itself. In fact, in many instances, the letters section of the magazine often proved to be the most entertaining and spiky section of all. Parker was here questioning the Arts Council's Contemporary Music Network (CMN), set up in counterpoint to the Musicians Cooperative "in order to compensate for the conservative tastes of regional arts associations". (Page 3.) In fact, a few editions later (*Musics* 6), it was noted that very few applications had been received for CMN grants. (Page 26.) Parker went on to make negative comparisons with the support systems available for applicants in West Germany, and to praise the work being done in Bristol by the Menters *et al*, which had been described in the previous issue.

I am reminded here, on a macro-level, of the forcing of Radio One onto the public's ear in 1967, a (successful) attempt to destroy the pirate radios. Once they had the public's ear, however, they weren't quite sure what to do with it. Many creative musicians were put off by the corporate shtick of the new station, hence the development of a self-conscious 'underground' scene, which wanted nothing to do with Auntie's portrayal of youth culture. Tellingly, *Wire* still calls the subject of its 2016 Xmas/New Year overview 'underground music', so the appellation appears to have stuck (whereas 'progressive' appears to have become mothballed).

On page 25, David Toop reviewed two future dub reggae classics, *Pick-a-Dub* by Keith Hudson, and *Ital Dub* by Augustus Pablo, which coincidently happened to be two of the earliest dub releases that this author had heard, at around the same time. Toop describes it as 'classical music' and, although people at the time (including this author) were somewhat baffled by the dub sound, he was soon proved correct in his estimation. The 'classical' trope was emerging strongly, even in this most rarified (at the time) of sub-genres.

Issue 5 (December 1975/January 1976)

This issue was mainly notable for a seven-page interview with Victor Schonfield, by Richard Leigh. In it, Schonfield, a very important early promoter of free music, explains his growing disaffection with the music. His Music Now organisation, started in 1968, had enabled tours from contemporary composers like John Cage and David Tudor to take place, and he had previously set up first-time gigs in this country by Ornette Coleman in 1965 and Sun Ra in 1970. He, too, had little good to say about the Arts Council, going as far as to call them "a bunch of shits" (page 5), despite having been in receipt of several grants, admittedly small, from them. That particular period he felt was "what the history books euphemistically call 'a period of consolidation'". I still see him at gigs in the here-and-now, though, so presumably his interest hasn't been completely extinguished.

Issue 6 (February/March 1976)

The first article was by Hugh Davies, the instrument builder, who gave us 'A Simple Ring Modulator' – a very detailed overview for those of us puzzled by Carla Bley's *Escalator over the Hill*, which was full of these devices. The article did, however, resemble an essay from *Practical Electronics for Beginners*, complete with circuit diagrams, which was a bit too much like O-Level Physics (at which I achieved a feeble Grade 5) for my humanistic tastes.

Pages 12-13 contained Peter Riley's rather prolix review of the era-defining *Teatime*, which posited a connection between the Gens One and Two improvisers: "It doesn't seem to be happening anywhere elsewhere: Germany, Holland, the banners are all flapping in the oily mud because no one is taking them up, and this could also be a sign of the virtual strength of our first generationers [sic], that they not only got there but got there first in such a way as to entail hope beyond their own ranges, so that their music leads us into an open universe because it has insisted on *revolutionary continuity.*" (Page 12, author's italics.)

Two influential, obscure (!), Obscure Records releases are also reviewed: David Toop/Max Eastley's *New and Rediscovered Musical Instruments*, which was a tie-in with Toop's book of the same name (Obscure 4), and Brian Eno's *Discreet Music* (Obscure 3), his earliest foray into ambient music, a style which, ironically, Toop and so many others would eventually be categorised under. *Musics* was certainly, in retrospect, identifying some of the most innovative records of the time for review.

A full account of the meeting of nine improvising musicians and three Arts Council members was featured, which proved very salient given the criticisms expressed by both Parker and Schonfield earlier. (John Cruft, the Arts Council Musical Director, had written a full, articulate, response to Parker in *Musics* 5, page 3.)

Page 28 contains a priceless statement by Colin Wood re: the above meeting. Now, I know that it is neither big nor clever to chide the actions of well-meaning people some 40-odd years ago, but I do feel that Wood's statement sums up some of the binary and dichotomous, or even just blurry, thinking that was at work at the time: "I include two versions [of the meeting] since my aim was to find a text agreed by all present, the musicians approved mine, which I then took to the Arts Council for corrections. They replied with their own version, which, while written in better English than mine, was not approved by musicians. To end this to-ing and fro-ing, here are both. The meeting is long past but issues covered by it cannot be dropped for that reason."

Wood had clearly not taken to heart the expression, "You can't please all the people all the time".

This is not the only occasion that I have quoted comments that now seem naïve or outdated, I'm afraid. They do, however, give us, from this safe vantage point in time, some idea as to why communication might have proved difficult between the various stakeholders involved in this music.

Issue 7 (April/May 1976)

Almost like 'breaking the fourth wall' in theatre, this edition's editorial decided to reveal its inner workings to the punters (an act that was, in itself, *very* 1977): "We all contributed £4 each to

Musics issues 7-12

provide the initial funds. Each issue costs around £85 for paper, plates, ink, stamps, etc. If there is more money available, we increase the print run (currently 800). The magazine is distributed to subscribers (about 100) through sympathetic bookshops, record shops, art centres and music places, and personal sales by the people involved with the magazine and their friends and contacts." (Page 2.)

Punk largely took the credit for this sort of demystification of the means of production but, as Steve Beresford has said, punk was a-historical in its Year Zero ideology. Although the likes of the Desperate Bicycles ("it was cheap, it was easy, now go and do it") and Scritti Politti (on the sleeves of their three early 45s/EPs in the late 70s) broke down their costs to demonstrate how it could be achieved, it had all been done before by *Musics*. The parlous position that *Musics* (and the LMC) were constantly in was hence a recurrent feature, and was worn almost as a badge of straight-talking transparency.

One of the most enjoyable aspects of a close reading of *Musics* is the small print. On page 30, tucked away in the bottom right-hand corner, is a small plea from Geoff Atkinson of Cleveland: "I've failed to find anyone else in the Cleveland area interested in free/improvised music. I wonder if you have some tiny space free you could insert a small blurb to the effect that anyone interested in the Cleveland area can contact me on Redcar 3336."

So, the improvisers in places like Redditch and Saffron Walden need not despair!

Otherwise, this was a 'Dutch Issue', from an idea by Peter Cusack, and need not detain us further, except to reflect on how genuinely international the scene was now becoming. Also, looking at the 'events' section, one is struck by how many Bristol gigs were advertised (five out of the total 15, to be exact), which shows how determined (and publicity savvy) the BMC had quickly become.

Page seven featured the Cracklebox Project, an instrument already discussed in these pages, written by the instrument's inventor, Michel Waiswicz. (Page 7.)

Issue 8 (July 1976)

On pages 29-31, there was a reprint of an antediluvian treatise by a C.J. Hyne ("author of *Sport Extraordinary*, etc", whatever that may have been), which appears to have been sourced from some font of colonial beneficence, beginning as it does with, "Many scores of years ago, a negro, who with his wife and family lived in the savage solitude of an African forest," and which eventually mutates into the praxis of "How to Build a Banjo". According to Richard Leigh, this originated from a jokey idea of John Russell. Today, it reads like a dodgy, miscalculated, PoMo prank.

This could be a rich source of Cultural Studies essays, I'm sure, and it's hard to say how to take this sort of thing in relation to any other magazine than *Musics*, where I'm sure it proved inspirational to the generation who would ultimately accept Harry Smith as their avatar. Here, in embryo, is the John Fahey's entire Revenant Records label mission, which was hot-wired by the reissue of Smith's *Anthology of American Folk Music*, as six CDs, in 1997. This was the equivalent of the Smithsonian jazz compilation of around 24 years earlier (1973), and it is very pleasing for me (as a numbers freak) to note the 23 motif again, as this is the number of years that separated the original Smith compilation (1952) from the first edition of *Musics* (1975).

Smith anthologised late 20s/early 30s blues and folk recordings (of staggering rarity, and hence further encouraging a whole industry of monumentally obsessive 78 shellac collectors). Read Amanda Petrusich's *Do Not Sell at Any Price* (2014), which will tell you all you need to know about near-psychotic 'collectors' of these aboriginal recordings, and who cartoonist Robert Crumb also so memorably and affectionately portrayed in his cartoons, which were also a sly dig at preoccupations which he very much shared. (Crumb, 2004; Crumb, 2008.)

Basically, this whole tranche of *faux* 'revivalism' could be said to have begun with these sorts of preoccupations. But what is also noteworthy is the Edwardiana of the Hyne article itself, which was surely more a reflection of post-hippie affectations than of pre-punk signatures?

Or maybe it was merely encouraging people to do it themselves, as apparently easy as constructing a ring modulator, playing the *shakuhachi* or operating a Cracklebox? After all, this was the age of DIY, according to the populist furore that followed Bill Grundy's 'interview' with the Sex Pistols on December 1st 1976. After which punk went viral, going on to produce some spectacular music, and gave practical examples of self-validation to so many people over time, up to and including, I hope, this self-published author. Those with long enough memories will remember how the DIY craze also even manifested in the domestic sphere of home and hearth, with DIY warehouses springing up everywhere, and (mostly male) would-be carpenters and plumbers spending their weekends self-improving their immediate living environments, with predictably mixed results.

Issue 9 (September 1976)

To be honest, not much of note in this edition. There was material, including some rather gross photos, about the Vienna Aktionists with their usual animal innards in tow, which my no doubt repressed tastes found both offensive and boring, including naked hippies with smeared beards (surely a horrid prospect in whatever modality?). 'Happy Entrails' perhaps? It looks like a precursor to the Bhagwan Rajneesh middle class hippie/yuppie unholy alliance, which was forming exactly around this time. (Milne, 1986.) Ho-hum and *euch* both.

Ultimately, this is perhaps the most boring *Musics* edition of all, imho.

Issue 10 (November 1976)

Pages 8-11 featured the history of the Stoke-on-Trent Free Music landscape, as alluded to in the previous chapter, with its telling headline of 'Good Morning Brick Wall'. Presumably this was a reference to the brick wall that surrounds the whole country in a Great Wall of China way, whenever and wherever free improvisation tries to 'get through' to people? Walls, nowadays, have received increased cultural currency thanks to Donald Trump's grandiosity, and they hence form a conceptual continuity, in however small a way, with the far-off days of Stoke improvisers.

On a more abstract tack, pages 16-22 concerned itself with 'What Happens to Time-Awareness During Improvisation', an experience that affects both players and the audience. A plethora of Gen One and Gen Two improvisers gave us their thoughts, from the erudite and lengthy (Phil Wachsmann and Simon Mayo) to minimalist contributions such as "Nothing, as far as I'm concerned," (Steve Beresford); "Time drags terribly, there must be more to life than improvisation," (Richard Leigh); "It passes," (Anthony Barnett) and "The ticks turn into tocks and the tocks turn into ticks," (Derek Bailey). Stand-up comedy had been robbed.

What I found probably to be the most interesting item in this edition was the 'Improgram' (these guys liked compound words, the first article in this edition was, for example, called 'Transcendprovisation'), which was a separate pull-out pod enclosed within the main mother ship, which told interested readers about forthcoming gigs in London for November 1976. This gives the historian a good idea of the venues of the time, then in operation. Most frequently cited was Action Space in Chenies Street, WC1; the Cockpit Theatre, NW8 (an LMC concert); Basement, Shelton Street, WC2; and, most poignantly, a Company duo of Bailey and Lacy at the Little Theatre Club then situated, very close to its original site, in 16-19 Upper St. Martins Lane. At that time it was known as the 'New' LTC (the final kiss-of-death, surely?), during its year-long tenancy, after which it was finally put to rest. Thus ended one of the holiest venues in the history of this music, in order to make way for the new Covent Garden that is now so beloved of tourists the world over.

The loss of both the LTC and the Unity Theatre (the two venues most associated with Gen One) made finding a new location to act as the centre of the music even more pressing. The discovery of the Gloucester Road premises, which became operational by February 1978, was a huge confidence booster. Before this, the HQ had perforce been at Battersea Arts Centre, where several important early events had been held.

It behoves me to describe, very briefly, because of their co-proximity and links to the LMC, the Film Makers Cooperative, which started in 1966, the *anus mirabilis* that saw the start of the Little Theatre Club, the SME and the Cardew-era AMM (all described in Barre, *op. cit.*). This Co-op ceased to exist in 1999, when it merged with London Video Arts to form Lux, one offshoot of which is still Hoxton Square's Lux

Cinema. Very much part of the London counter-culture, the Film Co-op was initially sited in Better Books at 94 Charing Cross Road (a key venue, which also featured live free improv), before moving to the Arts Lab in Drury Lane (a counter-cultural hotspot from the 60s also used, for a season, by the Cardew-era AMM). In 1971, the Co-op moved to an established squat at 13a Prince of Wales Crescent, Kentish Town, London NW5, before moving to Gloucester Avenue, which was its headquarters for most of the rest of its life before ending up at the Lux Centre in 1997, two years before the formal dissolution and merger.

Issue 11 (February 1977)

A rather pedestrian issue, but it does contain one very short note/communication from Evan Parker (page 26) that was a motivator for the Circadian Rhythm event in the following year, and that was stuck, obscurely, on one of the last pages (as was much of the most historically fascinating *detritus* in *Musics*): "I would like to thank Paul Burwell and David Toop for their long performance at Butlers Wharf. Their aims and achievements represent new benchmarks in the living music. They created another world and invited us in [another TAZ? *author*]. As a listener I was transported through the space they made, as a musician I learnt."

This was Rain in the Face, a mostly forgotten duo from this period of many duos.

Issue 12 (May 1977)

In the light of the Improgram LTC advert in Issue 10, it is especially galling to read the contents of a box inserted at the top right-hand corner of page 3: "SAVE THE LITTLE THEATRE SPACE: There will be a benefit for the Little Theatre, to be held at the Arts Theatre, Great Newport Street, London WC2 on Sunday May 22nd at 8pm…Donations are urgently needed…to Jean Pritchard [another forgotten female promoter, the woman who ran the LTC, *author*]…The theatre is closed at present but mail is being forwarded."

They should have had a larger and thicker black border around this announcement. The LTC had lasted for 11 years, a more than considerable achievement for this kind of endeavour and, if there is any justice, a blue plaque should be mounted on the wall of its original premises in Garrick Yard. As it should be on the site of the Unity Theatre, and at 42 Gloucester Avenue (both buildings unfortunately no longer exist). Oh well, one can but dream…

An LMC gig at Centerprise (yet another neologism) Bookshop, on February 11th, was covered by John Kieffer (page 26). This review made it sound like a later Company happening, teetering on the edge of chaos, but it does make one nostalgic for this sort of polymorphousness, which is somehow lacking in the current age, where such risk taking is mostly discouraged.

Issue 13 (August 1977)

The ever reliable letters section contains this observation from Richard Leigh: "The free music scene more and more resembles those mythical left wing organisations which vanish up their own factions. A degree of mutual respect, and articulation of what we have in common, might actually help the music, and I presume helping it is what *Musics* is for." (Page 3.)

Musics issues 13-18

Leigh signs off the letter "in a nasty mixture of sorrow and anger". This was a reflection of the problems that collectives, very much a product of their time, could create, especially with regard to leaders. Cooperatives had a clearer remit, i.e. to cooperate and work together towards a goal. Collectives were seemingly leaderless which, as anyone with some knowledge of group behaviour and dynamics knows, just doesn't work, and soon the collective mainly engages in 'anti-task' activities, as seems the case with the LMC. As Bell (*op. cit.*) acutely observed: "Open monthly meetings enabled the entire membership to participate in a lively criticism of any member who had actually done any work."

This was not active sabotage, I would surmise, but seems to have been unconscious large-group behaviour. The world famous Tavistock Clinic was just down the road from Gloucester Avenue, in Swiss Cottage, so it is a shame that the LMC didn't avail itself of their expertise in these matters. The Clinic runs a regular 'Consulting to Institutions Workshops', but these only began in 1980, sadly. (Obholzer & Roberts, *op. cit.*, p.xvi.) However, it is likely that the LMC wouldn't have been able to afford the consultancy fees, even if it had felt like having its unconscious group mind explored.

On page 5, there is another anthropo-musical piece, this time by Peter Riley, about a 'musical primitive' from the north of England called 'Neddy Dick' (1882-1926), who fashioned a row of stones laid out on a wooden frame, called a 'lithophone', and played it like a xylophone. This article is a fine feat of musical excavation that puts me in mind of (i) Harry Smith, John Fahey and Alan Lomax in America, and (ii) the free improvisers' new and reinvented instruments, some of which explored fire and water (as alluded to in Chapter Five) installations, as well as Annabel Nicolson's interest in the element of fire (the air element was presumably taken care of by the numerous reed and brass instruments?). The photo of Neddy himself could well have come from Smith's *Anthology*, timeless and mysterious, the 'old, weird England' to paraphrase Greil Marcus.

Meanwhile, back to 1977 and the Socialist Festival of Britain, which would have given Neddy Dick pause for thought, no doubt, and to which ten pages of this edition is devoted. There are contributions from many improvisers, but the one that stands out is from Cornelius Cardew, whose humourless Marxist polemic seems very much of its time. Cardew was sadly killed by a hit-and-run driver in 1981 (giving rise to several conspiracy theories, involving MI5, amongst other suspects, in its wake), so he was spared the revolution that did actually occur, i.e. the Thatcherite one.

Cardew criticises Rock against Racism (which he saw as a bourgeois Fifth Column within the labour movement, and a distraction from the class struggle as, of course, were supposedly secondary issues such as feminism and racism). 'The Clash Serve Imperialism', anyone? Johnny Rotten, the so-named 'spokesman' of Punk Rock, headed, according to Cardew, "a fascist cult associated with self-mutilation, exhibitionism and the glorification of decay and despair…virtually upheld as an example to the youth". Pretty spot on there, Corny, at least with regards to the superficial aspects of punk's reductionist attitudes, but otherwise entirely and spectacularly missing the point.

It is curious how Cardew echoes right-wing polemicists here – 'the youth', mentioned merely as a *lumpen* factor for 'the revolution', or as an inchoate force that must be controlled/contained, before it does any serious damage to the cause. Ironically, Rotten/Lydon never claimed to be a punk spokesman. (Just as Bob Dylan never claimed to be a spokesman for his generation.) Cardew's essentially ultra middle class elitism conveniently ignored the fact that punk was enjoyed and perpetuated (but *not* initiated) by the very working class youth that he claimed to be aiming to 'convert' to the notion of revolution.

It's very easy to mock these thoughts, many years on, but Cardew would probably turn in his grave if he could see how his old-fashioned image of the 'working class' had decayed, along with the industries that had fed and clothed it – coal, steel, shipbuilding – and how this class had voted for Margaret Thatcher and later, even more grievously, for David Cameron and George Osborne. Cardew's article reads like the death rattle of a particular way of thinking, managing to be unfortunately both pompous and self-righteous, especially in contrast to Will Menter's considered contribution to the debate (about the aims of the Festival) on page 13, on behalf of the 'village idiots' (Menter's phrase) outside London.

There is a piece on bio-acoustics (pp.24-7), e.g. seal and beaver sounds, which, before the inevitable trolls and mockers get going, has only increased as a credible sound-source. You heard it in *Musics* first (or at least, very early on), folks.

One Geoffrey Armstrong wrote a very stringent review of a March 17th LMC gig at the London Film Cooperative (page 29), in which he envisaged an end-day, a counter-factual of some power: "In a few years' time, there'll be nowhere to go to see the musicians who don't exist anymore, as they've become postmen or died or everyone will be complaining bitterly or nostalgically looking back at the 'good old days' of Albion Music at the Unity Theatre, the Film Co-op, etc."

Well, Mr. Armstrong was both right and wrong, and definitely rather presumptuous. Punk musicians as iconic as Vic Godard (Subway Sect) – postman – and Howard Devoto (Buzzcocks/Magazine) – librarian –both apparently happy in their occupations, offer a quotidian alternative to Armstrong's notional non-existence, of contentment in life post-'fame'. But Armstrong was certainly correct about the nostalgia industry – one of the many products of this being books like the one you are currently reading and, hopefully, enjoying.

Listeners could perhaps take a break here, to think about how improvisers make a buck outside of free improv practice (and unpaid rehearsal time), and what is the role of their (usually female) partners, which is almost certainly a significant one, and which involves them almost certainly in mundane work of some kind. There is probably a book to be written here, for anybody bold enough. "One thing that has remained constant is the virtual lack of money. John Stevens thought that this was a good thing, as it meant that people would only undertake this activity if they really wanted to, rather than as a way of getting rich." (Davidson, *op. cit.*)

The latter comment is an unintentionally ludicrous proposition, the idea of any serious financial secondary gain through this music, in this most precarious of careers (and most cynical of critical environments). Or maybe Stevens did have more noble aspirations….

Issue 14 (October 1977)

Now, I'm not the most qualified of cultural analysts and its signifiers, but the cover of *Musics* 14 does interest me.

But, first, I have to express my enjoyment, once again, of the letters page in this edition. A blunt contribution from Steve Beresford panning "the obsequious critic" Anthony Barnett, whose apotheosising of Leo Smith in *Musics* 13 truly potentiated Beresford's ire: "Leo Smith and George Lewis are good musicians who don't deserve deification: nobody does. The popularist [*sic*] idea of selling improvised music to people by dressing it up like a religious ceremony will eventually destroy the music." (Page 2.)

This was interesting, bearing in mind Beresford's experience in the Company Week just a few months before, but he needn't have worried – the music was neither popularised nor destroyed. *Catastrophisation* (my italics), however, was another regular defence mechanism regularly brought into play during this period, a dichotomous perspective that at times hindered more realistic assessments of the issues involved.

The irony here is, of course, that most of the public would never have heard of either Smith or Lewis, so the notion of them being populist is frankly preposterous in itself. It is interesting to note, however, the synchrony of Beresford's sentiments with those that punk supposedly espoused. 'No More Heroes' as The Stranglers said on their chart hit at around the exact same time (which proved to be punk's apogee) of this edition's publication.

The next sample is David Toop's response to a previous letter written by a correspondent called de Veres: "Any bone creaks that Mr. de Veres may have heard during my performance with Burwell at the Battersea Arts Centre must have been an accompaniment to the premature senility which he so perceptively singled out for attention." (Also on page 2.)

The attention to the micro-detail of sound from both punter and player is truly impressive.

The principal article of this edition is by the late Lindsay Cooper, the bassoonist, called "Women, Music, Feminism – notes", on pages 16-19. Cooper makes the observation that, in the recent Music for Socialism Festival essays that appeared in *Musics* 13, only three out of the 15 musician contributors were women, who were the most marginal group within this most marginalised of genres. The cover, ironic given the content of the article, features two men: one, who seems to be Steve Beresford, fellates an acoustic guitar *a la* Jimi Hendrix (a 'cock rock' cliché of the most stereotypical kind); the other, who I don't recognise, is standing by the sea, with a full beard, wearing a wet suit and carrying a deck chair. All fine and dandy, but perhaps a bit thoughtless, given the topic that the centrepiece concerns itself with, which also gets a major billing on the cover alongside our two blokes?

It could be said (certainly in my universe) that the 70s was the decade when feminism came into full blossom, in the guise of 'women's libbers' as they were, mostly scornfully, described by Joe Public, who tended to hate all the '-isms' that they blame the 60s for. The 60s were still really, in actuality, a wasteland for gender awareness (as graphically portrayed in the massively popular TV series *Mad Men*), but modern feminism began to find its feet around this time, and this was further actuated when radical feminists invaded the set of the 1970 Miss World (which my wife happened to have attended as a child, and that I witnessed on our own family TV). This came as a huge surprise to the average British household. Bob Hope, the *compere* of the event, memorably, and uncomfortably, blustered his way through the disturbance, and conservative opinion was both baffled and furious.

In her article, Lindsay Cooper, who had found a sort of fame with Henry Cow, the archetypical 'intellectual art rock' band, criticised the "sexist extremes of cock rock…a triumph for music's power to spread dominant and oppressive ideology in an easily marketable form". (Page 17.) A truism nowadays, but not so then, as the great hopes that many of us had for the popular music world after punk soon turned inexorably into 'business as usual'. This was, of course, well before the internet, and even before 'indie' embedded itself into rock music culture as an alternative attitudinal approach. Cooper pointed out that, "'Non-commercial' music constantly struggles against the monopoly control of record distribution and live performance, and therefore at least begins with a narrow and usually non working class and non female audience." (Page 18.) This was the situation that Cardew thought would lead to the proletarian revolt, but with the women (i.e. half of the former constituents) being conspicuous in their world historical absence (or, at the very least, taking a background role)?

Cooper described the practical and social restrictions that militated against female involvement in free improv: "Women are less likely to be in collective social situations where improvisation is possible…

'feminine' passivity and genuine powerlessness obviously inhibit the sort of confidence it takes to improvise." (Page 18.)

Which brings us to where women fit in the world of free improv, which is perhaps only a question a man would posit? Cooper quite rightly said: "To see some kinds of music as particularly 'male' is critically useful, but if carried too far can put women back where they started." (Page 19.) Or, as we would say in today's *argot,* 'back in their box'.

Issue 15 (December 1977)

One of the most interesting of all *Musics,* this one featured, on page 20, a review (by two female reviewers, by the way, as well as a photo by Val Wilmer, who also crops up later in this edition) of the first FIG live performance, arranged by Music for Socialism, at the Almost Free Theatre in London. The classic shot by Wilmer could easily have been of a post-punk band, with Liensol's lazy posture and Nicol's moody staring at the floor. This became an infamous gig, and the reviewers Susan Hemmings and Norma Pitfield describe well FIG's riposte to Cooper's stated concerns in *Musics* 14: "The insidious and generally held idea that women are biologically more emotionally chaotic than men was constantly hurled into the deliberately jumbled ears of the audience, where it exploded and shattered, one could vainly hope, forever." (Page 20.)

FIG's use of humour as a hammer may well be a point of distinction, as so many men are distinguished by their inability to effectively use such a weapon.

Moving on, page 3 contained an important piece of news: the obtaining of 42 Gloucester Avenue as an HQ for the LMC. On the same page were bulletins from the Manchester Musicians Collective, including "The Fall and other young punk groups", and the group "which improvises on tent poles, etc.," (one really wants to know what the 'etc' might have included), and the Bristol and Leeds Musicians Collectives. This was good news for the audience that lived outside London, and *Musics* consistently followed up on the extra-London narrative throughout its remaining issues.

The editors felt it necessary to tell us that "it should be made clear that *Musics* is not produced by either the London Musicians Collective or Music for Socialism – although members of the *Musics* group are involved with these organisations". (Page 2.) Confused? You have the right to be.

The entries on page 3 are among my favourites of the whole *Musics* series. They are DIY *in excelsis*. "We need someone with a little electrical knowledge to trace the lighting circuit and connect it with the mains." Sound squat-land principles at work here, the sharing of immediate resources, etc.? There are clear links to the 'improv lifestyle' of punk and post-punk, perhaps? "Some of the windows need to be sealed up with chipboard to exclude external noises from passing traffic and trains." (The venue abutted a major train line.) There were sections on this page about lighting, windows, heating, building, painting and cleaning, and there was much to be done. Unfortunately, the collective soon found out that their target audience seemed to be work-avoidant as well as impoverished, as we will soon see. "However, the space is COLD, so anyone with access to either temporary or permanent heating equipment (calor gas, studio heaters, etc.) is warmly [the latter word is an unintended irony, surely?, *author*] invited to get in touch." (Page 3.)

Pages 8-11 contained a disquisition on 'Echoes' – not the track that occupied the whole of the second side of *Meddle*, by Pink Floyd, from 1971, but of the acoustic phenomenon, by Michael Parsons, Hugh Davies and David Toop. *Apropos* of the emblematic *minutiae* that the magazine encouraged, is the letter/note that Martin Davidson sent in the next edition: "Your echo section omitted to mention the area of the Chislehurst Caves with a delay time of 30 seconds. I am sure someone could use it to make some interesting sounds." (Page 3, *Musics* 16.)

Equally obsessional/nerdy is my rejoinder to this communication, which was that the avant-rock Cleveland band Pere Ubu, in their first English tour, the 'UK Dance Party' of December '78, exactly one year later, did, in fact, play these very caves.

Pages 24-5 contained a piece on Pibroch, the classical bagpipe music of the Scottish Highlands, by Paul Burwell, who had the knack of writing on arcane topics in a knowledgeable, informative style.

The most controversial item in *Musics* 15 (pages 14-15) was, however, by future ECM label publicist-in-chief, and well regarded *Melody Maker* journalist of the time, Steve Lake. His acidic review of Val Wilmer's book *As Serious as Your Life*, about the African-American 60s Free Jazz musicians which, in time, quickly became a classic of Free Jazz literature, created a local shit storm, which reached out across issues 16, 17 and 18, and became somewhat of a *casus belli*. The very long assessment by Lake suggested that a reverse racism was at the heart of *As Serious as Your Life*, which he accused of giving scant credit to white pioneers such as Steve Lacy, Gary Peacock, Paul Bley and Charlie Haden, and other such iconoclasts. This book became in itself accordingly iconoclastic, and gradually began to be considered seminal, as did Frank Kofsky's earlier *Black Nationalism and the Revolution in Music*, which also received censure in Lake's piece. Lake's ire was particularly reserved for Wilmer's supposed fixation on black innovators of the 60s Free Jazz persuasion at the expense, as Lake saw it, of the white practitioner's contribution to the scene. This really gets to the heart of one of the most emotive of issues around this music, that of race. "In short, this work is not a history, but a fairly absurd piece of polemic." (Page 14.)

Without going into the heart of the matter, as it were, the concluding words will suffice to get across Lake's intent: "For me, it's a drag that a book as exclusivist and as separatist as *As Serious as Your Life* should be issued at a time when the natural inclination of improvisation-based musics is toward a kind of global consciousness. I thought we had progressed beyond the stage of hassling about who outsmarted whom." (Page 15.)

To finish, Lake provocatively stated: "Valerie Wilmer's blinkered arguments will serve only to erect more artificial barriers between the people who make the music and those who listen." (Page 15.)

These were arguments that inevitably touched upon white English free improvisers and their primary audience.

Issue 16 (February 1978)

This is the edition in which Bill Hutchins kicks off the letters pages by suggesting a re-launch as TOOPICS. (Page 3.)

It didn't take Val Wilmer long to respond to Lake's article, either, in an equally long missive on pages 6 and 7. It will come as no surprise that she disputes much of what Lake had to say, basically stating, for the record, that he, in actual fact, is the prejudiced one, ending the disquisition with the following barb: "Steve Lake will always be remembered by me as the man who, reviewing the 1974 Berliner Jazz Tage in the *Melody Maker*, described the veteran blues musician Robert Shaw as 'a gangling, wiry old *spade*'." (Author's italics.)

To be fair to Lake, that particular noun was still *au currant* at that time, being old *argot* from the Beat Era, which ageing white hipsters like Keith Richards still used (and continues to use), as well as his prehistoric fondness for the word 'chicks' as a catch-all for attractive young women. (I don't think it applied to women over the age of, say, 25.) A Rolling Stone was presumably above criticism, as regards anachronism.

On the next page (page 7), 'The Leveller' further puts the slipper in, by describing Lake's interest in the avant garde "as that of the *connoisseur/ dilettante*", presumably the worse insult that he/she could come up with at the time. "You…you…*dilettante*, you…!"

One of the most salient features, for the would-be historian, of the *Musics* letters page, was that it often consisted of arguments and counter-arguments between musicians themselves, and between them and journalists/writers, some of whom were also musicians. Thus the content of the pages consisted of a high degree of articulacy combined with a high degree of sensitivity to criticism. These dialogues, sometimes with other parties weighing in, made for some of the most entertaining (and *voyeuristic*) pieces in the whole output of the magazine.

The fact that Wilmer is both a woman and, furthermore, a feminist may have had a bearing: "Who else, apart from Lindsay Cooper writing in this magazine, has attempted to discuss the role that women have played in the world of creative music?" (Wilmer, *op. cit.*, p.6.)

Having reintroduced this topic, the 'events' columns on the back page of this edition seems to feature more female musicians than had been the norm up till then – for example the Company gig on February 17th featured Georgie Born and Cooper, alongside Terry Day and Bailey himself. Underneath the advert for a Benefit for Workers with Youth

Against Fascism at the North London Poly was this: "Women's Music Workshop at the Womens Art Alliance, 10 Cambridge Terrace Mews, off Chester Gate, off Albany Street, NWI. 9-11pm. 30p. Women only."

There was also an LMC concert: 'Improvisation with Lindsay Cooper and Friends' at Gloucester Avenue: "Women in Traditional Music" and "Women in Jazz", all part of the Workshop(s) described above. These were small steps, but indicated a sea change in attitude towards women in free improvisation.

Issue 17 (May 1978)

A rather paranoid editorial by Secretary (until June 4th) Paul Burwell starts this issue off on page 3, about how the LMC has been overlooked by the mainstream media: "There has been so much going on that one cannot help but feel that this is a deliberate policy."

The overlooking had apparently been committed by *Time Out*, *Melody Maker*, the *NME* and *Sounds*, but surely one of the points of setting up *Musics* in the first place was to act as a counterpoint to exactly these sorts of tastemakers, the sort that would inevitably sideline this sort of music? They, Burwell admits, "have carried information about the Collective's work, but one feels that, given the uniqueness of the venture, that the press could be more supportive and interested". I would have thought the uniqueness was one reason why the press fought shy of this type of venture? What did Burwell really expect these corporate organs to do, in the face of this deliberately anti-corporate project?

As if in support of the un-corporate, pages 8-11 covered "The Instruments or Spirit Cries played during Ommura Male Initiations (New Guinea)", three pages of ethno-musicology by Ragnar Johnson, an obdurately arcane bit of field research that would have been guaranteed to provoke the nay sayers but which, to true believers, represented one of the magazine's undoubted strong points. Sure enough, three years later, 23 Skidoo released their *The Gospel Comes to New Guinea* 12" single, 10.13 minutes of ethno-funk stew from the jungles of Kentish Town, no less, which was extremely lauded at the time.

Another node of controversy in these pages was provoked by Annabel Nicolson in her LMC review, on page 26, of a Toop/Burwell/Parker gig, a photo from which graces the front cover of this very book. Nicolson's coverage included a considerable dig at veteran photographer Jak Kilby, one of the few lensmen who covered the 60s free improv scene and has preserved, in his work, many timeless images from the first wave, and beyond, of this music. Nicolson, herself a photographer, seemed to believe that it was in her remit to excoriate Kilby because of his intrusive 'stage presence', to the point of actually photographing him at work *in vivo* with this trio, an 'intervention' that seems rather typical of the febrile atmosphere at number 42. Nicolson suggests a comparison to photographing in the wild, to boost her argument, with the 'affecting of natural behaviour' involved in filming animals. A mildly patronising reflection in itself, to say the least. Her piece does seem, at this distance, somewhat of a personal attack and is rather uncomfortable to read. Kilby told me that he approached all three musicians, who all knew him and his way of working, and who offered no opposition to his filming during their performance. "For someone in the audience [i.e. Nicolson herself, *author*] to attempt to deal directly with such a situation requires some rapid internal reasoning to justify threatening the performance further." (Nicolson, *Musics* 17, *op. cit.*, p.26.)

The sheer nonsense involved in the idea of someone "hauling the guy out of the way", as her instincts apparently told her to do, is rather fanciful. Kilby is a reasonably large man, as much as anything, but it was apparently only Nicolson's self-declared 'sensitivity' to the musicians' feelings that prevented her from wading in and presumably trying to physically eject him. But it is mainly the *tone* of Nicolson's piece that serves to demonstrate the sort of passive-aggressive affect that seems to have been around at the time. Nicolson was a Film Co-op member, and this organisation apparently had a sometimes uneasy and tense relationship with the LMC, whose premises they shared, so this conflict may possibly have been an acting out of repressed tensions between the two organisations. I only offer this because of the film factor involved, which is too obvious an aspect to ignore.

I have to say that this was one of the most highly personalised pieces of writing that I read in all of *Musics*, and it is doubly ironic that the photos that Nicolson herself took, which she claims, over-egging the pudding, might 'violate their space even further', are very amateurish (and not in a good way, seemingly more concerned with persecuting Kilby than anything else) as opposed to Kilby's highly professional portraits. In fact, Kilby has immortalised this particular gig with his photographs, which have appeared in several media, so I would have thought that the musicians involved have something to thank him for. Annabel Nicolson, on the other hand... The sarky epithet 'Jak Kilby and friends', which she appended to her three blurred and rather feeble 'portraits' of the trio, ultimately leaves a rather unpleasant taste in the mouth. This was one of *Musics* more ignoble moments, I'm afraid.

There was, finally, a much more helpful and positive piece (by Dave Panton, Jan Steele, Glyn Bush and Steve Raybould), which demystified the process involved in the Birmingham Musicians Collective's first grant application. (Page 29.) This was a genuinely helpful sample of the meta-language involved in dealing with institutions.

There was also an advert, in a box on page 32, for David Toop's 'Environmental Festival' (involving performances, environmental events, film/video documentaries, open music sessions and exhibitions), an event which was to take up a large part of issue 20 in December of that year.

Issue 18 (July 1978)

Violinist Phillip Wachsmann, in a letter on page 4, warned that, "*Musics* has incurred dangers of institutionalism [*sic*] and certain notions about what improvisation is about are becoming too firmly solidified amongst its regular writers".

This appeared to be a warning about absolutism and dogmatism in the music, features that we have seen highlighted throughout this book. He mentions the Bristol Festival held recently, where London chauvinism was brought up.

London may have been self-regarding, but its inhabitants didn't appear to be particularly supportive of *Musics*. A plea is made on page 2 for practical assistance (again) with producing the magazine. In the previous issue, a request was made for readers who could spare time to get in touch if they thought they could help. Sadly, and damningly: "We didn't get a single response to this request... Do you (this is especially addressed to London readers) support us or not?" (Page 2.)

It seemed, as is so often the case, that people were happier finding fault than offering to help in a practical way (anti-task, again). Further information was offered about the costs involved in producing the magazine and the role of (almost all unpaid) labour in getting it ready for the streets, but things were becoming critical, so it seemed.

As if to compensate for this crisis, edition 18 was mostly dedicated to extra-London activity. There was a supplement enclosed, 'The Unpopular Music Supplement', which covered the so-named Bristol Festival. "Other places represented (were) Essex, Devon, Cornwall, Leeds, Surrey, Bath, Luton, Warminster, Bridgewater, Nottingham, Connecticut (*sic*), Tamworth, London." [London at the end, I notice, *author*.] One family under an asymmetric groove?

Pages 30-1 outlined the choice of independent record labels then available, over 40 in total, which expands considerably the list of labels discussed in Chapter Six, although many of them were not solely concerned with free improvisation. This must have proved very helpful and informative at the time, which was well before the internet, we have to remember, so was doubly informative.

Issue 19
(September 1978)

This was another edition that focused on activities outside London, something that *Musics* was becoming adept at

Musics issues 19-23

(even so, the following list "is severely biased towards London, for which I apologise", a confession by Steve Beresford that was probably welcomed at the time). This comment was in connection with yet another supplement that was included, this time of 'useful addresses', covering the various collectives then in existence (11 were listed), other related organisations, periodicals/newspapers, radio stations, record companies and distributors, record shops and print facilities. All in all, this was an empowering breakdown for those interested in the free improv national network.

Pages 4-12 were taken up with the Technique and Improvisation discussion, which took place at the LMC on February 4th.

Issue 20 (December 1978)

Much of this edition concerned itself with David Toop's Music/Context Festival, which had, in actual fact, occurred five months earlier. Toop himself seems, by his own reckoning, to "have made no more attempt to create coherence in it than I did in planning the Festival itself". (Page 4.) Which is less than informative and inspiring for the historian, to be honest. Furthermore, "many of the early ideas were orientated to community involvement on a large scale, but unfortunately the majority of them had to be abandoned through lack of funds and time". (Page 4.) All in all, despite these *apologia*, the events have sometimes been presented as some sort of English free improv Woodstock (as has the ICES event), with Toop playing Michael Lang.

The photographs on pages 6 and 7 look like neo-realist portraits of urban *ennui* (with flares), gangs of kids being interviewed by bearded, balding middle-aged men, pedestrians poking their heads in car windows, small groups on wet pavements shooting the breeze. One Albert Mayr (presumably the follicly challenged man involved) receives very direct feedback from one member of the Essex Road community that he is trying to involve in his action research (apparently about everyday sound/noise), which he calls 'Available Amplification', for some reason and to the bafflement of his research 'participants':

Male Interviewee: "Eh…the states is paying millions of pounds out to people like you…why don't you fuck off!!" (Page 7.)

(*crunch*) Tape recorder thrown to the ground at this point and broken

Or, when interviewing the younger members of the N1 area:

Mayr: "I am doing this for – so people can be louder; can be heard. Is there anything you would like to say to the people living here?"

Boy: "Nah." (Page 6.)

There you have it – the Voice of the People, like it or not.

Even good old Lol Coxhill looks disaffected and weary somewhere on the Lock towpath, being observed by A.N. Other bloke, who looks equally jaded. Boredom, boredom everywhere, which is a tad unfortunate, given that 'boredom' was very much the previous year's thing.

There is something quintessentially English about all this (despite the fact that Toop and Burwell had apparently taken part in similar festivals in Florence and Milan), displaying a wartime spirit or whatever. The terrible puns of 'whirled' and 'wheeled' music ("anyone with a 'wheeled' instrument welcome to participate", p.16); the fact that the hubristic 24-hour improv-athon only lasted just over half that time, before weariness set in; the 'canal walking piece' – "walking the length of the canal there and back two times: first time recording, second time – playing back" (page 14); what looks like one of those council road-marking devices, "this instrument seems to attract a positive curiosity and interest" (page 14), i.e. the "Multiple Wheeled Ratchet" (page 12), by John Taylor (which is beyond parody, to be frank); the 'euphonium tunnel' piece, which was basically euphoniums played in the Camden Lock canal tunnel on various rowing boats (page 17). These all smacked of English eccentrism and derring-do, and were no doubt great fun to do. It sounds like the public stayed away in droves, probably more interested in the Lock Market, which was beginning to establish its now worldwide reputation.

None of this was particularly original but, somehow, Toop's mission statement had become: "The focus of the festival as it developed became increasingly centred upon the idea of presenting an overview of sound work specifically concerned with contextual problems and relationships." All of which sounded increasingly woolly and is increasingly difficult to relate to, in terms of the seemingly bathetic events in and around Camden Lock.

The AEC percussionist Don Moye offers a converging viewpoint from St. Louis' Black Artists Group: "We used to have concerts called the Sunrise Series. We'd start one day at noon and play all the way through till the sun came up the next day with continuous music featuring all the different groups and combinations." (Lewis, p.260.)

Annabel Nicolson excels herself once again with a rather fanciful Huck Finn comparison vis-à-vis the euphonium thing-y: "His (Mark Twain's) descriptions of piloting along the Mississippi at night are on my mind for a performance that evening."

This is Camden Lock in 1978 we're talking about, not the two-and-a-half-thousand-mile chief river of the largest drainage system of the North American continent. I'd love to try whatever it is that she'd been taking in that tunnel. Those of us with long memories might recall the detritus that filled the London canal system at that time. "It is very dark and full of things floating about," enthused Nicolson, as her skiff no doubt bumped against a dead dog or two.

Nick Cave eventually recorded a much less fanciful take on Twain's hero, on the first Bad Seeds album, six years or so on from Nicolson's odyssey:

"O you recall the song you used to sing-along
Shifting through the river-trade on that old steamer
Life is just a dream
But you trade on the mighty ol' man River
For the dirty ol' man Latrine
The brothel shift
The hustle 'n' the bustle and the green-backs rustle" (*Saint Huck*, 1984)

Now, I want to make it clear that I am not trying to issue some sort of a sneery retrospective condemnation of these Cage-ian events of nearly 40 years ago. They sound challenging enough, though I remain unclear about Toop's overall intention, if there ever was one (apart from the notion of 'environment' and the 'contexts' thereof), but one does get the impression that perhaps much of it took itself just a *teeny weeny* bit too seriously? One of the lessons of the first generation was that it was possible to temper the avant garderie with a *soupcon* of levity, but I can't find much of this quality in pages 4-27 of this edition of *Musics*. Perhaps it's just me, but I suggest it was probably more rewarding for the performers than for whatever audience was present. The proletarian audience in the Essex Road, so sought after by the likes of Cornelius Cardew, Keith Rowe, Green and Chris Cutler were clearly less than impressed, and knew when they were being patronised. This was ultimately Cardew *et al's* tragedy, replayed as farce, in the face of a 70s audience more interested in spectacle than revolution.

Page 3 featured two regional collectives, a new one in the East Midlands and the York massive. But the most alarming item, '*Musics* Benefit', was surrounded by black edging, which intimated perhaps the beginning of the end: "*Musics* has a financial problem…Because of rising costs…we've accumulated a few hundred pounds of debts…The money to pay for producing this issue has been lent by friends."

An all-day Benefit Concert was to be held on December 16th at No. 42, including a very successful 'musical jumble sale', which made around £400 for the collective, according to Richard Leigh – a tidy sum at that time.

Meanwhile, back in Squabbleland (a separate TAZ to Environment/Context), Charles Noyes sent in a letter bemoaning the 'Evan-versus-Steve climate', which had allegedly arisen from the article in *Musics* 19 on 'Technique and Improvisation', within which Messrs. Parker and Beresford had, somewhat predictably, expressed differing views. Personality/ideological clashes, Lake vs. Wilmer, Nicolson vs. Kilby, Parker vs. Beresford, seemed essential to the magazine's sense of itself, however manufactured these might have been, or perhaps it was just an accurate reflection of what was going on at the time in the rarified culture of free improvisation?

I would also like to add, as a Barre family post-it, that my wife has just retrieved a memory (clearly repressed for decades!) of a visit that she and her mates made to (as she remembers it) the London Film Makers Cooperative at No. 42 Gloucester Avenue, on New Year's Day 1979. An afternoon gig, which clearly featured a collection of DIY bands. Headlining were the North London Invaders (who were a direct precursor of Madness and obviously already both competent and ambitious) and an unlikely bunch calling themselves The Millwall Chainsaws, whose well deserved descent into musical oblivion is only halted, briefly, by the fact that among their membership was one Spider Stacey who, a few years later, gained fame and presumably some fortune as the tin whistle player of Poguemahone, who in time became The Pogues. These are more of the bizarre linkage/coincidences that I love to unearth. Gloucester Avenue's matrix was indeed an extensive one. Mrs Barre also recalls how distressed (an adjective yet to be fully exploited in the world of commercial public venues) the venue was. She now requires full psychoanalysis.

Issue 21 (March 1979)

The most significant article in this edition (several have been covered earlier) is Beresford's evisceration towards the end (p.30), of *The Boy Looked at Johnny* (1978), which was almost certainly the first book published about punk rock music in this country, by the so-called *kinderbunker* hacks Julie Burchill and Tony Parsons, then at the early height of their iconoclastic approach to pop culture, which was basically a rather clumsy updating of the main thrust of Nik Cohn's seminal *Awopbopaloobopalopbamboom* from 1969.

Beresford certainly put it up 'em (as they say), however: "If you're a fat, gay old Arab housewife or any of these things, according to B/P, you're a write off. But then, the book is dedicated to Menachem Begin – even Pluto (the publishers) blushed at that."

Burchill went on to become one of the most famous self-promoting philo-semites of the day, as well as being, ironically, a rather overweight lesbian at one point, it must be added. Consistency has never been one of her most striking qualities. "It's a nice package to sell: Dress it up in neo-RAR/neo-punk layout and fill the pages with petulant put-downs of anyone who ever sneered at you at the Roxy." (Beresford, *op. cit.*, p.30.)

One does, however, get the impression that it was B/P who were doing most of the sneering. It is a book that concerns itself with the very subject of that most popular of pastimes, hence Burchill's future huge popularity and influence. "The moral tone of the book is carefully linked to heterosexual monogamy – there's a soppy section on a rock and roll wedding." (Beresford, *op. cit.*, p.30.)

This latter comment is, retrospectively, dated and, once again, rather ironic, given Burchill's later hyper-mediated (and medicated) discovery of her inner lesbian, and her very personal attacks on her then ex husband Parsons, only a few years after this book was published. But this is exactly the sort of squabbling that sells, folks! No one ultimately gave a damn about the in-fighting of free improvisers (something that I will try, in a small way, to rectify).

Whatever, Beresford's corrosive review demonstrated that *Musics* continued to concern itself with trends outside of its immediate orbit, which gives it much retrospective kudos.

Issue 22 (June 1979)

The only comment that I would like to isolate here is one made by John Russell, who appeared to be expressing further concerns consequent to those of Wachsmann, made earlier (Issue 18), regarding the ossification and intellectualisation of the magazine into a single viewpoint product: "The academic parcelling off of things implicit in the area of improvisation and their subsequent shift to a dominant position, has put a distance between the contributors and the music/musicians as a whole. A magazine has been created that has become an institution outside the business of playing the music, and can only be seen in the same light as similar magazines, eg. *Melody Maker*, *Jazz Journal*, etc. The only difference is that *Musics* whines incessantly about its open structure." (Page 2.)

Given that Russell was one of the original editors of the publication, this was of concern. However, events soon took an inexorable turn.

Issue 23 (November 1979)

The reading of this final issue of *Musics* as a narrative conclusion to a story (as I did), felt like saying goodbye to an old friend (as any good story should). I used, earlier, a comparison of the cover picture of *Musics* 23 to the Cornelia Parker installation *Cold Dark Matter*, somewhat fancifully, but the apocalyptic nature of both images is unavoidable with everything being flung about and away from the centre, which clearly cannot hold, by an immensely powerful centrifugal force. An apt image for this, the final round.

Features on (again) the Bristol and York Collectives bode well, as does one by Paul Burwell on his Actual Music project (page 29), another organisation formed to promote a nationwide network of free improv musicians, one which, ultimately, after five years of activity, ended in 1984.

On page 5, Peter Cusack optimistically stated: "The number of Musicians Collectives and Cooperatives…has risen from two to 15 at the last count…Much of the change comes from the vast increase in activity outside London…it is a music and a musical organisation of growing size, strength and diversity. It is still expanding." (As the magazine's cover was perhaps hinting at; that, or apocalypse, take your pick, *author.*)

Paul Burwell died in 1997. He contributed majorly to the first edition of *Musics* through to the last and to most in between, and was always a passionate proponent of free music in all its guises and disguises, and his immense contribution to the magazine needs to be recognised. Thank you, Paul.

At the very end of this final *Musics*, Richard Leigh contributed an enthusiastic review of the first Alterations album, which is as good a point as any to bow out. No other hints were provided, apart from the rather specific 'FINAL ISSUE' that was embossed into the lower left-hand corner of the cover, apparently added controversially by who-knows-who, as the Wikipedia entry states.

So, *Musics* ended in a slightly downbeat fashion, with unknown fifth columnists (possibly, maybe) declaring the corpse officially dead. But it had a very good life and its absence would soon be noticed, in the next decade. But the latter almost immediately proved to be even less friendly to this sort of musical endeavour than the 70s had been, which is not saying much.

To end on a more positive note, the importance of *Musics* was reinforced by Ian Menter of the Bristol Musicians Cooperative: "*Musics*…was more or less the staple of improvising and collective musicians…at the one-day festival, organised by us at the LMC last November, a discussion was held to consider ways of replacing *Musics*." (Bristol Musicians

Cooperative magazine, No.3, July 1980, p.2.)

Unfortunately, it appears that attempts to set up a replacement floundered at an early stage (as did the attempts to set up a countrywide improvisers network that we heard about in the preceding chapter) and these hopes were transferred, bathetically, to expanded editions of the LMC's newsletter.

However, veteran jazz critic Kenneth Ansell, later a founder member of *Wire*, was able to say, very positively, in connection with the above festival: "The gig went a long way towards dispelling the myth that, to create a valid music, a musician must live in London." (BMC, *op. cit.*, p.55.)

CHAPTER 9

Epilogue
Endings and New Beginnings

"Over the past four or five years, the 'improvised music scene' has radically changed. Many more musicians are now involved, the range of music to be heard is much wider and there is a far greater exchange of ideas, both musical and theoretical, with other areas. Indeed, this makes the notion of an 'improvised music scene' impossible to define: it may well be passing into history". (Peter Cusack, *Musics* 23, 1979, p.5.)

Cusack was both right and wrong. The music had indeed changed, and in ways that no one could have predicted, but the improvised scene was far from becoming a historical curio or an anachronism, it being as healthy in our modern era as it was back then, if not more so.

By 1980, there were many more free improv collectives across the country, as we have seen, compared to the sorry state of the extra-London situation in 1972. *Wire* magazine started in 1982, *the* successor to *Musics* in many respects, but one that proved to have longer legs. Company and LMC gigs/festivals continued in the live arena, and Derek Bailey's book on improvisation eventually proved to be the scene's literary backbone. All these factors, small though they might have been, ultimately gave the music a heft that it just hadn't had at the turn of the 70s, when absolutely nothing of any written significance had emerged except for individual magazine articles.

Derek Bailey and Evan Parker were, without doubt, the two leaders of this time continuum (as Anthony Braxton would no doubt describe it), and I am sure that the recorded evidence bears this out. Derek Bailey having left the original Iskra 1903, the new version of the group, with Phil Wachsmann added, formed part of a *fin de siècle* gathering at the Notre Dame Hall in March/April 1980. This was Actual Music's 'A Final Resolution', which featured the scary American soprano vocalist and composer Diamanda Galas, as well as post-punkers This Heat and an Instant Composers Orchestra, which included Parker, Bill Dixon, Steve Lacy, flautist James Newton, Keith Tippett and Han Bennink. This was a very good representation of the international 70s legacy, a mix and match combination of all the talents, which boded well for the next decade in terms of adventurous and varied programming.

However, an LMC newsletter (May 1980) pointed out that: "Since the demise of *Musics* magazine, there has not been a 'traditional' channel for discussion."

The newsletter, which some had huge hopes for (see the conclusion to Chapter Eight) continued to convey the usual unromantic realities: "The water bill of £439 is being queried by Peter Cusack," which is a reflection on the latter's true community spirit. Thirty six years later, Cusack deserves to get a retrospective acknowledgment for these efforts alone. So, take a bow, Peter Cusack, and thank you.

Another newsletter (July 1981), a year on, merely deepened the gloom: "In all, we need something in the order of £4000 to bring the performance space up to the standards that performers and audiences deserve… we *need* to make these improvements." (Paul Burwell.) £4000 was a *lot* of money then.

The big event of 1979, however, in the UK, occurred on May 3rd when Margaret Hilda Thatcher, later Baroness Thatcher, became the first female British Prime Minister. An achievement of sorts, it has to be admitted. This was *not* the revolution that Cornelius Cardew and others had anticipated. Thatcher was subsequently to become popular with many working class voters, from whom Cardew had expected great things, and whom she shamelessly courted with stunts like selling off council properties, one of the major factors that has contributed to the housing problems of our current era. Her election victory is now seen, historically, as the beginning of the end of post-war consensus politics in this country, based as that was on full employment and Keynesian economic management principles. It is strange to consider that, only 20 years earlier, the word 'Butskellism' had been coined to describe the relative similarity of the Labour and Conservative Parties of the time – Hugh Gaitskell was the Labour chancellor and Rab Bailey the Conservative. (Wheen, 1982, p.70.)

Over the next decade, public funding received a hammering, to put it bluntly (but nowhere near our modern day standards of parsimoniousness). Previously undreamed of financial strictures began to be imposed on the NHS. The arts budget also soon fell under the beady eye of Conservative scrutiny, and the notion that the 60s was the decade that allowed permissiveness and promiscuity in through the front door was birthed around this time, and still remains a powerful trope today (even though the 70s was the more likely culprit). All this highlights the limitations of 'decade-ism'.

The 70s, despite the complaints of free improvisers, was a decade of relatively generous central arts funding: "Business patronage for the arts reached a record £6 million by 1979, while Arts Council funding for regional arts associations more than trebled in ten years." (Sandbrook, 2011, p.20.)

By the 1980s, however, the new Conservative government had begun pursuing one of the party's favourite tactics: to invoke the will of the new demigod, the 'marketplace', otherwise known as creeping privatisation. It was made a condition of public funding that arts organisations look for money from sponsorship, corporate donations and charitable trusts. Only during the Labour 'Cool Brittania' era of 1995-7 was former Tory minister George Walden able to reflect that: "To my knowledge, no Cabinet minister…had ever given official approval to what is conventionally regarded as avant garde art." (Sandbrook, 2015, p.115.)

This was with reference to John Major's National Heritage Secretary Virginia Bottomley's espousal of Damien Hirst's half-sharks in formaldehyde and suchlike, the work of the Young British Artists, or YBAs as they were acronymed. Politicians of that era were hardly friends to marginal material, unless it came with Nehru suits and Lennon/ McCartney chords as standard (as featured in the infamous No.10/Brit Pop Love-In in July 1997). The comparisons of Harold Wilson and Tony Blair were too obvious to miss. We don't need to think too hard to imagine, however, how much corporate *largesse* remained for free improvisation, as opposed to the sex, sensationalism and shock tactics that the YBA provided in abundance. There was very little private patronage from the likes of Charles Saatchi for free improv, unfortunately. Oh well...

Organisations were encouraged to set up fundraising departments, but it is difficult to imagine the LMC, for example, being cohesive, or politically compromised enough, to operationalise such a venture. Jumble sales were one thing, but we were entering a more ruthless period, retrospectively known as the 'me decade' where 'greed is good' (according to Michael Douglas's infamous character Gordon Gekko, in the 1987 film *Wall Street*). The fact that *Musics* refused to countenance adverts would have baffled 80s monetarists, who would have seen the decision as incomprehensibly naïve and self-defeating. We were entering much tougher and more cynical times.

The 60s, and even the 70s up to a point, were ultimately optimistic years with idealism to the fore, either from beats, hippies, post-hippies or post-punkers. No one could say this about the succeeding decades, which is one reason why I would ultimately lump the periods of 1966-72 and 1973-79 into one conglomerate unit of progressive modernism, with the 1979/80 caesura as a most important breach between that and the period that followed. Things were never the same after 1979.

Even the Bristol Musicians Cooperative, which had proved itself to be one of the most robust and confident entities to have emerged from the entire matrix of self-help theories (and praxis) of the mid/late 70s, had to admit to a degree of depression by 1981, as indicated in that year's self-produced BMC magazine (page 50): "The excitement had disappeared. With a few exceptions, the tales that follow [i.e. updates of the various collectives' fortunes, *author*] are of desperately treading water to keep one's head above the surface, and swimming would be out of the question. Despondency – sometimes with a façade of philosophical stoicism or sarcastic carelessness, sometimes without – but always with the grim reality clearly discernible."

To put another spin on this, from the perspective of another discipline: influential psychoanalyst Melanie Klein (Hinshelwood, pp.138-155) would suggest that a depressive position is, in fact, put in very simple terms, an appropriately mature stance to adapt, insofar as it is one that faces reality, and one that acknowledges both the gain and the pain involved in life's vicissitudes. Eventually, free improv's fortunes did, indeed, improve and, at the time of writing, seem to be waxing, however minutely. But in 1981, these fortunes did seem to be waning, as can be seen by the above BMC description.

The reasons put forward by the Bristol Co-op for these doldrums, which were no doubt applicable to other collectives across the country were threefold – the perpetual difficulties with getting adequate funding from the local arts bodies; the closure of important and (mostly) welcoming venues; the drifting away of the less committed (and perhaps more practically ambitious) musicians towards other forms and/or genres. (Bristol Musicians Cooperative, *op. cit.*, p.50.)

Steve Beresford told me that he doesn't think that *Musics* was ever satisfactorily replaced as an organ of mature free improvisation, perhaps because it was such a product of its times, and their laissez-faire libertarianism. One of the reasons that the *Wire* magazine has lasted so long (34 years and counting) is that it *does* do advertisements and presents as a highly technically assured, and confident, journal, with professional designers and art directors. It still offers a reasonable coverage of free improv interviews, articles and gig listings, but this is leavened by coverage of many other genres. It has an 'advertising sales team' even, which would have been anathema to the *Musics* DIY-ers. In fact, the latter's relative amateurism, and its concomitant enthusiasm, was part of the appeal: "This was contemporary with punk, of course, yet running in a parallel universe. Some of this earnest material is turgidly epitomised, yet it honestly reflects another aspect of the times, that people could parch stirring subjects to a degree of desiccation barely imaginable in an edited world." (David Toop, in his Foreword to the *Musics* 2016 reprint on Ecstatic Peace.)

In other words, more simply put, there is no real contemporary equivalent to *Musics*. It was history, even by 1979.

Free Improvisation was heading for a rough ride, under a government that had little time for the avant garde. The 80s were, in many ways, the doldrums for the music, which the BMC article referred to above reflects, but it did recover strongly over time through both an influx of younger 'generations' and the continuing maturation, and influence, of the older improvisers, the survivors of whom are still playing at an incredible level of purpose and intensity. They have always set a fantastic example.

The opening of Café Oto, in 2008, finally provided a secure base for experimental music in our capital, although our other major cities are not so lucky. The election of Margaret Thatcher, back in the far-off days of 1979, was followed by an interregnum, a pause or 'phony peace', which slipped by before the full Conservative agenda became gradually clear a few years into her regime.

The 70s now seems to be another world, a separate reality, but the years of 1966-79 were very much the years of discovery in this particular creative sphere. That of the exploration of a new world of sound, a world that has remained one of the most imaginative sonic environments ever engendered in this country.

REFERENCES

Bibliography

Albertine, V.
> *Clothes, Music, Boys*, Faber and Faber, 2014

Anderson, I.
> *This is Our Music: Free Jazz, the Sixties and American Culture*, University of Pennsylvania Press, 2007

Atwan, B.A.
> *Islamic State: The Digital Caliphate*, Saqi Books, 2015

Bailey, D.
> *Improvisation: Its Nature and Practice in Music*, Da Capo, 1992

(Making sure not to outstay its welcome, Bailey's classic study acts as a codex to what came after, *author*.)

Barre, T.
> *Beyond Jazz: Plink, Plonk & Scratch, the Golden Age of Free Music in London 1966-1972*, Compass, 2015

Bell, C.
> *The History of the London Musicians Collective*, on www.variant.org.uk, originally published in *Variant* magazine Issue 8, Summer 1999

(An invaluable early guide to the LMC, written by one of its earliest members, *author*.)

Blake, A.
> *The Land Without Music: Music, Culture and Society in Twentieth Century Britain*, Manchester University Press, 1997

Bristol Musicians Cooperative.
> *Co-operative Music*, self-published magazine, May 1979
> *...And Music*, self-published magazine, July 1980
> *Bristol(s)cream*, self-published magazine, 1981

Burchill, J. and Parsons, T.
> *The Boy Looked at Johnny*, Pluto Press, 1978

(Probably the first book published about English punk rock, and one of the first that emerged whilst the phenomena was still (just about) current. The hippie equivalent would be Mick Farren's *Watch Out Kids!*, *author*.)

Carr, I.
 Music Outside, Latimer, 1973
(The first book that covered, in some detail, the then current free improvisation scene in England, *author*.)
Cohn, N.
 Awopbopaloobopalopbamboom, Paladin, 1969
(This short book prefigured much punk musical attitude. Cohn's dad wrote the essential *In Pursuit of the Millenium* (1973), which was a much-loved text in the 60s about 'revolutionary millenarians and mystical anarchists in the Middle Ages'. I love these two books so much I have to mention them somewhere, *author*.)
Cohn, N. & Peellaert, G.
 Rock Dreams: Under the Boardwalk, Pan Books, 1973
Cook, R.
 Jazz Encyclopedia, Penguin, 2005
(A micro-version of Cook's other encyclopedic work, this is its highly simplified sibling and still useful for its reference facility. Again, English free improvisation is given significant attention, *author*.)
Cook, R. and Morton, B.
 Penguin Guide to Jazz on CD, Edn.7, Penguin, 2004
(One of the few encyclopedias that covers free improvisation in impressive (and how) detail, *author*.)
Corbett, J.
 Extended Play: Sounding Off from John Cage to Dr. Funkenstein, Duke University, 1994
(This has some great interviews with international improvisers, at a time when the music was starting to get significant attention on the world stage, *author*.)
 A Listeners Guide to Free Improvisation, Chicago University, 2016
Couldry, N.
 Turning The Musical Table: Improvisation In Britain 1965-1990, Rubberneck 19, 1995
Crumb, R.
 The R. Crumb Handbook, MQP, 2005
 R. Crumb's Heroes of Blues, Jazz & Country, Abrams, 2008
(If only Crumb had been interested in free improvisation, artist Mal Dean might have had some competition. Dean needs a significant reappraisal with regards to his portraits of late 60s/early 70s English improvisers, and is in danger of being forgotten. His *Melody Maker* work is priceless and captures the essence of improvisers in ways that photographers would be hard pressed to emulate, *author*.)
Daly, M.
 Gyn/Ecology: The Metaesthetics of Radical Feminism, Beacon Press, 1978
Du Noyer, P.
 In the City: a Celebration of London Music, Virgin Books, 2009

Eyles, J.
> *Biosphere* review, www.allaboutjazz.com, October 2006

Fischlin, D. & Heble, A. (Ed.)
> *The Other Side of Nowhere: Jazz, Improvisation and Communities in Dialogue*, Weslyan University Press, 2004

Freud, S.
> *Civilisation: Society and Religion*, Freud Library Vol.12, Penguin, 1966-8

Gluck, B.
> *The Miles Davis Lost Quartet and Other Revolutionary Ensembles*, Chicago University, 2016

Heining, D.
> *Trad Dads, Dirty Boppers and Free Fusioneers*, Equinox, 2012

Heller, M.C.
> *Loft Jazz: Improvising New York in the 1970s*, University of California Press, 2016

(This describes, in detail, the 1970s 'loft scene' in New York. Heller very helpfully posits, for consideration, four discourses for the loft community, those of 'pay, play, place and race', i.e. economics, musical practice, geographical location(s) and of the black experience. The latter of which was much more important in New York at that time than in London. The other three are equally applicable to our own shores, *author.*)

Hepworth, D. *1971:*
> *Never a Dull Moment*, Bantam, 2016

Heylin, C.
> *All the Madmen*, Constable, 2012

Hinshelwood, R.D.
> *A Dictionary of Kleinian Thought*, Free Association Books, 1989

Joynson, V.
> *The Tapestry of Delights: The Comprehensive Guide to British Music of the Beat, R & B, Psychedelic and Progressive Eras 1963-1976*, Borderline Productions, 1995

(Both AMM and the SME get entries in this mammoth encyclopedia, an indication of the openness of those times, *author.*)

Kofsky, F.
> *Black Nationalism and the Revolution in Music*, Pathfinder Press, 1970

Lanza, J.
> *Elevator Music: A Surreal History of Muzak, Easy Listening and Other Moodsong*, Quartet Books, 1995

(A book very much of its time, *author.*)

Lash, D.
> *Metonymy as a Creative Structural Principle: J. H. Prynne, Derek Bailey and Helmut Lachemann*, Brunel University PhD, 2010

(And we wonder why free improv is considered a rarified – to put it politely – genre? The music could benefit from complementary analyses and discourses to these that academia demands, but which appear to be thin on the ground, unfortunately, *author.*)

Lewis, G.E.
> *A Power Stronger Than Itself: The AACM and American Experimental Music*, University of Chicago, 2008

(An essential primer on the collective that was such an influence on a generation of English organisations, it is surprisingly readable for such a weighty tome, *author.*)

Lilleker, M.
> *Beats Working for a Living, the Story of Popular Music in Sheffield 1973-84*, Juma, 2005

(There are plenty of books on Manchester – and some on Bristol and Liverpool – but few on this most receptive of cities for experimental music. Focuses mainly on rock/pop/electronic music, *author.*)

Lock, G.
> *Chasing the Vibration*, Stride Publications, 1994

Mann, T.
> *The Magic Mountain* (trans. John C. Woods), Everyman Library, 1995

Marcus, G.
> *In the Fascist Bathroom*, Harvard, 1999

Martinelli, F.
> *Evan Parker Discography*, Bandecci & Vivaldi, 1994

McKay, G.
> *Senseless Acts of Beauty*, Verso, 1996
> *Circular Breathing*, Duke University, 2005

(These are two highly recommended books that identify and explore race and gender issues, which most studies shy away from, *author.*)

Menter, W.
> *The Making of Jazz and Improvised Music: Four Musicians Collectives in England and the USA*, PhD dissertation, University of Bristol, 1981

Milne, H.
> *The God That Failed*, Sphere Books, 1986

(The Bhagwan phenomena explored from an insider's viewpoint. Still fascinating and disturbing, at least for anyone over 50 years old who can remember it all, *author.*)

Morton, B. and Cook, R.
> *The Penguin Jazz Guide: The History of the Music in the 1001 Best Albums*, Penguin, 2010

Morton, B.
> 'Far Cry' column in *Point of Departure* e-zine, No.47, June 2014

(A very good American site on free jazz and improvisation, including usually very informative and discursive editorials by Bill Shoemaker, *author.*)

Nisenson, E.
> *Blue: The Murder of Jazz*, Da Capo, 1997

Nuttall, J.
: *Bomb Culture*, Paladin Books, 1971
: *The Bald Soprano: Portrait of Lol Coxhill*, Tak Tak Tak Books, 1989

Obholzer, A. & Zagier-Roberts, V.
: *The Unconscious at Work, Individual and Organisational Stress in the Human Services*, Routledge, 1994

(Highly recommended as a very readable introduction to the psychology of groups – which would include co-operatives and collectives – so relevant to this book, *author*.)

Paulo, J. & Wiedemann, J. (Eds.)
: *Jazz Covers*, Taschen Books, 2008

Pekar, H.
: *Swing as an Element of Jazz*, Vol.11, No.11, Coda, September 1974

Petrusich, A.
: *Do Not Sell at Any Price*, Scribner, 2014

(Essential for any readers concerned that they might have developed a vinyl dependence. File next to Burroughs' *Junkie*, *author*.)

Prevost, E.
: *Historical and theoretical precedents for the workshop* (written on the occasion of concerts and events arranged to mark the 50th anniversary of AMM), Unpublished, November 2015

Quantick, D.
: *The Making of the Beatles White Album*, Unanimous, 2002

Reynolds, S.
: *Rip It Up and Start Again*, Faber & Faber, 2005
: *Shock and Awe: Glam Rock and Its Legacy*, Faber & Faber, 2016

(The Dominic Sandbrook of modern popular music, Reynolds' books are unfailingly informative and fun, mostly free of academic jargon, and invariably make one want to return to the source material, *author*.)

Richards, K.
: *Life*, Weidenfield and Nicolson, 2010

Rod, J.
: *Free Jazz and Improvisation on Vinyl 1965-85*, RBK, 2014

Sandbrook, D.
: *State of Emergency*, Penguin, 2010
: *Seasons in the Sun*, Allen Lane, 2011
: *The Great British Dream Factory*, Penguin, 2015

(The Simon Reynolds of modern English history, *author*.)

Sassienie, P.
: *The Comic Book*, Ebury Press, 1994

Savage, J.
: *1966*, Faber & Faber, 2015

Scott, R.
> *Free Music, Improvisation and the Avant Garde 1965-90*, PhD Thesis, London University, 1991 (see www.richard-scott.net)

(Scott's thesis contains several superb interviews with British free improvisers who deserve to be better known. He tells me that he may consider trying to publish this work in the future, *author.*)

Speaks, J. (Ed.)
> *A Dictionary of Philosophy*, 2nd ed. Pan Books, 1981

Strongman, P.
> *Metal Box: Stories from John Lydon's Public Image Ltd.*, Helter Skelter, 2007

Tilbury, J.
> *Cornelius Cardew: A Life Unfinished*, Copula, 2008

(In some ways, the English equivalent of George Lewis's book on the AACM, in terms of academic rigour and sheer enjoyable reading – and length, *author.*)

Toffler, A.
> *Future Shock*, Random House, 1970

Toop, D.
> *New and Undiscovered Instruments*, Quartz/Miriliton, 1974
> *Sometime During the Night the Gods Had Left*, Unpublished document, 2012
> *Into the Maelstom: Music, Improvisation and the Dream of Freedom*, Bloomsbury Academic Press, 2016

(My thanks to David Toop for access to the latter document, one that increases our knowledge of this most infamous happening in the streets and waterways around the LMC HQ in Summer 1978, *author.*)

Various
> *Longman's History of the Twentieth Century*, Longman, 1998
> *MUSICS: A British Magazine of Improvised Music and Art 1975-7*, Ecstatic Peace, 2016

(Absolutely key to understanding this era of British experimentation, presented as a huge doorstopper of a book, *author.*)

> *New Musical Express* (magazine supplements) *Jazz from the 50s to the 70s*, IPC, June 20th & 27th 1981

Watson, B.
> *Derek Bailey and the Story of Free Improvisation*, Verso, 2004

(Flawed, but still essential for its insights into the pre-'fame' Bailey early years. Over 20 years old now, it still remains the only significant biography of any of the first generation players, *author.*)

Wheen, F.
> *The Sixties: A Fresh Look at the Decade of Change*, Century Books, 1982
> *Strange Days Indeed: The Golden Age of Paranoia*, Fourth Estate, 2009

Wickes, J.
Innovations in Modern Jazz, 1960-80, Soundworld, 1999
Wills, G.
Zappa and Jazz, Matador, 2015
Wilmer, V.
As Serious As Your Life, Quartet, 1977
Wright, S.
AMM and the Development of Free Improvisation as a Musical Practice, Open University PhD, 2013
Young, R.
Electric Eden, Faber & Faber, 2010

Discography

Adderley, C.
   Somethin' Else (with Miles Davis), Blue Note CD 95392-2, 1958

Alterations (group).
   Alterations, Bead 9, 1978
   Up Your Sleeve, Quartz 006, 1980
   My Favourite Animals, Nato 001280, 1984
   Live At Frankfurt 1983, Unpredictable Series (limited edition), 2016

(There is now a myriad of live Alterations albums, from past to present, thanks to the effort of Blanca Regina and Steve Beresford, and the Unpredictable Series. So take your pick… *author.*)

AMM.
   AMM 1966, Elektra LP EUK 256, 1967
   At The Roundhouse 1972, Anomalous Music ICES 01, 2003
   To Hear and Back Again, Matchless MRC 03, 1994
   It Had Been an Ordinary Enough Day in Pueblo, Colorado, Japo 60031, 1980
   The Nameless Uncarved Block, Matchless MRC 20, 1990

Bailey, D.
   Improvisations for Guitar and Cello (with Dave Holland), ECM 1013, 1971
   Live At Verity's Place (with Han Bennink), Incus 9, 1972
   Taps 1-4 (solo) Incus iv and vi, Reel-to-reel tapes, 1973
   Lot 74 Solo Improvisations, Incus 12, 1974
   First Duo Concert (with Anthony Braxton), Emanem 601, 1974
   The London Concert (with Evan Parker), Incus 16, 1975
   Improvisation (solo), Diverso 2, 1975
   Duo (with Tristan Honsinger), Incus 20, 1976
   New Sights, Old Sounds (solo), Morgue 03/04, 1978
   Time (with Tony Coe), Incus 34, 1982
   Arch Duo (with Evan Parker, recorded in 1980), Rastascan BR 0045, 1999
   Compatibles (with Evan Parker), Incus 50, 1985
   Notes (solo), Incus 48, 1985
   Balance (with Brighton, I., Wachsmann, P., Malfatti, R., Perry, F., Wood, C.), Incus 11, 1973

Barrett, S.
   Barrett (contains *Effervescing Elephant*), Harvest SHSP 4007, 1970

("A 90-second long piece of Lear-like nonsense…a fitting end to the recording career of a man who had made the nursery rhyme such an integral part of the late 60s pop sensibility," *Clinton Heylin, 2012.*)

Bedford, D. *et al.*
 The Garden of Love (with Coxhill, L., Wyatt, R., Ayers, K., Oldfield, M.), Voiceprint VP180CD, 1997
Beresford, S.
 The Bath of Surprise, Piano 003, 1980
Beresford, S., Toop, D., Zorn, J., Marshall, T.
 Deadly Weapons, Nato CD 950, 1986
Braxton, A.
 For Alto (solo, recorded in 1968), Delmark DE-420, 2000
(One of the earliest freely improvised solo albums, a form that became popular in the next decade. And a double album, what's more, *author.*)
Bryars, G.
 The Sinking of the Titanic, Obscure 01, 1975
Buzzocks (group).
 Spiral Scratch, New Hormones, 1977
Cave, N. & the Bad Seeds (group).
 From Her to Eternity (contains *Saint Huck*), Mute Records CD Stumm 17, 1984
Circle (group).
 The Paris Concert, ECM 1018/9, 1971
Company (shifting personnel).
 Company 1 (with Bailey, D., Parker, E., Honsinger, T., Altena, M.), Incus 21, 1976
 Company 2 (with Bailey, D., Braxton, A., Parker, E.), Incus 23, 1976
 Company 3 (with Bailey, D., Bennink, H.), Incus 25, 1976
 Company 4 (with Bailey, D., Lacy, S.), Incus 26, 1976
 Company 5, Incus 28, 1976
 Company 6 &7 (rec. 1977 with Bailey, D., Smith, L., Altena, M., Honsinger, T., Braxton, A., Lacy, S., Coxhill, L., Parker, E., Beresford, S., Bennink, H.), Incus CD 07, 1991
 Fables (with Bailey, D., Parker, E., Holland, D., Lewis, G.), Incus 36, 1980
 Epiphany/Epiphanies, Incus 46/47, 1985
Coxhill, L.
 Ear of the Beholder, Dandelion DSD 8008, 1971
 On Ogun (from 1977/8), OGCD 008, 1998
 Ictus (solo), Ictus 11, 1978
 Spectral Soprano: Solo and Group Improvisations 1954-1999, Emanem 4204, 2002
Davis, M.
 Kind of Blue (featuring Cannonball Adderley), Colombia CK 64935, 1958
 Live At Fillmore, CBS LP 66257, 1970
 Live/Evil, Columbia 65135 2CD, 1970
 Tutu (contains *Perfect Way*), Warner Brothers 925 490, 1986

Day T.
: *Interruptions* (from 1978-81, mostly solo), Emanem 4125, 2006
: *The Fairly Young Bean* (rec. March 1981 with Maarten Altena and John Russell), Emanem 4036, 1999

Desperate Bicycles (group).
: *Smokescreen*, Refill Records, 1977

Dolphy, E.
: *Far Cry*, New Jazz 8270, 1960
: *Last Date*, Mercury LP 6433 550, 1964

Durutti Column (group).
: *Eponymous* 'Sandpaper' solo album (Vini Reilly), Factory Records FAC 14, 1979
: *Endgame* (with Guy. B., Riley. H., Stevens. J., Watts. T.), Japo 60028, 1978

Guy, B.
: *Statements V–XI for Double Bass and Violine* (solo), Incus 23, 1976.
: *Assist*, Jazz & NOW 4, 1985

Just Music (improvising group).
: *Just Music*, 4-LP box set, ECM 1002, 1970

Lacy, S.
: *The Crust* (with Potts, S., Carter, K., Stevens, J.), Emanem 304, 1975
: *Saxophone Special* (with Watts. T., Parker, E., Potts, S., Waisvisz, M.), Emanem 3310, 1976

Manchester Musicians Collective.
: *A Manchester Collection*, Object Records Obj 003, 1979

Martyn, J.
: *Live At Leeds* (with John Stevens and Danny Thompson), Island Records, 1975
: *One World* (with John Stevens and Danny Thompson), Island Records, 1977

Mitchell, R.
: *Sound*, Delmark DL-408, 1966

(A considerable synchronicity saw this highly original release being recorded at around the same time as early stirrings by the Spontaneous Music Ensemble and AMM over here. All three explored 'silence' – or at least a drastic reduction of free jazz 'kineticism', *author*.)

Morning Glory (group led by John Surman), *author*)
: *Morning Glory*, Island Records ILPS 9237, 1973

Osborne, M.
: *All Night Long*, Ogun OGCD 029, 1975

Oxley, T.
: *The Baptised Traveller*, CBS 52664, 1969
: *4 Compositions for Sextet*, CBS 64071, 1970
: *Tony Oxley*, Incus 8, 1972
: *February Papers*, Incus 18, 1977

Parker, E.
> *Three Other Stories (1971-1974)* (with Lytton, P.), Emanem 4002, 1995
> *Two Octobers (1972-1975)* (with Lytton P.), Emanem 4009, 1996
> *At The Unity Theatre* (with Lytton, P.), Incus 14, 1975
> *Ra* (with Lytton, P.), Moers Music 01016, 1976
> *Saxophone Solos*, Incus 19, 1975
> *The Ericle of Dolphi* (with Rutherford, P., Holland, D., Lovens, P.), Po Torch 13/14, 1976 *The Longest Night, Volumes 1 and 2* (with Stevens, J.), Ogun OG 120-140, 1976
> *Monoceros* (solo), Incus 27, 1978
> *At The Finger Palace* (solo), The Beak Doctor 3, 1978
> *Vaincu Va: Live at Western Front 1978* (solo), Front 003, 2013
> *From Saxophone and Trombone* (with Lewis, G.), Incus 35, 1980
> *Zanzou* (solo), Jazz & NOW 1, 1982
> *Tai Kyoku* (with Barry Guy), Jazz & NOW 3, 1985
> *The Snake Decides* (solo), Incus 49, 1986
> *Hall of Mirrors*, MM & T CD 01, 1990

The Passage (group).
> *Pindrop*, Object Music OBJ 011, 1980

The People Band.
> *The People Band*, Transatlantic TRA 214, 1970

Pink Floyd.
> *Meddle*, Harvest SHLV 795, 1971

Pink Military (group).
> *Blood & Lipstick*, Eric's 002, 1979

Promenaders.
> *The Promenaders*, Y records 32, 1982

Riley, H.
> *Angle*, Columbia 494433-2, 1969
> *The Day Will Come*, Columbia 494434-2, 1970
> *Synopsis*, Emanem 4044, 1973
> *Singleness* (solo), Jazzprint 110CD, 1974
> *Overground 1974-5*, Emanem 4054, 2001
> *Improvisations Are Forever Now 1977-9* (with Guy, B. and Wachsmann, P.), Emanem 4070, 2002

Rip, Rig & Panic (group).
> *God*, Virgin Records VS 2213, 1981

(This post-punk album led many rock groups towards free jazz and its ramifications, one of which was free improv, *author.*)

Rutherford, P.
> *The Gentle Harm of the Bourgeoisie* (solo), Emanem 4019, 1974

Scritti Politti (group).
- *Skank Bloc Bologna* EP, St. Pancras Records, Scrit 1, 1978
- *4 A-Sides*, Rough Trade RT027, 1979
- *2nd Peel Sessions*, Rough Trade 034, 1980
- *Songs to Remember*, Rough Trade RT 20, 1982
- *Oh Patti (Don't Feel Sorry For Loverboy)* 45 Single, Virgin Records VS 1006, 1988
- *Cupid & Psyche* (contains *Perfect Way*), Virgin Records V2350, 1985

Shepp, A.
- *In the Tradition*, Horo Records 13-14, 1978

(An early example of vanguard 60s leaders, of which Shepp was one of the most prominent and vocal, making recordings that directly celebrated their forefathers. Anthony Braxton and Sun Ra were two of the many other leaders who opened the gateways [floodgates?] to the past, *author.*)

Smith, H. (Ed.)
- *Anthology of American Folk Music* (6-CD set), Smithsonian Folkways Recordings, 1997

Soft Machine (group).
- *Number Three*, CBS LP 64079, 1970

Spontaneous Music Ensemble.
- *Challenge*, Emanem 5029, 2001
- *Withdrawal*, Emanem 4020, 1997
- *Summer 1967*, Emanem 4005, 1995
- *Karyobin*, Island 979, 1968
- *John Stevens Spontaneous Music Ensemble* (aka *Oliv*), Polydor 2384 009, 1969 (initially on the Marmalade label)
- *Face to Face*, Emanem 4003, 1973
- *Quintessence 1 and 2*, Emanem 4015 and 4016, 1974
- *Biosystem*, Incus 24, 1977

Stevens, J.
- *No Fear* (with Guy, B. and Watts, T.), Hi 4 Head Records HFH 001, 1977
- *One Four and Two Twos* (with Rutherford, P., Guy, B., Parker, E.), also known as *4,4,4,4*, Emanem 5027, 2012
- *Live at the Plough* (with Osborne, M. and Rogers, P.), Ayler Records ayl 007, 1979

Talking Heads (group).
- *Speaking in Tongues* (includes *Slippery People*), Sire Records 92-3883-1, 1983

Taylor, C.
- *In Berlin*, 11 CDs, FMP 0,2,3,4,5,6,8,9,11,16,18, FMP Records, 1989 [get 11 and 16, *author*]
- *Teatime* (with Todd, G., Coombes, N., Beresford, S., Russell, J., Solomon, D.), Incus 15, 1975

Three and Four Pullovers.
Three & Four Pullovers (recorded in 1975 and 1978 respectively), Emanem 4038, 2000

Toop, D. & Eastley, M.
Buried Dreams, Beyond Records cassette, 1994

23 Jewels (group).
Playing Bogart, Temporary Records Temp 145, 1979

23 Skidoo (group).
The Gospel Comes to New Guinea 12" single, Fetish Records FE11, 1981
Seven Songs 12" mini-LP, Fetish Records FM 2008, 1982

23rd Turnoff (group).
Michaelangelo Deram 45", DM150, 1967

(If you ever see this item – which is highly unlikely – do yourself a favour and buy it, *author*.)

Ulmer, James Blood.
Are You Glad To Be In America?, Rough Trade Records Rough 16, 1980

(An era-defining combination of *the* hip English rock label and an innovative African-American jazz modernist, just on the cusp of the decades, recorded on 17/01/80, *author*.)

Various.
Circadian Rhythm (with Lytton, P., Toop, D., Eastley, M., Burwell, P., Nicolson, A., Parker, E., Davies, H., Lovens, P.), unreleased in CD format, Incus 33, 1978
Electric Muse: The Story of Folk into Rock, 4-LP box set unreleased in CD format, Folk 1001, 1975
Imitation of Life 4 LP box set, Beresford, S., Honsinger, T., Kondo, T., Toop, D., Y Records, Y13, 1982
Jazz/Actuel: a collection of avant garde/free jazz/psychedelia from the BYG/Actuel catalogue of 1969-71, Charly Records 707J, 2002
Messthetics D.I.Y 77-81 Midlands 1, Hyped2Death # 103, 2007
Messthetics 1977-82 D.I.Y. Bands, R-to-Sh, Hyped2Death # 1, 2006
Messthetics The Manchester Musicians Collective 1977-1982, Hyped2Death #106, 2008
1980: The First 15 Minutes, Neutron 45 EP 003, 1980
Sept Tableaux Phoniques: Erik Satie (with Beresford, S., Coe, T., Cornford, R., Coxhill, L., Hacker, A., Holland, D., Wachsmann, P.), Nato 39, 1983
Smithsonian Collection of Classic Jazz 6-LP set, Smithsonian Institute, 1973
Street to Street: A Liverpool Album, Open Eye Records OE LP 501, 1979
Tougher Than Tough: The Story of Jamaican Music (limited edition 4-CD set), Mango Records, 1993

(There is an absolute plethora of reggae compilations. This is one of the best. Really!, *author*.)

Hey Ho! Let's Go! Punk and New Wave 1976-79 5-CD set, Universal MCD 60066, 1999

Wildflowers: Loft Jazz New York 1976 3-CD set, Douglas AD 10, 2000

(A small snapshot of this musical network that unfolded over the same years – approximately 1973-80 – as those discussed in this book, *author.*)

Watts, T.
    Dynamics of the Impromptu 73/74 (rec. 1973/4 with Bailey, D. and Stevens, J.), Entropy ESR 004, 1999

Wheeler, K.
    Song for Someone, Incus 10, 1973

Zorn, J.
    The Parachute Years 1977-80 7-CD set, Tzadik 7316

(These were a product of the emergent, mostly white, Lower East Side scene in New York, which developed, initially, in parallel to that of the lofts, *author.*)

Filmography

Jazz: A Film by Ken Burns
Dir: Burns, K., 4-DVD Box Set documentary, 2001
(Exhaustive, except for its treatment of free jazz, which is rather cursorily swept away from the 'classic jazz' floor plan. Not that this deviates from the by now accepted canon of key figures and events. Wynton Marsalis plays a key presentational role (which he does with his usual immaculate professionalism). The sheer weight of archival footage is incredibly impressive and the film is a must for all interested in the music. *author.*)

Taking the Dog for a Walk: Conversations with British Improvisers
Dir: Prum, A., DVD documentary, NVNC-DVD002, 2015
(An engaging film about British improvisers, but with some puzzling omissions – Evan Parker being only the most obvious. *author.*)

Withnail & I
Dir: Bruce Robinson, DVD film, HandMade Films, 1987